Girl, Don't You Jump Rope!

Girl, Don't You Jump Rope!

A MEMOIR

Betty Anne Hennings Jackson

GIRL, DON'T YOU JUMP ROPE!
A MEMOIR

iUniverse books may be ordered through booksellers or by contacting:

iUniverse LLC
1663 Liberty Drive
Bloomington, IN 47403
www.iuniverse.com
1-800-Authors (1-800-288-4677)

ISBN: 978-1-4917-3585-5 (sc)
ISBN: 978-1-4917-3586-2 (e)

Printed in the United States of America.

iUniverse rev. date: 09/30/2014

PREFACE

As one of the elders on my father's side, and the oldest living relative on my mother's side, this book meets my obligation to our family tradition of passing on the stories told to me, along with stories told by me—from my own life—to our younger relatives.

The purpose of this work is to make these vignettes available to our descendants and to anyone who wants to read true and often dramatic stories.

I have employed the soothing salve of retrospection in fulfilling my compulsion to record my life experiences. On occasion, I have called upon knowledgeable family members to supply and corroborate facts and dates.

Faithfully, without embellishment, I have recorded these life occurrences just as my memory has presented them to me.

Each recall is written in 'chapic' form. "Chapic" is my made-up word (combining 'chapter' and 'topic') in which each episode is described. A chapic may be as short as one paragraph, or it may go on for a few pages.

The title of this book is a directive from my childhood which my mother often gave to me.

My reference to Chicago's West Woodlawn Community as a "tight little island" is borrowed from a book of collective recollections published in 2008: TIGHT LITTLE ISLAND by Robert L. Polk, in which an excerpt from this work is included.

Some of the chapics may contain wisdom to be passed on, some may possess truths from which lessons may be gleaned, and some may simply entertain.

Very often, a favorite grandchild solicits stories from Grandma; asking, "What was your life like, Grandma, when you were growing up? How were things in the olden days when you were young?" A strengthened bond between grandma and grandchild results when Grandma shares her memories with that grandchild, and the grandchild becomes richly endowed as the repository of Grandma's vivid life narrative. I have not had the good fortune to be blessed with grandchildren, thus: THIS BOOK IS MY GRANDCHILD!

DEDICATION

This book is dedicated to my son and my nieces and nephews. Some have expressed gratitude for having this family record. Karen, Cecile, Renee, Bobby, Jeffrey, Chuckie, Andrea, Byron, Rodney, Arnold, Alison, Kenny, Joy and Frederick; this is for you and your families.

I am enormously grateful to Grace F. Edwards, Director of The Harlem Writers Guild, for her 'fine tooth comb' final editing work, friendship and generous sharing of creative ideas. Thank you, to Olinda Simon for her heartfelt critique and expert editing work.

A special thank you, to members of The Harlem Writers Guild for 'hearing me out', including M. Angela Lynch Clare, for her valuable suggestions, friendship and guidance.

Relating and sharing family stories were invaluable to this work. When it was a mere concept, I was blessed to have my uncle Rick and my brother Ted (both deceased) act as sounding boards. I am eternally grateful to them. Thank you, to Cousin Kathleen Marie Humphries for permission to use an excerpt from your carefully researched, "Humphries' Family History". Thank you, Aunt Mary Henning Moore, for providing, "Precious Memories" (the 1992 Henning's Family Reunion booklet) from which I obtained information about my great-grandfather, Leonard Henderson Henning.

I am very grateful to my dear sister, Sandra Laroc, and my loving nieces, Karen Sowu and Andrea Boston for reading and suggesting changes and corrections (which I heeded) to my manuscript. Thank you, Ed Dancy for spell check. When technical problems arose, my 'Lil brother' Dan Bolling, saw me through them. Thank you, Dan. And a very special thank you, to Eric Coleman, without whose prompting this work would not have been completed at this time.

CONTENTS

PART I

MY VERY EARLY YEARS

A HOME IN WEST WOODLAWN

Even though Chicago's West Woodlawn community was a tight little island—with Cottage Grove as its eastern border and South Park, (now King Drive) its western, and Sixty-third to sixty-ninth Streets its north/south boarders—it was not a closed little island. It was a place where aspirations could be realized, a place where role models were abundant, where lawyers and laborers lived on the same block, where day-workers and doctors worshipped at the same church, where stockyard-workers and school teachers shared the same seat on the streetcar. It was a place where a person had a chance to fulfill his potential, where not being white was not an excuse for not being successful. West Woodlawn was an oasis in a sea of black migrants from the south.

Population density in West Woodlawn was half of that in other black-belt communities. Houses were generally large and spaced apart so that there was room for growth in vegetation as well as in human development. The crime rate in West Woodlawn was as low as it was in white communities. Adult neighbors were respected authority figures for all of the children in the neighborhood, and juvenile delinquency was something you read about in white newspapers that seemed to try to convince readers it occurred only in black neighborhoods.

The few months between the time when the first 'colored' family moved into a neighborhood and the last white family moved out could be called "Racial Integration, Chicago Style". Generally, there was a buffer zone of white homeowners, who—after holding out as long as they could from selling their homes—finally gave in to pressure and moved so that the area became all 'colored'. The buffer zones fell, (to the delight of real estate companies) like placed dominos, one after the other, in the community known as West Woodlawn.

When my family lived there, a few white families (probably too poor to re-locate) remained scattered throughout this lovely community where its non-threatening atmosphere nurtured creativity and upward mobility.

There were some Negro families who, long before its repeal, had managed to find white sellers who would ignore the restrictive covenant provisions written into all house deeds. The covenant stated that a property could not be sold to a person of the 'negro' race. These provisions were enacted into law in 1920 and not removed until 1948 by the Shelly v. Kraemer Supreme Court ruling.

Negro families who had purchased multiple-dwelling property in West Woodlawn rented spare apartments to other Negro families anxious to move out of over-crowded black-belt neighborhoods. This is how my family, The Hennings, came to Woodlawn—moving from 48th and St. Lawrence (which was squarely within the black-belt)—not as owners, we came as renters.

In the spring of 1936, The Beard Family leased the first floor, five-room apartment in their two-flat building to my family; Theodore (Ted) and Elizabeth (Betty) Hennings and their four children; ages eighteen months to seven years. It was the corner house at 6600 Marquette Road that headed the row of houses where the road curved, and automobile accidents were frequent. A spacious wooden porch jutted out from the first floor and extended up to the second floor. Like all porches of that era, it was painted battleship gray. Mr. And Mrs. Beard lived upstairs with their two children; ages five and seven.

Most of the houses on the block were sturdy, large, one-family homes, but there was a sprinkling of multiple dwellings too. There were even a couple of three-flats, which were brick, in compliance with Chicago's strict building code enacted after the great Chicago fire of 1873 when almost all of Chicago was destroyed.

Schooling for the two older Hennings children began a little outside of Woodlawn. St. Anselm's Catholic School, at 61st Street and Indiana Avenue, placed seven-year-old Theodore in second grade, five-year-old Betty Anne, in kindergarten. Three-year-old, Daphne, attended Mrs. Carlos' Nursery School program housed in a neighborhood church. Not yet two-year-old Bubby did not attend school.

PORCH CHILDREN

The porch was our playground. After school, we would head for the porch usually joining the Beard children in play. We didn't have many toys on the porch, maybe a ball, or some jacks, or a yo-yo. We played a lot of verbal games, like "I'm Thinking Of a Word" (where caller chooses the initial letter of an object and the correct guesser becomes the caller), and we did a lot of rhythmic hand-slapping games such as "Mary Mack all dressed in black." My older brother would sometimes sneak off the porch and join some of the boys in the neighborhood for a game of marbles, but in those early years we were mostly porch kids.

I don't remember how long we lived at 6600 (as we, in later years, referred to our home), but I know that it was long enough for my baby brother, Robert, (the one we called 'Bubby' (thanks to sister Daphne's pronouncement of 'Bobby') to grow from baby to boy, and my brother Arnold, to be born.

Mother had definite ideas about raising her children; she taught us the correct terms for body parts and bodily functions. The book from the library told the story of the sperm and the egg and how their unity would produce a new little baby. We were intrigued by the story even though it didn't tell how the egg and sperm got together.

Mom was pregnant with my brother Arnold (the fifth Hennings child) so I am sure that was her motivation for the sperm and the egg story. I remember playing on the porch and calling my little brother, "You ol' sperm!", and he, responding with, "You ol' egg!" We bantered these terms back and forth, giggled, and became very loud. I remember quite clearly that the Beard children were called in by their mother and I don't remember playing with them again on that porch.

MOM'S BACKGROUND

My mother's mother, Anna, died when Mom was eleven years old and that loss had a profound effect on her personality. Mom was the eldest girl of nine siblings. Her brother, Mitchell, was a year older but Mitchell never grew any bigger than a ten-year-old boy and his size dogged his lifestyle and influenced his life's choices. Sensitive to the point of being downright hostile, Mitchell fought his way through life to prove to the world that he was as much a man as any six-footer. The writer, Walter Moses' famous character, 'Mouse' (Easy Rawlings' sidekick) is the perfect embodiment of my uncle Mitchell.

Being the biggest, Mom's seven brothers and one sister regarded her as the oldest and therefore leader. In fact, Anna (the grandmother I never knew) had also looked to her for leadership because, on her deathbed, she made my Mom promise to . . . "Take care of your brothers and sister!" My mother took that oath very seriously and when her two youngest brothers (Rick and Solomon) had problems with their foster home, she took them in to live with her family. That totaled four children, two teen-agers, a dog and two adults, with a new baby on his way in that five-room apartment.

Mother's other brothers; Mitchell, Sidney, Robert, Alphonso and Clyde were out of school and working. They were pretty much on their own but regarded our home as headquarters. They visited very often, brought their girlfriends by and always spent the holidays at our big oak dining table. My mother's father 'Papa' came by on occasion. All mirth subsided when Papa visited and a lot of praying took its place. No card-playing was allowed, no joke-telling, no music (that was not of a religious nature) was tolerated and by no means was any dancing allowed because Papa was now ordained to the Baptist-Spiritualist Ministry. Mother's sister, Anna Mae, was married and producing children at a faster rate than my parents, so we didn't see her and her family often. Another person that we saw

5

too little of was my father. He worked an average of two-and-a-half jobs all during the time that I was little. Daddy made his presence felt when he was home; he helped groom the boys, cooked and did most of the house cleaning.

ST. ANSELM'S: NOT A HAPPY SCHOOL

By the time I was six-years-old, we were attending McCosh Public School. We had been thrown out of St Anselm's because of my older brother's behavior and my Dad's refusal to disclose intimate information to the priests during mandatory instruction classes. Dad was, later, to tell that the priests wanted to know about his sex life and he told them, "Don't ask me what goes on between me and my wife, I'm not asking you what you and these sisters do in this parish house!"

At the time we were excised from the enrollment list, I was not aware of these things. I thought I was responsible for our expulsion because I had wet on myself during play time. I had asked the nun for permission to go to the bathroom and been denied. The usual procedure was to take discarded paper from the waste basket and blot up the urine, instead, I was spanked.

The spanking wasn't the first hostile act I'd experienced at St. Anselm's. During the priest's weekly visit to our kindergarten class, he asked questions to see how well we'd learned our Catechism; a correct answer earned a medal. My hand shot up at each question. Our teacher was the one who designated which child got a chance to answer. She never called on me. I was so determined to win one of the medals, that on the next question, I got right up in the priest's face, waved my hand in a wild frenzy and the priest, himself, pointed to me. I answered the question and got my medal.

The fact that my brother and I were, perhaps, the most "Negroid" looking children in attendance at St. Anselm's, with our tan skin and kinky hair, was what probably set us up for scrutiny. I remember my kindergarten teacher calling other nuns over to observe my hair.

It was on a hot sunny day during the May Procession. We were lined up in our bride-like finery, waiting for the signal to march into the church. I'm sure the nuns had never seen straightened hair revert (from my profuse sweating) to its original kink. They shot each other glances that even a five-year-old could understand. I must have displayed my discomfort because one of the nuns covered up by complimenting me on my headband (an ordinary rigid barrette-like band that covered some of my hair in the front). When I got home, my mother asked me why the nuns had gathered around me. I masked my feeling of being uncomfortable, and told her only about the compliment. There were other 'Negroes' who attended St. Anselm's, but they did not stand out from the white children. They were, on the whole, light-skinned, curly, or straight-haired, and most of the girls had long tresses, unlike my short (it didn't grow long until puberty) kinky hair that my mother straightened with the hot comb once a week or more.

Michael was my favorite kindergarten friend. He was as close to being 'Dick' from our "Dick and Jane" reader as he could be. He had yellow hair and pink skin which were the colors I always used when I colored people in my workbook. It didn't take long to figure out that pink skin and yellow hair was the way people were 'supposed' to look. In fact, all of the children in all of the books had pink skin, even those with brown hair. I'm sure that's why I always chose Michael when it was time for a partner. One day, I wanted to take Michael home with me, but his mother frowned at me and jerked his hand away from mine. I had no idea what wrong I had done, but that didn't keep me from having a funny feeling that I HAD done something wrong.

VISITORS FROM THE SOUTH

My father's sister, Effie, and her new husband arrived from Tennessee with nowhere to stay, so our dining room became their home until they could find a place of their own. That took at least two major holidays. On more than one occasion, the adults had to clear out Effie's belongings and stash them in the room that I shared with my sister so that we could celebrate a big holiday in the dining room. Their clothes and bedding crowded us out of surface space. One night we piled their things on top of our double bed and slept on them. In the morning, there was damp adult clothing on our bed because we had not outgrown our bedwetting years.

DAD'S BACKGROUND

Dad could not have been more than five years old when his parents left him in charge of two younger siblings. Baby Edward cried so much that my dad, Teddy, thought he must be cold. He moved the baby closer to the fire and the baby's blanket caught fire. Teddy put the fire out, but Eddie's toes were burned away.

That's how the stigma of 'Crazy Teddy' got applied to my dad in that farming town of Denmark, Tennessee. When he was thirteen, his parents sent him to live with an uncle in St. Louis hoping a new start would erase the stigma of 'Crazy Teddy' and that he would get an education.

In St. Louis, Dad's country ways didn't endear him to the guys on the block. Dad said that his parents had bought him new clothes to take with him to the big city; three pairs of identical bib-top overalls. He told me, "I wanted to impress the guys so I sported all three pairs of my new overalls on the same day. I wore one pair outside, and nobody said anything about them, so I went back in and changed to another pair. Then I changed again. When there was still no one telling me how sharp I was, that's when I started to notice that none of the boys wore overalls. In fact, some of the boys laughed at a boy on the street because he had on faded raggedy coveralls."

Dad also told me about the class assignment that got him kicked out of school.

"When the teacher said it was time for art, and said to draw something that you are familiar with, some kind of scene, like a sunset; something that made you feel excited. Here I was a great big boy, thirteen-years-old, in the fourth grade. I remembered one scene that I had seen many times on the farm that excited me, so I drew two donkeys mating. That was the end of my schooling I was taken to the office and expelled."

Dad's final effort at trying to become 'citified' in St. Louis was, "All the boys were flipping milk wagons. That's when we'd grab on to the back of a horse-drawn wagon and flip our bodies up over the back of the wagon's end. Oh, you could get a good ride with the driver probably not knowing you were there, or,

9

if he knew, until the driver stopped the wagon to make you get off. Then you would run off. But by then you would'a had your ride and all the guys would praise you and tell you how swell you were. Well, one day, I was determined to make my mark, so I flipped the first wagon that came along, before any of the other boys could get to it. As I flipped my body up and over, I started sliding down into the wagon and couldn't stop. I slid on down to the bottom of the wagon, and I was completely covered in garbage before the driver stopped the wagon and got me out. It was a good thing the driver saw me, 'cause I might have suffocated. Man, how the boys laughed at me! Everyone but me knew you didn't flip a garbage wagon!"

Dad said that he heard about Chicago, and struck out for that 'promised land' by the time he was seventeen.

Six of Dad's younger siblings are college educated and I grew up with the idea that I, too would attend college, but in those early days, any thought of higher education would have been a pipe dream for Dad, not only because he wasn't able to attend high school, but because he had to work. And work, he did! He was very enterprising.

As often as he could, Dad would buy produce from the wholesale market (usually corn and string beans) and with his melodic baritone he'd call, "ST-RING, ST-RING, ST-RING, BEEEENZZZ", or, "C-C-C-C-ORN", and sell his produce up and down Chicago's alleys. He did this only part-time since he had two other manual labor jobs in restaurants. He would take my brother Theodore along to pull his little red wagon full of corn or beans and to run the pail up the stairs when a purchase was made.

After the vegetables were sold, Theodore would wash out his wagon and take the pretty girls in the neighborhood for rides.

LEONARD HENDERSON HENNING (L.H.) DAD'S GRANDFATHER

Daddy's grandfather was born into slavery in 1850, yet during his lifetime he acquired over five hundred acres of farmland, and ran a successful blacksmith shop and furniture-making business. He was a genius at organizing newly freed black people into a community of landowning farmers and he provided a newly-built farmhouse and acres of land as a wedding present for each of his six sons. He also passed down to them his blacksmithing, furniture-making and farming skills.

Although the dealer refused to sell him a new one, L.H was the first black man in his county to purchase an automobile. He was so successful that he donated the land for the church and for the cemetery where many of our relatives are buried. L.H. was so progressive that his was the first house in Denmark, Tennessee to install carbide lighting. Thanks to L.H., none of our relatives had to become sharecroppers. Some of the houses L.H. built for his sons are still standing and occupied today. Some of my cousins rent out their land to tenant farmers. It is interesting that the tenant farmers have all been white; sort of sharecropping in reverse. Today, over one hundred acres of land are still owned by our family; land that my great-grandfather, Leonard Henderson Henning bequeathed, as his legacy to us.

BACK ALLEY ENTERPRENEURS

My parents and my uncles had learned how to make Mexican tamales from Papa, who had picked up the skill from one of the many jobs he held over the years. Papa had been part owner of a hand cart from which he sold shrimp, tamales and roasted peanuts.

At night, Baby Arnold's buggy was converted to a vendor's cart; equipped with warming charcoals and steam pans, and the tamales that were prepared in our kitchen during the day, were sold on the streets of West Woodlawn at night. They were sold to people who strolled around the neighborhood in their daily, after-dinner ritual of being 'out walking'. Some were sold to the crowd as people left the Langley theater on 63rd and Langley where the whole family got to see a double feature movie, plus newsreel, for just twenty-five cents. Upon leaving, each member of the family—child or adult—was given a saucer, or a bowl, or a plate to complete the family's set of milk glass dishes. Every dish in our home, for many years, was milk glass.

There was a huge crock that occupied space in our pantry. If one of the grown-ups in our family didn't replace the heavy lid properly, standing on tiptoe, I could lean over the crock and smell a pungent odor coming from the purple liquid in that crock. It was something like old grapes which had been left out in the sun. I loved smelling the fumes from the crock.

One day, I saw Rick—my sixteen-year-old uncle; whose friend was visiting—dipping a cup down into the crock. I told him, "I wouldn't drink that if I was you". He said, "You'd better not tell, girl, it's only for my company!" Again, I told him, "You shouldn't be drinking that stuff from the crock, because I broke a glass and the pieces fell down in there because the lid wasn't on right!"

I never saw my people bottle and sell the wine from that crock, but I believe it was for more than just their personal use.

OUT WALKING

Few people had cars so life in West Woodlawn included a lot of walking. A large part of family socializing was meeting people who were 'out walking' while we were 'out walking'. Children would never go 'out walking' before they 'got cleaned up' for the evening. Getting 'cleaned up' consisted of washing up and changing out of the clothes you wore all day and putting on a nice outfit. When you were 'cleaned up' no heavy play was allowed which might dirty your clothes, because these were the very clothes you'd likely wear to school the next day. My family went 'out walking' with whomever was living with us at the time, and since we almost always had extended family, we must have resembled a parade going around the neighborhood. Our group would often end up at my parents' friends' bakery and sweets shop.

DePILLAR'S

Althea and Hilton DePillar were "Negroes" who owned their own business; DePillar's Bakery and Sweets, on 67th street between St. Lawrence and Rhodes. Althea was a close friend to my mother. The candy she had for us was no match for the chocolate peppermint patties we could buy at Cunningham's store. The fact that many shops and stores were black-owned was no big deal. Scores of people who impacted our lives held positions of importance—African-Americans who serviced our community as insurance men, door to door salesmen, doctors, grocers, ice men, postmen, laundrymen, and teachers. However, all civil servants; bus drivers, milkmen and bread delivery men were still all white. After the war, Uncle Rick became one of the first 'Negroes' to work the Silvercup bread truck. It was a big deal.

Cunningham's store was located across the street from McCosh School, where my favorite peppermint patties were filled with either white or pink peppermint cream. If you got a pink-filled one, which was quite rare, you could have another patty for free. Cunningham's was also headquarters for buying kosher dill or sour pickles and the penny peppermint sticks which we used like straws, sticking them down in the pickle and sucking up the juice. For some reason, I never saw boys partake of this treat, but all of my girlfriends enjoyed peppermint and pickles together, and we all smelled like pickles and peppermint most of the time. Cunningham's was also black-owned.

Another treat Cunningham's offered was potato chips cooked in the store where we watched them frying in clear-colored oil and then put into little brown bags that would immediately become oil stained. I rarely had enough money to buy potato chips, but when I tasted one, I was hooked on that flavor and crunch. One day, I tried my hand at making them at home. No one had told me that the clear-colored liquid wasn't water. It looked like water. I cut up my potatoes and dumped them in water that hadn't even boiled, and I was really baffled when the stuff turned to mush.

In later years, I found out that there were other treats that could be obtained from those candy stores. These treats didn't get put in greasy little brown bags, these treats didn't depend on getting a pink-centered patty. You would have to be an adult and you would have to have known terms like; 'bolita', 'green gold' or 'high rider'. You would probably own a 'dream book', and you would have 'placed your bet' in the morning, if your 'treat' was to be collected after the afternoon or evening 'drawing'. The treat was referred to as; 'Winning at policy', or' Playing the Numbers'

AUNT EFFIE

My Aunt, Effie, and her husband had found jobs in Chicago's Loop (the downtown area). Effie considered hers a temporary job because she was a recent graduate of Lane College in Jackson, Tennessee and expected to start teaching school in the near future. It wasn't easy for a black woman, educated in the south, to walk into a teaching job in Chicago, so it was many years before she finally landed a teaching position in the Chicago Public School System.

BONDAGE BY BABIES, BUT FEELING SPECIAL

By the time Arnold was born, I was beginning to figure out that every new child Mother had cost us four years of not going anywhere special. I don't mean on vacation, that idea wasn't even a thought then, not away trips, just in-city trips, like down to see

Buckingham Fountain spurt out its multi-colored waters, or to Riverview Amusement Park (our favorite), or even on picnics. We had stayed close to home until Bubby was big enough for us to get out as a family, then along came Arnold to spoil all the fun!

My uncles, Sol and Rick, were off to Civilian Conservation Camp (CCC), so they weren't living with us then but Effie was still there. Effie's husband must have liked me a lot because he used to tickle me under my arms. I was so glad to have extra attention from an adult that I couldn't understand why Mother gave him those funny looks and stopped him from tickling me. I thought, at the time, that she just didn't want me to have fun and that she didn't want me to feel special. My brother, Theodore, could feel special because he could run errands and earn money. Daphne could feel special because she was so small and so pretty. Bubby could feel special because he was so cute and so smart. He could write his name and read words at 4-years-old. I know because I taught him. Arnold was special because he was the baby and he had been in the "Beautiful Baby Contest' at the community centre and he had come in second.

FIGHTING CHICAGO'S COLD

"Betty, do you know anyone with an extra winter coat that I can borrow? This November weather goes right through this light coat of mine." Effie asked my mom.

"I'll ask Althea. She has lots of clothes. I'll bet she has an extra coat." Mother told Effie.

Althea was very happy to give Effie a coat. In fact it was a fur coat. She said, "I'm glad someone could use it. It's been hanging in my closet ever since my aunt died. It belonged to her."

Effie was toasty warm the day she wore that coat. She waited for the trolley or streetcar (as it was referred to) on Cottage Grove Ave. which took a long time to come. The wind was doing its usual Chicago thing . . . blowing hard. Effie reported that as a big gust of wind blew especially hard, she noticed that something was irritating her eye. She tried picking out whatever it was, by pinching her eyelashes. Then, it was in the other eye. Then, it was in her nose. She blew her nose with her handkerchief but by then, she was having trouble seeing and breathing. She said that the other people near her, also waiting for the streetcar, began moving away from her, flailing their arms, holding their noses, spitting and picking stuff from their eyes. Effie reported that by the time she got to work, she was wearing a skin coat. The fur coat was dry rot, and that famous Chicago wind was all that was needed to whip every bit of fur off of it!

THEODORE; INDIAN WARRIOR

One day, Mother got Mamie McGee, friend, baby-sitter and my Uncle Bob's eventual sister-in-law-to take care of me and my three younger siblings while she, my older brother, Theodore, and Daddy—who just happened to be home as we came in from school at lunch time—rushed downtown to the Loop on the streetcar. When they came back, Theodore was carrying a big brown box and wearing a big grin. He seemed so very happy! In the box was an Indian outfit, consisting of a large feathered headpiece, a neck bandana, matching pants and vest with fringe. He quickly dressed up in the outfit, and we all—Mom, Dad, Theodore, Daphne and I—went back to school for whatever was left of the afternoon session. Since this was a special occasion (according to Theodore) we went to Theodore's third grade class. We expected to see all of the children dressed in their cowboy or Indian outfits, because Theodore had rushed home at noon and announced that he just had to have an Indian outfit that very afternoon. He declared, "All the children in the class will be wearing cowboy or Indian outfits for the play at school!" When we walked in, the third grade was quietly doing class work. The teacher was helping one group of children with a workbook assignment. The five of us stood in back until the teacher tore herself away from her pupils. Theodore, still wearing that grin, proceeded to his seat and sat down. There was not another child wearing an Indian or a cowboy outfit. There were many children wearing Indian-outfit-envy-expressions on their faces as their eyes followed my big brother to his seat.

Daddy was so angry at Theodore that he spanked him in the class coatroom. We walked back home and our parents made another trip to Chicago's Loop to return the Indian outfit.

In later years, I asked my brother what was he was thinking to tell such a whopper? All he could say was, "I wanted that Indian outfit so badly, that it's the only thing I could come up with that I thought Mom and Dad would fall for. I got the idea that I wanted to dress like an Indian, from my friend, D'arcy Edmonds, who wore his Indian suit to Cub Scout meeting on the Saturday before I came up with that lie."

CAR ACCIDENTS

Woodlawn was very beautifully kept. Almost every house had a lawn and there were many tree-lined streets. Our street was also well kept, but the trees were few and far between on the curve. Since it was a fast street and we lived on the corner, we had a wide view of much that happened in the neighborhood and somewhat of a view of what happened in the alley. Few families in our neighborhood had cars but many cars raced by on the curve that sent Marquette Road west bound from its north-south course.

White people drove the cars that sped past our home. Many of the cars were two-seaters which seemed to be quite suitable for racing. There was no traffic light on the corner and we often heard the heavy screech of a skid before hearing the thud of the crash.

If the accident happened during the daytime, my big brother was often the first one at the scene. The most common type of accident was overturned vehicle. He would often take water to the passengers in the cars. I thought he was very brave to help the victims even though he was a total pain around the house.

In later years, Theodore confessed to attending the scene of those accidents for what he could get from them: loose change, a stray purse, money sticking out from a dazed motorist's pocket.

My brother; the businessman! He would sell us children anything. I took the small end table from our living room to my bedroom and put my toys on it. When Mother came and took it back I got a lesson in economics 101: you can't sell what you don't own! My brother had sold the cute little end table to me for about a nickel.

One of his most popular treats, which he made and sold to us, was 'snowball ice cream', made out of snow with sugar sprinkled on it and some evaporated milk from our refrigerator poured on top. These ingredients were available to all of us but it took many purchases of Theodore's 'ice cream' before I realized that I could make the same 'snowball ice cream' without giving my big brother my money.

In one particularly brutal scene, an open-topped coupe overturned and threw all three occupants out onto the pavement. The two young men and one woman lay out there in the sun for what seemed like hours before the police and ambulances came. Theodore made no attempt to go near the victims or their car. I believe he was traumatized by that accident. We watched the scene through our living room windows from the time we heard the screech until the bodies were taken away.

MY UNCLES

Of my five uncles (on my mother's side who did not live with us) four lived in West Woodlawn. Sidney and Alphonso (Al) second and fourth eldest uncles, both in their early twenties, before they married, rented a room together. Bob (third eldest) after reaching his eighteenth birthday, continued to stay with his foster family; a working photographer, his wife and two sons, Bob's status changed from foster son to renter-boarder. Clyde, (third from the youngest, barely out of his teens) drove a taxicab for the black-owned Daigre Cab Co. He stayed with Sidney and Al sometimes, with Papa sometimes, and with Bob.

Almost every day, at lunchtime, Clyde parked his taxi in front of our home. Mom would heat up whatever was left over from our dinner the night before, even cabbage—which I hated—and Clyde would pay her twenty-five cents for the meal. She was happy to get the money. Clyde was very ambitious, he always talked about opening a business, in fact, all of my uncles and my dad, talked about going into business, but no one talked about it as much, or with such passion as Clyde. During off-hours, when he was not driving the taxi, Clyde worked in a cleaner-tailor shop where he learned so much that he was soon able to successfully run his own business. These uncles, and their (eventual) wives were a prominent part of my young life and I loved them dearly. They always made me laugh because they all told jokes all the time. They all had the same kind of great sense of humor. Ours was a family of comedians.

When they were in high school, Sidney, Al and Bob worked at Theresa's Grocery Store as part-time help. When they were no longer in school Theresa hired them full time. The store was at 64th and Langley. Theresa was an older white woman who had continued to run the store when she no longer had family working there. Theresa was fond of my uncles because she could trust them. My mother's family had a reputation for honesty. Papa had put a lot of emphasis on being truthful and honest. His mantra was, "No matter how hungry, no matter how poor, a Humphries never takes anything that isn't his!" Papa spoke these words often and his boys developed a reputation for living by these words.

Theresa relied on her hired help to do everything; ordering, inventorying, cashiering, clerking and bookkeeping. Her store became the training ground and model for the grocery and butcher shop the Humphries Brothers would open in a few years. In addition to the store, the brothers would eventually create an air-conditioning and heating installation business, a cleaner/tailor shop (Clyde's), a liquor store and an I-HOP (International House of Pancakes) franchise (Rick's). Clyde's block-long strip mall, with a Popeye's and other lucrative businesses was taken over by his widow when Clyde died in 2007. My dad's restaurant, in the late 30's proved not to be a good investment since he wasn't able to be there full time. He folded within months.

The next generation of Humphries and Hennings would expand the entrepreneurial spirit, started by my uncles in West Woodlawn during the 1930's, '40's and 50's, by establishing businesses, which, in the year 2013, operated well and employed over 30 people.

Among the businesses launched by these second and third-generation family members are a soul food company in Chicago, which my brother Kenneth owns, a production company that produces documentaries is owned by my cousin Kathleen Humphries. Real estate holdings and a strip mall are businesses run by my nephew Byron Hennings. There are other recent ventures which I've heard about, but haven't checked out yet, including a sports and entertainment agency in Arlington, Virginia.

MORE VISITORS

In addition to the relatives who sometimes bunked with us in our rented apartment, my mother's friend, Helen Brown and her family—husband and two children—often came from

Washington, D.C. where they lived most of the time, and stayed with us for a while. Helen's daughter, Rosemarie, was a year younger than I. She would sleep with Daphne and me, in our double bed, and although it was usually fun to have company, they sometimes stayed too long. Helen was married to Harold Brown whose brother was, (I was told) Edgar Brown, the well-known lobbyist for the NAACP and equally well known as a tennis player. I can remember when the Browns were with us, there would be brochures and leaflets to pass out, and people making statements through bullhorns from cars that drove slowly through the streets with posters attached to their doors.

By the time we were totally settled into 6600, we had become part of the neighborhood. We participated in all of the juvenile activities of Woodlawn A.M.E. Church; our recreational and educational activities were at McCosh School. We were enrolled in Cub Scouts, Brownie Scouts, and Thimble Theater. Evangeline Morris was the leader of the Girl Scouts and the driving force behind the Thimble Theater. She was one of the few Black teachers at McCosh School. Miss Morris worked tirelessly serving our community.

Thimble Theatre was a very active children's theatre group that produced plays to which the public was invited. The performances were first rate and the costumes were elaborate. I remember being an elf, with my sister as a flower, for a production called 'Fairyland". There must have been 50 children who were members of Thimble Theatre and the school was used for performances as well as for rehearsals. Miss Morris became my and my sister's role-model. It was because of Miss Morris' example that my sister, Daphne, became inspired, at a very early age, to become a teacher. It was a goal that she attained in spite of being overtaken by a severe illness when she was in her early twenties.

COMRADE ROBERT JOHNSON

My parents belonged to an organization which sometimes met at our house, and it had so many people in attendance that rented folding chairs had to be set up in the living and dining rooms. Almost half of the people who attended the meetings were white and all of the people were named 'Comrade'. They even called my father 'Comrade Robert Johnson', but his name was Ted Hennings. They were very nice white people, not like the ones Daddy often talked about that he encountered on the streetcar, or on one of his jobs, or the white people who were always trying to cheat Daddy out of his money at the stores. These white people smiled at us and said nice things, not like the white people whom we'd sometimes see on the opposite side of 63rd Street, who'd make fighting gestures with their fists just to scare us. They did this to make sure that we stayed on our 'south' side of the street. The only thing wrong with these white people was that we never saw them any place other than at the meetings. They didn't visit, they didn't bring their children over to play with us, and we never saw them when we were 'out walking'. And if we had seen them, would their children also be named 'Comrade'?

They shook my dad's hand and shook the hands of all the other people, black or white, attending the meeting. My dad's smile became an affixed grin at this acknowledgement of his humanity in an era when custom dictated; white people did not shake hands with 'Negroes'.

WE HAVE TO MOVE

Maybe it was the meetings. Maybe it was the visitors. Maybe it was the overnight guests. Maybe it was the commercial activities, or maybe it was that mean old dog named Hitler, who came to live with us while we still lived at 6600. He was supposed to replace Tyler, the dog we loved, who got killed, but we hated Hitler.

My sister and I were taking turns giving each other rides, by scooting the baby's high chair across the kitchen floor. Daphne accidentally dropped the chair when it was my turn to ride, because I was too heavy for her. The chair landed on Tyler and broke his back.

Maybe it was the loud noises made by five children, several child guests, and two teenage boys. Maybe it was Mom and Dad fighting, and Mom venting her terrible temper with the vilest of curse words which she would utter at the top of her lungs! Whatever the reason or reasons; I saw Mother crying, and when I asked what's wrong, she told me that we had to move!

I think my time sequence is in order as I recall the day, shortly after mother telling me we had to move, when we were all kept home from school (my dad was at work, as usual). The police, neighbors, and Mrs. Beard came into our apartment to hastily drag us onto the porch for fresh air because we all had been overtaken by gas from the oven and stove. This was another time that I noticed my mother's tears.

TYLER vs. HITLER

Our dog, Tyler, was a large, gentle, mixed-breed who had been with us before we moved to 6600. He was a good watchdog, very tolerant of our childish rough play, but very protective.

Uncle Rick tells the story of the time, when we lived in the black belt, a rent collector came to our apartment. The rent collector was sent by the owner. He was an overweight white man wearing a toupee who'd never collected rent at our home before. Mother had given him the money and was waiting for him to write out the receipt. The man—probably overtaken by Mom's beauty, and probably thinking, like so many white men, that this Negro woman would be 'easy'—started making strong advances toward her. Tyler pounced on the man with such speed and force that the man left his rent money, receipt book and toupee behind, as he ran for his life.

We buried Tyler in the back yard, under the shade of the Four-o-Clock bushes. We all missed him greatly. Someone gave us another dog right away before we fully mourned the loss of Tyler. He was fully grown, all black with medium length hair. I thought he was ugly and he sure didn't like us much. He would bark and snap at us for the least little thing. Someone started calling him Hitler and the name stuck. Hitler didn't stay with us long. By the time we moved to 6503 Rhodes, where no pets were allowed, he was gone. I never found out what happened to him, nor did I care.

OUR NEW HOME

Our new apartment wasn't nearly as nice or as spacious as 6600. It was a yellow brick building two flat, with a front façade that made the house look taller than it was. Again, we occupied the first floor but that apartment wasn't made right because we had to stand on chairs to look out of the living room windows. There was no front lawn, just cement everywhere and no porch at all. I'm sure this environment had a lot to do with my developing perception that cement was natural formation. Our front door had a cement stoop that was very close to the sidewalk, and our house was much too close to our neighbor's house. The only attempt at an aesthetic yield to compliance with the tone of the community, was a cement window box—which spanned the width of the house—in which nothing grew.

There was only one staircase. It was located right next to our front door. We could hear the clump, clump, clump noise that the second floor tenants made every time they used the stairs, and there was no porch, but we were still in West Woodlawn, and still able to attend McCosh School, which was considered, at the time, to be the best elementary school for 'colored', in Chicago. The new home did have a yard, however, it too, was mostly cement.

We had formed some friendships during our time at 6600, but nothing like the number of friendships we would make while living on Rhodes Ave. There were loads of children our ages living on our block and we took full advantage of their friendships. They were often in our apartment and we were often in their homes.

Mother would not permit any 'overnights' at our home, nor were we allowed to overnight outside the home. She would come and get us if she thought we were out too long. Another 'Mother no, no' was the beach.

JACKSON PARK BEACH

We were not permitted to go to Jackson Park Beach with other people. If Mother and Daddy were not able to take us, we couldn't go. Jackson Park Beach (which we called 'the sixty-third street beach), being the closest beach to us, had strict segregation rules, but no signs that said 'For Colored'. It was known which section was ours and we were pretty content to stay in our section. It really was the best part of the beach because it was where the land curved and afforded a great view of the entire beach. I was to learn later that Mother had an abhorrent fear of water and of us catching polio, called infantile paralysis, at the time. My siblings and I joked that Mom was so scared of water that she bathed in only one cup of water.

On those very hot Chicago days when our playmates were at Jackson Park Beach, we were practically the only ones left to play on the block. Sometimes Ronnell Bright could be heard practicing his piano lessons. Ronnell lived next door at 6505 Rhodes, and all he seemed to ever want to do was play the piano. He was very good at it. He and Theodore were the same age, about 10 at the time we moved there, and Ronnell could play 'Flight of the Bumblebee' without making any mistakes. Ronnell was the only child in his family. Rev. Bright, his grandfather, was the minister who (fourteen years later) performed my marriage ceremony. Ronnell went on to become a fine musician with a great career and for many years he was Sarah Vaughn's accompanist. It was usually one or two mothers who would take several children to the beach, but we were never among those several.

The only time that I went to Jackson Park Beach as a kid and without my parents, was after my family moved out of West Woodlawn. It was on the rare occasion when Mom allowed Daphne and me to stay overnight with the Overstreets. There was Doris, my age, and Jeannie, Daphne's age. Their mother was cousin to my Uncle Al's wife, Norma. Norma and Mrs. Overstreet (cousins) had an aunt (their mothers' sister) who was married to Mr. Fuller, the well-known Fuller Products "millionaire". The Fuller Products Line was sold from house to house, thus employing many workers. Like Amway today, the products were of the highest quality. Sometimes people would get Mr. Fuller confused with the Fuller Brush people, but that didn't prevent him from becoming highly successful, in fact it may have aided him.

Allowed to spend the weekend with the Overstreets, we awoke that Saturday to a record hot morning. We went to the beach in borrowed bathing suits, and along with the Overstreets and the childless Fullers, we enjoyed the heck out of Jackson Park Beach! In glowing terms, they discussed their recent vacation. They had actually stayed in a hotel in one of the Caribbean Islands.

It was the first time that someone, with whom I related, had shared travel experiences (other than children who went south to grandparents) and it was the beginning of a feeling that I was missing something which I should have. I secretly promised myself that someday I would travel and see the world. Whenever I think of Jackson Park Beach, I think about that particular occasion. And even though I have visited that beach many times since (as a teen-ager and as an adult) when I recall my time there, the most vivid image is the visit with Doris and Jeannie Overstreet

When Mother learned of our visit to the beach, she simply said, "I hope you girls don't come down with infantile paralysis!" Her words struck fear in my heart that lasted for days!

DRESSED UP AND STEPPING OUT

Daphne and I sat on Mother's bed transferring the contents from her everyday purse to her evening purse and watched Mother put on her new dress. It was, by far, the most beautiful dress I had ever seen. It was white satin, had long sleeves, a high cowl neckline, a train, and the back was completely missing. There was a big pink rose that was sewn to the left side of the dress and, when Mother leaned over to kiss us goodnight, the rose dangled down and winked at me. Mother's hair was waved all over and she looked prettier than any princess in any book from the library. The smell of Mother's perfume must have been the reason why, after Mom and Dad left, I had such a happy dream about Daddy and Mother, like Cinderella and her prince, dancing at the ball.

In the middle of my sleep, I was startled by loud shouts and screams in my parent's voices. I shot into the dining room to find my parents fighting each other! I started crying and screaming for them to stop. I managed to stand between them but several blows continued to be exchanged, and I got bumped and banged as they struggled against each other. At first, they didn't seem to notice me. Then, when Daddy ordered me to go back to bed, I could smell the 'drinking' smell on his breath. Daddy's speech wasn't clear, his words were slurred as he ordered me again and again to go back to bed. I usually obeyed my Dad, but this time, I didn't. Even though I was terrified, I stayed between them until they stopped fighting! Mother didn't look pretty any more. Her hair was flying all over her head, her lipstick was a mess on her face, her dress was hanging off, and the big pink rose was almost torn off her dress. She took me back to my room and she slept in the bed with Daphne and me. We both cried all night.

The next day, Mother told me, "Thanks for helping me last night. Your father had been drinking. You were brave to stay there between us, you probably kept me from getting hurt really bad, I'm proud of you!" I was six years old.

Shortly after the fight, I began to have a recurring dream. It started out with seeing huge dark red balls that moved and changed shape as they got nearer. The closer they got, the smaller they became, until they became recognizable as the bumpy raspberry Christmas candy that cut my tongue when I sucked too hard, but when I eased up on the pressure, the liquid center flowed down my throat and burned my tongue and the inside of my mouth. In the dream, the candy turned into the white part of Daddy's eyes—now as red as the candy—and I could smell the 'drinking smell' on his breath as he swept each of us children up in his arms and kissed us, squeezing us tight and calling us his baby, the way he never did when he wasn't drinking. It was a frightening dream.

AUNT HATTIE AND UNCLE LEE

For a long time after the fight, Daddy said very little to me. I thought he was mad at me because I didn't obey him when he had told me to go back to bed.

Soon, Mother started talking to me about my father. She told me Daddy was mean.

Mother said that he was a cruel man, that he had lots of faults; drinking being the worst one. I knew that Mother probably didn't mean all that she said. She just had to have somebody to talk to. Mother didn't have a mother but she had Aunt Hattie. Aunt Hattie and Uncle Lee lived near 43rd Street. The neighborhood was not nice but it was their love that made me want to go there. Uncle Lee was often in bed. He wasn't a strong man like Daddy. Aunt Hattie never had children. She was my mother's mother's youngest sister, just a few years older than Mother. Aunt Hattie had a high-pitched voice and my family teased me by saying I talked just like her and looked like her. Aunt Hattie was always kind to us children, and sometimes my mother's sister, Aunt Anna, and her children were visiting at the same time that we were there. This way we got to see our cousins; Nathan, Catherine, Christine, Daniel, Donald and Lillian. By the time Aunt Anna and Uncle Joe were through producing children, the cousins numbered 16. I still don't know all of their names.

Aunt Hattie's apartment was on the second floor over the garage where they kept their big black car, and off of a courtyard that was all cement. I am told that when I was a toddler, I had gotten my foot lodged in the drain-opening in that courtyard. It was at Aunt Hattie's that we spent the night on one or two rare occasions. When we had to go the bathroom, we always had to go downstairs to a small bathroom at the foot of the stairs in the basement. We were not allowed to use the bathroom on the same level as the apartment. We didn't question this, but in later years, I figured out that the bathroom on the second floor was for Uncle Lee, only! He died of tuberculosis when I was nineteen.

Most of the furniture in Aunt Hattie's apartment was old, smelled of furniture oil, and seemed too large for the room. Hattie and Lee had probably seen better days because they had a radio / record player console that had a setting for television, and this was long before television as we know it today, was available. Aunt Hattie and Uncle Lee did not attend the family gatherings at our house, nor did we eat at their house. Aunt Hattie was an average-size, light-skin woman who was attractive, but not nearly as pretty as my mother. She had a lot of black hair which she wore in a knot at the back of her head. She had little sense of style. Her husband still had traces of having once been quite handsome. He was dark brown and very tall, with well-proportioned features and limbs.

It was at Aunt Hattie's house that I saw my mother cry and tell her aunt about the fight. Daphne and I were ushered out of the room and sent to that barren courtyard before I could hear all that was said. I listened as intently as I could but all I could hear was an exchange of voices with Hattie's high-pitched one doing most of the talking. After the visit to Aunt Hattie's, Mother no longer talked to me about my father's faults. In fact, she seemed to go out of her way to mention that my father loved us children. Her mood improved, she seemed almost happy, but the new mood did not stop her from singing those morbid songs about losing one's mother. The one she sang the most was,

"Last night as I was sleeping, in my own small bed, an angel came from Heaven, and told me my mother was dead . . ." or she would sometimes sing,

"My mother, she's dead, she's gone away, and I wish that she was with me today . . ." Mother's voice wasn't nice to listen to like Daddy's. She made me feel sad when she sang those songs, because I knew that she was feeling sad and she sang them very often. I was constantly on the lookout for Mother's mood. I took her emotional temperature whenever I was in her presence and I generally matched my mood to hers. If she was sad, I became sad.

I continued to have the dream about the raspberry Christmas candy and it was at this time that I started making up stories in my mind. The stories were about a girl, and like a radio series, continued each day. I would tell myself 'my story' mainly when I was trying to get to sleep at night, but on occasion I would supply an episode during nap time or in the morning. Sometimes, I would lie down during the day in order to tell myself my story. In my story, the girl was not afraid. She wasn't anything like me because she was very brave. She didn't jump every time her father raised his voice, or her mother made a wisecrack comment that 'scored' on her father, and caused her to be on guard to defend her mother from him. And the girl in the story didn't wet the bed almost every night. The girl in the story didn't get demoted from the 'Robins' reading group (the most advanced) to the 'Blue Jays' (the second highest) in her class, and the girl in the story didn't have stomach aches and 'throw-up' many times during the week.

IMMUNIZED BY CATCHING IT!

It was around this time that I changed from being a healthy little girl to being quite sickly. It was probably due to having one childhood disease after another in quick succession. I missed several weeks of school and became the sickest child in the family.

My older brother, Theodore, was the one who brought home every childhood disease that we caught. Theodore seemed to have an iron clad constitution. He would get sick for a few days and shake off the illness right away—whereas I would be bed-ridden for a week or more—as each disease ravished my body. Chicken pox was the first of the childhood diseases that Theodore brought home. He had a few bumps, scratched and recovered. I had so many chicken pox bumps that they were touching each other. I even had them on my upper and lower eyelids. Before chicken pox had finished infecting all five of us, Theodore brought us measles. I became desperately ill with measles, and lost more than ten percent of my body weight. Mumps soon followed, and ran through the family in birth order; with me catching the disease from Theodore, Daphne catching it from me, and so on down the line.

Children were immunized by having caught each disease, so it was considered necessary to have the major childhood diseases while young so that one couldn't catch them in adulthood where they would be serious and cause greater harm.

Chicago's Department of Health provided large quarantine signs that were placed on our front door to warn visitors that there were communicable diseases at our house. The signs, resembling bull's eyes, were usually yellow and black (the loudest color combination, before day-glow colors were invented) and had large lettering that started out with the word, 'WARNING'. Our family 'earned' several of the signs, and did they come in handy! Long after we were no longer contagious, Mom and Dad would put the signs on the door to discourage the bill collectors from ringing our bell. I can remember those signs becoming tattered and torn but still being used. Occasionally, we would forget to remove the sign before the milkman came in the early morning and so we'd have no fresh milk that day; with the cream at the top—frozen and sticking out of the thick glass bottle as much as an inch and-a-half—in response to the frigid Chicago weather.

CLIMATE CONTROL

As much 'Out walking' as we would do in the late spring, summer and early autumn, we did no walking for pleasure during the cold days which, in Chicago was from about the second week in October until the third week in May. For more than one half of the year, we hovered in our homes and went out only when necessary. In very cold weather (several degrees below zero) the only way I could recognize my neighbors who were standing at the streetcar stop, was to recognize their clothing or voices, because everybody had on as much covering as possible and all faces were covered with scarves.

Inside our home, radiators hissed day and night drying heavy, hand-washed corduroy pants into mountainous sculptures that, in the morning, Mother ironed back into knickers or long pants, in time for them to be worn to school. And all the while, we children scratched designs into the beautiful white frost patterns we found anew on the inside of our windows each day.

The knickers belonged to my big brother who always pulled them down around his ankles. We called them knee pants because they were supposed to be worn just below the knees with heavy long wool stockings. Theodore wanted to pretend that he was already twelve years old (the age at which boys got to wear long pants) so he always stretched them down to his ankles making them into hip-huggers that wouldn't fit the hips because they were made to fit the waist. He would unbutton the top two or three buttons and freeze his unprotected mid-section. When he made it home, his belly was the first thing that he'd try to warm up.

DADDY FALLS, INJURES BOTH KNEES!

Very late one night, two policemen came to our house and took Mother and us children to the hospital. Several days before, my father had suffered an accident. While running to catch the streetcar, he'd fallen on both of his knees. He had waited for the next car, boarded it, with his knees bleeding, and gone on to work. He had not gotten any first aid for his injury, just some iodine and a crude bandage that he applied when he got home. His knees had gotten worse but he had ignored the pain and swelling.

On the day that the police came, he had been at work for several hours when he passed out and was taken to Cook County Hospital. He had developed a very high fever, was delirious, and not expected to make it through the night. The police had been summoned to bring his next-of-kin to see him one last time. Mom brought the four of us; Theodore, me, Daphne and Bubby. This happened before Arnold was born.

I can still remember the quietness of the hospital, the bleakness of the setting, the antiseptic smell and, most of all; the gripping, lingering fear that visited each of us and engulfed us like a bad spirit. Most of us were too young to grasp the full implication of why we were in that hospital room or what it meant when the doctor told Mother that Daddy might not make it through the night. The fear we felt, I am sure, was a reflection of the fear emanating from her.

Everything in the room was white. The bed was made of iron and in places the white paint was worn off to show the bare grey iron. There were many other beds just like Daddy's, in that large room and almost every bed had a man in it. Our dad was the only one who had visitors. Daddy, like most of the other men, was sleeping. He didn't wake up to give us a hug. Mother wasn't crying, although I'm sure I had heard her crying when we were in the car with the policemen, but we were so crowded in that car, that I couldn't see her well. She was up front and we were in the back seat. Now, she just gritted her teeth. She gritted her teeth a lot whenever she got mad or upset, she gritted her teeth. All of her brothers—and her sister too—gritted their teeth when they were upset about something. I later learned that Papa also gritted his teeth.

There was a crank at the foot of Daddy's bed. It looked a lot like the crank that my uncle Clyde and some other men had used on Clyde's car to make it start. That was on a day in the summer, when Clyde was taking our whole family for a ride, and the car hit a big bump in the road. The car jumped off the highway and landed on the sand near the water.

All of the people who had come to help us then were white. The beach people spoke very kindly to us and gave us soda pop to drink. Soon, after cranking it, and cranking it again, the men had the car running and lifted back onto the road. We were on our way with Theodore, Daphne and me sitting in the rumble seat. The car must not have been badly hurt because Clyde was able to drive us home in it.

Mother always told us never to go off with strangers but now she made us go off with the two white ladies, wearing white. They must have been nurses. This reminded me of our rescue from the beach.

The nurses took us to another room where there were no beds, only some hard chairs and a few small tables. We were left there by ourselves with a few old magazines. Pretty soon; two of our uncles came with Margaret (mother's best friend) and Earl (Margaret's husband). All four of us children were so scared that we were totally quiet. Theodore didn't even tease or hit us. He was perfectly still.

DADDY COMES HOME

When he got out of the hospital, Daddy didn't look the same. He had hair growing all over his face, he wasn't big anymore and his walk was very slow.

For a while Daddy was in the house a lot and it was really strange to see him at home when we came back from school, and to see him in bed in the middle of the day. But as soon as he was able to walk well again, he went back to work. Just like my brother, he had an ironclad constitution, nothing kept him down for long.

A lot of friends and family members came to our house when Daddy was sick, and at first, they were very quiet. Later on, when they would visit, there was a lot of laughing, teasing and joking. Mother, who was really good at making people laugh at her witty sayings, would tell everybody, "Yes, Ted almost died from falling on his knees. Who's ever heard of dying from hurt knees?"

Then everyone would laugh—even Daddy—and offer their own jokes or comments, such as, "Ted just wanted to get outta havin' ta spend his whole Sunday on his knees in church listening to those long-winded preachers."

This kind of humor was what our family and our extended family did best. We were all comedians. This was a case where the jokes were a way of letting us children know that Daddy was better and that things would get back to normal. Joking and teasing were ways that my family used to cope with problems. It was our major survival mechanism.

The accident had happened after Halloween, but before Thanksgiving, so it must have been in early November. Mother was very much pregnant with my brother, Arnold, who is almost eight years younger than I. In fact, Arnold was born on my sister, Daphne's birthday; December 14. They were both born on Wednesdays—six years apart.

Dad's accident must have taken its toll on our income, because that Thanksgiving, we could not afford a turkey, and the usual collection of relatives did not attend. Mother made a big meatloaf, which she tried to fashion into the shape of a turkey, but it looked more like a football. She took a feather off one of her hats and stuck it in the meatloaf, and just before Daddy blessed the table, she said, "Gobble, gobble, gobble. Happy Thanksgiving!

OH NO! NOT MY LITTLE BROTHER!

We children were playing on the pavement when I saw a man frantically carrying someone to the door of my house! Mother opened the door and the man—one of our neighbors—went in. I ran in too, along with my other siblings and several playmates. My brother, Bubby, whom I dearly loved and felt responsible for, was unconscious, but I just knew that he was dead! I screamed and cried with such fury that Mother had to leave Bubby to be attended to by neighbors while she quieted my hysteria. Bubby didn't have the ironclad constitution of my father or my brother, he was very sensitive to a lot of things but he survived that falling out, and by evening he was asking Dad to; "Park my hair and shine my shoes, so I can look like a big shop", and we were laughing at his mis-pronouncement of "part my hair" and ". . . big shot".

Bubby was teased a lot, not only by us, as older children who tease younger children, but he was also teased by Mother. We told him that we found him in the alley and that we were going to put him back in the alley. This terrified him so much that he would run like mad across all alleys when we were 'out walking', and instead of anyone trying to soothe the terror he must have been feeling, we would laugh. I can't ever remember feeling sorry for him or wanting to tell him that it was just a joke. I learned later that this kind of teasing was quite common with people from Georgia, and my Mother was from Georgia. I never found out why Bubby had fallen out!

CHRISTMAS

It was a few days before Christmas when our doorbell rang. When we answered it, no one was there. Instead, there were some un-wrapped toys on the stoop; a doll cradle, a pair of juvenile roller skates that strapped on, a spinning top and a jig saw puzzle in a box. There were five children in our family, but there were only four presents. Since Arnold was just a baby, we decided that the presents were for the four of us and there was no present for Baby Arnold. Mother's reaction to these gifts was strange. She seemed to not want us to have the presents. She kept repeating, "Who would give gifts by leaving them on the doorsteps?" She knew that we had probably been identified as a needy family and I think that she was embarrassed by this discovery. Mom talked about the gifts for days, (supposing) they came from the nursery school that Daphne and Bubby had attended. Then she did some 'maybe-ing' that they came from the church but the deliverers were too busy to come in for a visit. She even suggested that the gifts may have been left on the wrong door step. Eventually, she stopped talking about it and let us pass the gifts among ourselves.

Daddy was working more and more and was almost never home. The apartment was never well lit, even when the sun was shining directly on it, because the windows were so high. We didn't see our uncles as much as we used to since some had married and some were in the armed services. Aunt Effie and her husband had moved out, had a baby and did not visit often. Holiday dinners were still occasions for family gatherings but they had lost some of the old sparkle since they were held in that small dining room with windows up near the ceiling.

Christmas was not the time when we gathered around a tree that had been decorated for days like those pictured on Christmas cards or those at the homes of friends. In our house, the Christmas tree suddenly appeared on Christmas morning, decorated and lit, with presents, mostly unwrapped, under the tree. When I was a little older, and had been included in the process of helping to provide the magic of Christmas, I found out why Christmas wasn't ready until Christmas morning. Daddy absolutely refused to spend money on a Christmas tree. He always waited until late Christmas Eve, went out to the tree lot and got the vendors to practically give him a tree. One year, he must have been too late because all he was able to get were several branches. He rigged those branches up to resemble a tree and decorated them. They looked O.K. as long as the tree lights were on. Another time, he came home with two small trees and strung them together with wire. He said he was not going to pay good money for something that would be thrown away in a few days

For Christmas, our parents tried to get whatever we asked for. An understood rule was that we could ask for one big thing and three small things. I must have been eight years-old when I requested a desk as my big thing. I got the desk but it didn't resemble any desk I'd ever seen before. It was so thin that it looked to me as if it were made of cardboard. I was very disappointed. Somehow I knew this was probably the best that my parents could do so I masked my disappointment and pretended to like it. I don't know if I ever believed in Santa Claus. I think that I did not. From a very early age we were taught that Mom and Dad had to pay Santa Claus. Since I was one of the older children, I enjoyed bringing the Santa Claus Myth to my younger siblings. The things I got the most for Christmas were books. Most of the books were dull and on a reading level that I had not as yet attained, but I prized them, and my collection grew every year. My reading skills also grew, but I did not go back and read the old books that I had put aside because they were either still too difficult or, by the time I could read them, I wasn't that interested in them. In my mind they had become stale, but I felt they still had value.

MY EARLY SCHOOLING

When I was transferred out of St Anselm's Catholic School and enrolled in McCosh School, I had to take some tests. I remember being treated with great respect after taking the I.Q. test. I was also given a reading test simply by having the basic reader thrust into my hands and being asked to read from it. That was no problem. I easily finished the first reader. I had read it in kindergarten. I was advanced to the next basic reader (all from the Dick and Jane series) and I read that one with ease. When I was given the next one and breezed through it, the placement teacher was so impressed that she wanted to skip me to second grade. My mother could not be persuaded to skip me. In her wisdom, she felt that I should stay with my age group.

Not to skip me was a wise decision, because when I was given other material to read, which contained the same vocabulary as the Dick and Jane readers, I wasn't able to master it with such ease. My skill was reading the Dick and Jane readers because I had memorized the copy in those books from my grade level on through my brother's third level reader. Today, I can still recite from memory, the Dick and Jane primary readers.

When I worked in my high school's office, I sneaked into the files and looked up the I.Q. score on my cummulative record (the record that follows students from kindergarten through high school). I was very disappointed to learn that it was no more than 98. Average was 100 on the Stamford Binet`, which was the most popular test for measuring intelligence given to most school children during my era, and beyond. But the score didn't justify the enormous amount of respect I had received all during my school career from teachers and other educators. Also, the score had a percentage mark above it which I didn't understand. I was as a fourteen-year-old high school student sneaking a peek at forbidden records. Sure, I knew percentage and how to figure it, but had no idea how it applied to my score. I learned later I had scored in the ninety-eighth percentile, a much higher score than I had originally thought. A percentile score of 98 is a far more elevated rating than a 98 on the Stamford Binet`. The highest possible percentile score is 100. I had not been given the Stamford Binet` as the measurement test for my intelligence score.

This explained, after the fact, why my teachers—through the years—always let me know that much was expected from me, why such phrases as, "I think you can do better . . .", or "I know you can handle this . . ." were phrases with which I became familiar. And when, ". . . not living up to your potential" was another phrase that bombarded my ear, I became alternately challenged, bored or, conversely (at times) motivated—just to show that I could—but usually with little desire to sustain high achievement scores because the motivation was rarely intrinsic.

COUSIN TEDDY DIED, AUNT HATTIE CRIED!

I was almost ten years old when my cousin, Teddy, died. He was a second cousin, the child of one of my mother's uncles. I didn't know him. I don't remember him ever coming to our house to play with us. What I do remember, was feeling very sad when I saw how sad my mother became when she told us about Teddy.

A few days after hearing about Teddy, Mother had us all dressed in our best clothes, and sitting on folding chairs at Teddy's funeral. I guess the reasoning was, 'children should attend a child's funeral, just as children attend a child's birthday party.' I remember how still Teddy lay, there in his thin little brown casket, which looked somewhat like the desk I had gotten a year ago, for Christmas. I am sure it was made of the same stuff. Teddy had on a suit and a tie and his face was dark with rough-looking skin on his cheeks. He was on full view. I could see his shoes. They were brown and looked like they were made of cardboard. They looked very stiff because there was not a crease or a wrinkle in them. Teddy was near my age, but a bit older, because he had already turned ten when he died.

A lot of our family members were there; most of my uncles, my aunt Anna Mae and her family, and, of course, Aunt Hattie. There was organ music which sort of came in waves and made my heart beat faster. Then people started to speak and some started to cry. The organ music did not take its turn and stop. It continued to play all during the time that people were speaking. Sometimes the organ music got loud and that's when more people would cry. When someone was up front talking to everybody, it would get softer. I felt more frightened when the music became loud because that was when people did the most crying.

About the time I was feeling that I wanted to definitely not be here in this place anymore, somebody moved Teddy and his casket closer to us. People started to get up from their seats, go up, one-at-a-time, to take a closer look at him in his brown suit with those stiff cardboard shoes! Some of the ladies had to be helped up to the casket because they were crying so much. When I saw Aunt Hattie go up, I tried to wave to her, but she was crying, too. Then, when she got right up there next to the casket, she started to scream and make a barking kind of noise. Her arms were in the air and she stumbled so that two men had to hold her up and all the while she was screaming, "No! No! No!"

Pretty soon she stopped and just went limp. People had to help her sit down in a chair in the front row. Her hat was off her head and she looked strange. Two women were fanning her with paper fans that had wooden handles, while men held her in the chair to keep her from falling on the floor. I was afraid Aunt Hattie was going to die, too. Her eyeballs had rolled around in her eyes before she went limp. I was more frightened than I had ever been in my entire life. I looked to my mother but she was crying and almost falling out, too. Then I began to cry! My sister started to cry when she saw me crying, and the little boys, Bubby and Arnold, got into the crying business as well.

There are no words in the English language I could use to express the fear that I experienced that day. Almost everybody in my world, that I looked to for strength and protection, had been at the funeral, and they had all broken down and shown helplessness in the presence of grief. My young mind interpreted grief as terror. Aunt Hattie's grief was especially hurtful to me because she had ignored me! Nobody put arms around me to comfort me. It was a form of rejection with all of the attention going to a dead boy. A boy who couldn't even give her a hug. A boy who couldn't even give her some 'sugar', which is what she called those big wet kisses on her cheeks.

This new terror would not allow me to go to sleep in a dark room, or to have the bedroom door closed, or to have the heavy blanket removed from our bed, no matter how warm the temperature became. Daphne seemed to experience the same intensity of terror because she exhibited the same fears. Wetting the bed had always been a problem for my sister and me, usually happening one or two nights a week. After Teddy's funeral, it occurred almost every night. In fact we became bed-wetting champions. This fear remained with us for years after attending Teddy's funeral.

When Daphne and I reached the period of our lives, that all young girls go through, where everything is funny, and we'd literally fall down laughing—unable to control our mirth—we would quiet each other's laughing binges by reciting, "Teddy died and Aunt Hattie cried."

Like throwing cold water on a fire, that statement would sober us up from the mirth-convulsions we experienced as we went through the silly period where almost everything provoked laughter. But, "Teddy died and Aunt Hattie cried" would recall such terror that the laughter would immediately stop.

SPEAKING 'DOG AND CAT'

Mother and Daddy discussed many things that were mature subjects right in front of us children. They did it in a language they called 'dog and cat'. It consisted of some neutral words, with some other juicy words spelled out in 'dog and cat'. The initial consonant is used and 'us' is added, so that a word beginning with the letter b would be spelled 'bus', along with its remaining letters. The exception was that the letter H was pronounces 'hash'. Vowels were pronounced with no change. For example: Mother might be telling Daddy about an encounter with a saleswoman: ". . . so the old bus-i-tus-cus-hashs says, "I'll wait on you after I see what this gentelman wants. ". . . and you know that he was an ol' cus-rus-a-cus-kus-e-rus that she was waiting on; when it was my turn, and she knew it!"

It didn't take us long to figure out how to talk in dog and cat. I was the one who interpreted it for my older brother, who didn't seem to care about wanting a translation unless he heard,. ". . . tus-hash-e-o-dus-o-rus-e", then he was all ears! Daphne only cared when I indicated she should. Bubby was also quick to pick up on dog and cat. He seemed to have no filter on the things he could learn. He was so bright and quick, that even though he was almost four years younger than I, he was my peer in learning. He and I were the children most concerned about interpersonal relations, scoring (called 'playing the dozens', today) and assessing the moods of our parents. Bubby became a very nervous little boy. His breathing sometimes became panting and he developed a tic. He did everything extremely fast and became the best game-player in our household, especially in checkers. Bubby and I practiced dog and cat for long periods at a time. It took Mom and Dad only a little while to find out that we knew their secret language.

I don't remember liking dolls all that much. I had dolls, some soft ragdoll types, and some that were hard bodied, but none of the dolls I owned could compare with the real live babies that Mother brought home from the hospital. I knew that they grew inside her 'stomach' and they came out in the hospital, but I really did not know how those babies got out of my mother's body until I was in my late teens. I had seen my mom in the bathtub (in her 'cup of water') so I knew there was no scar on her belly where she had been cut open. I reasoned that the babies came out below, but I just couldn't believe it. There was no sex education in school or at home that taught this. The only sex education my sister and I received was, "Don't EVER let a boy so much as TOUCH you!"

These words were repeated often enough to become Mom's mantra. We knew that being 'touched' by a boy would result in pregnancy, for certain, and we had been thoroughly brain-washed to consider pregnancy the worst thing that could happen to us. When Daphne was about twelve years old, we were with a group of children, laughing and playing, and one of my brother's friends just happened to touch her on her arm. Daphne worried for weeks that she was pregnant. I did not take the 'touch' warning so literally. I knew what Mother meant.

MAKING GOOD USE OF TIME; BEFORE T.V.

During the more carefree days of my very young life, there were always many people around and always lots of things to do. Some of my favorite activities were: giving pennies to the organ-grinder's monkey and watching him tip his cap in a salute before he put the money into his master's tin cup. Some organ-grinders didn't bother to cut their monkey's fingernails and the monkey would scratch us as it took coins from our palms.

On rainy days, drawing pictures on the stiff cardboard that came with shirts returned from the laundry was a fun way to spend the time. I don't know who supplied the cardboards. My father didn't wear starched dress shirts to work every day but we always seemed to have the cardboards. Often, we would draw something and ask Mother to identify what it was. Whatever she replied, was what it was in my mind too. I would ask Mother to draw a picture of me, and she always drew the same picture. It was a girl with two long braids, with a wide-skirted dress and arms stretched out to either side. In one hand, she is holding a bag of candy with a candy cane and a lollipop protruding from the top of the bag. The drawings were so precious to me that I would sleep with the pictures. Although my hair was short and stubby, mom would always make it long in her pictures. Hair signified beauty. My mother's hair was long and crimpy, not kinky, and she wondered aloud why her daughters had short hair that would not grow. These musings on my hair gave me an inferiority complex about hair. Daphne's hair was also short, but since it was curly-crimpy, somewhat like Mother's, ending in ringlets which framed her face, it was kind of pretty. According to my mother, and, of course, to me as well (because

51

I learned that if something was O.K. with Mother, it was O.K. with anything in my world) the hot straightening comb was the only way I thought I could look decent.

Roller-skating on the street, with my skate key on a string around my neck, was another favorite activity. We didn't know that there were rinks where we could skate inside until I was almost ten-years-old. When the roller skates become old, we'd take them apart with a plier and use them to make a scooter or a milk box derby racer. An old milk box, which was an eighteen inch cube, would be pressed into service and have a wooden plank or a two-by-four nailed to it. One skate section was nailed to the end of the plank to form the section for foot operation. The other skate section was nailed under the milk box as the steering section. The result was a scooter that really worked.

The derby racer employed almost the same materials, but would need two skates, or, if you were lucky enough to have some doll buggy wheels, they would make a better racer.

I was very excited to make my first (and only) scooter, Theodore was helping me nail the skates onto the wood. Because the wood was so thick, he got tired and quit. I was so determined to finish the job that I banged on that long nail until it bent. Testing the skate section to see if it would hold, I determined that it would. Though more than half of the nail was not secured and sticking out dangerously, I launched my new scooter for a test run. I don't think the skate wheels got a chance to make three revolutions before they fell off and the bent nail made an ugly gash in my leg. Crying, I ran to Mother, but she gave me no sympathy. She scolded me and said, "I told you about always trying to do what the boys do. Those scooters aren't for girls!"

The truth is that Mother never told me not to make a skate scooter and she sure surprised me with her response. She made me do my own first aid of pouring iodine on the wound and wrapping a clean rag around it. It bled for quite a long time and took very long to heal. Today, I still have that ugly, gouged-out scar on my right leg, just above my ankle.

After my leg injury, I looked for quieter activities. I had never thought doll buggy parades were much fun. Daphne was always joining one, but I was usually looking for something more exciting. Now the parade had a new appeal. Doll buggy parades were held in and around the school. Bicycles and buggies were decorated with crepe paper by the children who owned them. Every child did not own a bicycle. No one in my family had a bike before my older brother, Theodore, was twelve-years-old and came home with one that he claimed he found. In fact, there were always more buggies in the parade than there were bicycles. The idea was to parade around the neighborhood and show off the creative work you had done to your doll buggy. The adult judges awarded prizes for the best decorated. I joined the parade by helping my sister with her entry. We didn't win a ribbon but we got a box of Cracker Jacks just for participating. Only one box was given for each buggy. I remember thinking how nice it would be to have a whole box of Cracker Jacks. This was as stingy as going to the park with my family. We always had to share the box of Cracker Jacks with a sister or brother. For once it would have been nice to have a whole box all to myself.

Sharing with a sister or brother was for Cracker Jacks or Cream sickles, not for ice cream bars or popcorn. Every day, the ice cream man came to our street peddling his white bicycle cart, and ringing his tingling little bell. When there was money for each of us children to get a whole ice cream bar, we would choose the chocolate-dipped, single stick, vanilla bar. When money was tight, Mother would ask for two Cream sickles. Cream sickles had two sticks, with the frozen goodies topping each stick. Mom would break each in half and serve the four of us. Sometimes Theodore had his own money. He was very ambitious about running errands and would sometimes hire me, Daphne and even Bubby, to do some of his chores. We would clean up his room, wash out his tub, do dishes, shine his shoes, or any other work he was avoiding. Then he would sell us something and get the money back, in those rare instances when he paid us what he promised.

More than the ice cream man, I looked forward to the popcorn man each day. The popcorn cart also had bicycle mechanisms attached to it, but it was much larger than the ice cream cart. The popcorn cart had a calliope built into it. It would park at the end of the block and send out its loud bursts of sound, along with its wafting scent of popping corn, carried on the Chicago winds. It didn't try to make a stop at every house, like the ice cream man, it didn't have to, we all headed to the popcorn cart like metal filings near a magnet.

MOTHER, MY HERO!

My mother was my hero. I admired how brave she was. She never let the white people who worked in stores, or as service people, insult her dignity. She was always ready to tell somebody off when she thought she was being wronged. One day, she saw the perfect dress in the window of a store on Sixty-Third Street.

She went into the store and asked to see the dress in her size. The sales woman was very nasty to her. She replied that there was no size fourteen in that dress. Mom went over to the section that contained the dresses and immediately found her size. The woman wouldn't let Mom try on the dress, so Mother stood over to the side, where she couldn't be seen from the street, and slipped the dress on over the dress she wore. It was tight, but she could tell that it would fit. All the while, the saleslady was protesting and spewing out epithets about, ". . . you people!"

Mom reached in her purse and counted out the money to pay for the dress and the sales woman became quiet and even supplied a box in which to put the new purchase. After all, it was the depression era (which, for our people, lasted a lot longer than it did for others) and the store clerk was not about to pass up a sure sale. I'll never forget that dress. It was made of powder blue rayon crepe with cap sleeves, shoulder pads and a skirt that had a side drape and flounce. Mom wore it many times before it started to fade. She was in the habit of giving her dresses away to Daddy's sisters, when they came to visit but she never gave that one away! For many years, it served as catalysis for re-telling the story of how it was acquired.

MY UNCLES GO TO WAR

Four of my uncles served in the armed services during World War 2. Sol, Rick and Sidney were in the infantry and Bob was in the navy. Al had hurt his leg and was not eligible. Clyde had lost a leg when he was about ten-years-old, and Mitchell did not meet the size requirement.

UNCLE MITCHELL

Uncle Mitchell was rarely part of our family gatherings. He would show up sometimes with that drinking smell on his breath, and he would sometimes bring his lady, Tillie, with him. Mother would let us see just enough of the disapproval that she would register to inform us that Mitchell's life style was not something to which she wanted us to aspire. Mitchell was very generous. He would dole out money to us, and grab us around the neck, in the crook of his arm and ask us (in that sing-song-y, high-pitched soprano voice of his) how our lives were going? He would ask about girlfriends, or boyfriends, and then he would make promises: "I will come and take everybody to Riverview." Or, he would promise, "I will bring my friend, who owns a car, to take ya'll on a ride." I don't think he ever fulfilled any of his promises but, in his way, he let us know that he cared about us.

Uncle Mitchell was the toughest cat on the south side. He may also have been the smallest. Though Mitchell never grew to be any larger than a ten-year-old boy he was perfectly formed; no dwarfism or deformities. In fact, Mitchell was a very handsome miniature man. He had a smooth olive complexion and coal-black wavy hair, a thin mustache and fine features. He must have had his clothes tailored, because he always dressed in the latest style. He sometimes wore a two-toned light brown jacket with a built-in belt in the back. The jacket had a leather collar and leather buttons. The shoes he wore with the jacket were brown and white pointed-toe spectator oxfords. He also had a zoot suit made out of a hard menswear grey flannel. The reason I remember these particular outfits so well is that he handed them down to my little brother. My brother, Kenneth, still boasts that he was the only boy in kindergarten with a zoot suit and brown and white pointed-toe spectator oxfords.

Mitchell was every inch a man, being small in stature didn't seem to take away any of his manhood; in fact, it probably aided in his tough, self-image. Being small provided him with a chip for his shoulder that was, (in his imagination) constantly being knocked off by the biggest man in any gathering (usually a bar). In Mitchell's mind this called for defending himself, always uttering the declaration, "Just because you're the biggest one here, don't mean I can't beat your ass! I may be little, but I can whip men twice my size."

When Mitchell made his threat, he was prepared to carry it out. It all depended on the response to his brazen talk and how much alcohol he'd consumed. If the man didn't respond with a challenge—which was usual, most big men were amused by his threats—Mitchell would poke at him, or attempt to shove him until he became angered and said something like, "Aw, get away from me, Shorty. I don't want to have to hurt you."

Then Mitchell would whip out his knife or razor and show the blade. This would elicit a response from the big man to show that he capitulated to the power of the weapon carried by the little man. The verbal response would be something like, "O.K. you win, you're the toughest!"

Usually this would satisfy Mitchell and he would seek other challenges, but not always. By vocation, Mitchell was a butcher and when my uncles opened Humphries Brothers' Food and Butcher Shop, Uncle Mitchell left his job at a meat market to become butcher in the store. There are many stories which accumulated in our family-stories' lexicon about how his pugnacious temperament played out in a business setting.

The story repeated most is the one about Mitchell, one spring day, eyeing a certain customer in the store. He was a big man, probably over six feet—just the kind Mitchell liked to challenge—and weighing over two hundred pounds.

As Mitchell weighed up pork chops for another customer, then wrapped the order in butcher's paper, he kept his eyes peeled on the guy. All of a sudden, Mitchell darted from behind the counter, wielding a huge butcher knife, and caught up with the man who was just about to step out of the store! Mitchell slashed the front of the man a few times with his knife—shouting obscenities at him—and a whole ham fell from under his overcoat! The ham was cut to the bone!

Clyde, who was in charge at the cash register, thought Mitchell had gone berserk and was killing a customer. The man was unharmed but his coat was destroyed.

Later, when Mitchell was asked how he knew the man was stealing, he said,

"He had to be up to no good. He was wearing a heavy wool overcoat and it's too hot for that!"

HALLOWEEN

My Baby brother, Arnold, was beginning to talk, even though he hadn't taken his first step yet and wouldn't until he was about 20 months old. The Halloween when I was eight, we all marched around in the schoolyard to show off our homemade (for the most part) costumes and then went home to a party at our apartment. We bobbed for apples in spite of the fact that Angela's little brother had a runny nose and snotted up the water in the pan of apples. No one managed to snare an apple with his or her mouth but Nellie got one by grabbing onto the stem with her teeth.

After the party and dinner, we were put to bed. I don't know how long we slept, but we were awakened by my Mom and three uncles. We got dressed again but not in our costumes. We walked to the local vacant lot where a huge bonfire raged; burning up lawn furniture (mostly wicker) and other things that had been left on stoops and porches. This was the custom for Halloween since 'Trick or Treat' had yet to be established. Everyone knew that you should take inside anything of value that you didn't want on the Halloween bonfire. Someone raked white potatoes out from the fire and passed them around. I can still remember trying to hold onto that hot potato by passing it from my right hand to my left, over and over, and how it warmed my hands against that cold Chicago night and how good it tasted when it finally got cool enough to eat.

GIRL, DON'T YOU JUMP ROPE!

Most of our ailments were treated with home remedies. For colds, mom would grate onion and mix it with honey. Minor burns were treated with a mixture of soap and baking soda (which never left a mark). The box of baking soda was also brought out to dose stomach aches. Oil of clove dulled a toothache and smelled up the house. If the toothache was so severe that the sufferer kept everyone in the house from sleeping that night; in the morning, he or she would be taken to the dentist for an extraction. Most of us had weak teeth like my dad's, not strong ones like my Mom's. By the time we were grown, all of my siblings, except my baby sister, Sandra, had experienced tooth loss. In those days before fluoride in toothpaste, we had no decay-prevention program and we did not brush regularly. My brother, Ken, took his partial denture out of his mouth and absent-mindedly placed it on the passenger seat of his car. When he picked Mother up to give her a lift to the doctor, she sat on it and swore that Ken bit her in the place where the "Sun don't shine".

Dr. Beasley came to our house when someone was sick, and he also came about twice a year to check on everyone's health. When Dr. Beasley examined my chest with his stethoscope, I became embarrassed when I saw mother's reaction. The tiny nipples on my chest had expanded. They no longer looked like the nipples on my sister Daphne's chest. My mother's reaction to the examination showed how embarrassed she was when she asked me,

"Where is the new undershirt I gave you to wear? You are to wear it at all times, do you hear me? At all times! Day and night! Do you understand?" And she said it in such an accusing manner that I figured I must have done something wrong by taking it off.

The 'undershirt' was a pretty white cotton camisole with tiny vertical pleats and three tiny buttons. It was supposed to hide the fact that I was beginning to sprout bosom. Breasts, growing on her not yet eight-year-old daughter, was not something Mother wanted to happen. She wasn't able to stop them but she sure didn't want the world to know. In her mind, girls who developed early tended to be 'fast'. And 'fast' girls got bad reputations and needed watching when they were around boys. I didn't wonder, at the time, 'who watched over you, Mom? You must have developed early because you've got big breasts!'

The breasts continued to develop and by the time I got fitted for my first brassiere, at nine years old, before I was allowed to go outside each day, Mother was cautioning me,

"Girl, Don't you jump rope!" Mom was not about to have any 'bosom-bouncing' child of hers being stared at by men and older boys in the neighborhood.

My sister, Daphne, could jump rope. In fact, she became quite good at it. She was naturally athletic, small for her age and very aggressive. Whereas, I was big for my age, very clumsy and shy. Daphne loved telling the story of the girl who was choking me when she came to my rescue by dropping to her hands and knees and biting the girl on her leg. People who didn't know us well assumed that there were at least four years difference in our ages but we were only a year and nine months apart.

Mother was my hero but I knew at an early age that she had faults. She often used foul language, she had a terrible temper and talked about people in a way that I was later to label 'gossip'. Her good traits greatly overshadowed her faults; she was enormously generous, if Daddy brought home an order of barbecue ribs for her—the smell having awakened us—she'd give each of us a rib, and sometimes there'd be none for her. She was very hard-working and washed all of our clothes by hand. I was twelve years old before we got our first clothes washer (with the manually operated wringer). Mom was extremely witty; she could always come up with just the right retort or snap. Her intelligence was respected by her many friends who sought her counsel. Mom was highly principled in the Biblical style she learned from her religious father. She was ambitious about 'getting ahead'—taking in sewing projects and doing hair—earning money by working at home. Mother was also very creative she could make a meal out of what seemed like nothing. She could create a new dish that was quite tasty out of a few scraps of ingredients. She invented a recipe that didn't have a name. It was canned tomatoes with bread baked in it. I'm sure it was invented out of necessity but it became a hit with us and she served it often.

DESSERT? DESERT THE TABLE!

Mom tried to always finish off a meal with something sweet, but when she had made no dessert and we would ask, "What's for dessert?" She would answer, "Dessert? desert the table!" And if we complained about something she served us, she let us know that we didn't have to eat it. We always had a choice. We could eat it, or we could, not eat it! Those were our two choices. Daddy would punctuate the choice idea by repeating, "When you get hungry enough, you'll eat anything!" And make us sit there until we, . . . 'got hungry enough!'

Dad also knew his way around the kitchen. He would prepare the meals when Mother was in the hospital bringing us another boy. He even had the opportunity to prepare the holiday turkey one year. It was a tradition in our home to have slivers of turkey, in gravy, served over grits, for breakfast the day after the holiday. We all loved and looked forward to this treat.

Searching the pantry shelves, Dad found no grits. He served turkey and gravy over oatmeal, and then tried to bully us into eating it. When he tried to make an example out of his own axiom of, 'When you get hungry enough, you'll eat anything!' by tasting it himself, he sputtered and spat, and dismissed us from the table.

BESSIE—BESS—BETTY

Mom had many friends and more people were attracted to her than she could ever have had the time to befriend. She had a very soft heart for children who had a tough time. She had grown up the hard way—losing her mother at age eleven—and taking on the responsibility of seeing after her eight siblings. She had a first-hand understanding of what it meant to be under-privileged.

Although her name was Elizabeth, my mother's family called her Bessie. My dad called her Bess. She told me Bessie was the name assigned to her at an early age because she used to stare at the cow whose name was Bessie and imitate the mouth motions the cow made while chewing her cud.

MY MOTHER'S VERY ROUGH YOUTH

When Mom's mother was in the hospital and knew she was dying, she asked my mother (who had sneaked up to see her, against hospital regulations) to bring all of the children to her bedside so that she could see them one last time. Mother complied. She was somehow able to show up at the hospital with eight children; ages, a few months (Solomon) to twelve-years-old (Mitchell). It was during this visit that Anna Humphries (my grandmother) said, "Bessie, I want you to promise to always take care of your brothers and sister. Keep them all together and ya'll always live together in The Lord!" Shortly after this promise was made, Anna died.

After losing his wife, the mother of his nine children, Walter was so distraught that he kept Bessie home from the little bit of school that she had been able to attend before losing Anna. Bessie became the cook, housekeeper and surrogate mother to the whole brood.

Before going off to work each morning, Walter gave Bessie fifty cents, instructing her to buy food for the family for the day. Mom told me that she would almost always buy the same things; twenty cents worth of 'streak-o-lean' (salt pork), a head of cabbage for ten cents, five cents worth of okra, a five-cent bag of corn meal, to make corn bread, two eggs at a penny each, a five cent bottle of milk for Solomon the baby, and the three-cent box of vanilla wafers that she would reward herself.

She knew to start cooking the salt pork long before putting in the cabbage, otherwise the meat would be tough if she put them both in the pot at the same time and she'd have to cook the cabbage down to slime before the meat softened. Then she would put in the cabbage and okra and make the corn bread. When she had the corn bread baking in the oven, she would wet the vanilla wafers by pouring water down into the box so that the wafers became mushy, then she'd scrape her hand into the box, and, with great delight, eat the mushy reward.

As Mother told me this story, I asked, "Why would you wet the cookies, why didn't you just eat them plain?" She answered, "I don't know. I just liked them wet. Remember, I was only eleven-years-old."

Mother continued the story of her youth by telling me about the period when her father, Walter, didn't come home from work.

"We hadn't seen Papa for several days and we had eaten all the food in the apartment. Solomon was crawling around on the floor in a soiled diaper trying to drink from a baby bottle that had been empty all day. He would sit and cry for a while but seemed to realize that there was no use crying. He would shut up and start again when one of the hunger pains hit him."

"What about the other kids, how did they deal with being so hungry?" I asked. "They did a lot of sleeping I think some may have been beyond hunger." Mother said. She continued, "I told the two oldest boys, Mitchell and Sidney, 'Ya'll better go out and steal us some food! I don't care what Papa say! We ain't gon'a starve just 'cause Papa gone!'"

"After a while, Mitchell and Sidney came running up the stairs shouting, 'Bessie, open the door!' They were carrying a peck basket of okra, that's one of those cone-shaped baskets—it doesn't hold as much as a bushel basket—that's all they had managed to steal and two Irish cops were right behind them, running up the stairs too."

"When the cops saw our apartment and all nine of us children, with the baby crawling around in his dirty diaper, sucking his empty bottle, and the rest of us huddled together, scared almost out of our skins, they wanted to know where our mother was. We told them she's dead. We told them that we hadn't seen our father for many days and those big strong cops looked around our almost empty apartment, went from room to room, poked around our kitchen, opened and closed our empty ice box (with no ice or food in it), and one of them sat down and cried."

"They took money out of their own pockets and gave it to me so that I could get something to eat for all of us and some milk for the baby. The next day, people from The Children's Aid Society came and took us all to foster homes."

Throughout my childhood, my mother told me stories about her young years after the death of her mother. Life was very hard for her and her sister, Anna Mae. The foster homes where they were placed left much to be desired. The biggest problem was trying to avoid being raped. Since Mom and her sister were always placed together in the same foster home, the two of them looked out for each other. Sometimes they had no idea where their brothers were. All nine of the children joined in the search for their siblings at one time or another. Anna Mae and Bessie became known to the placement agency as run-aways because they had to escape in the night, many times, to get away from the advances of men or older boys. The girls always wore all of the clothes they owned at the same time, which wasn't much, as a way of guarding against rape. That solution worked because they were able to protect themselves with layers of ragged clothes. They slept in many a door-way and many building vestibules.

Before home conditions forced her to leave school, Mother had made friends with two sisters, Margaret and Helen Allen. When the Chicago weather became too cold to sleep outdoors, Margaret and Helen would sneak Bessie and Anna Mae into their big spacious home at 4444 Vincennes Ave. and allow them to sleep on the floor in their bedroom. Their mother, Mrs. Allen, a widow with 5 teen-agers, took in two roomers as a way to make ends meet. She certainly didn't need any more responsibilities. Nevertheless, when she found out about the extra two girls living in her house, she couldn't evict them; they became part of her household. Mrs. Allen even enrolled the girls in school. Life became almost normal for Bessie and Anna Mae.

The boys had been placed in two separate foster homes. The two older ones, Mitchell and Sidney became wards of the court for juvenile delinquents and spent some time in a group home. The three youngest boys were placed in the home of a married couple whose last name was Humphrey who lived on 47th and Langley. Since the boys' last names were Humphries, Mrs. Humphrey tried to pass these cute, curly-haired boys off as her nephews. She really seemed to love them. She was childless, had never taken in foster children before and wanted to be a good mother to them. Mrs. Humphrey fed them well, enrolled them in school when they became of age, and even supplied them with piano lessons. The two middle boys (Al and Robert/Bob) were in another court-appointed foster home.

Mrs. Humphrey had some kind of abcess on one of her legs; with a gaping sore that would not heal. She kept it covered with a white bandage, and she would often sit and rub it. Someone reported this to the Division of Social Services, saying that the sore might be contagious. Without hesitation, the children were taken from her home to another foster home down the street, run by a man everyone called Dr. Miles

One day, just as mysteriously as he had disappeared, Papa reappeared. I don't know whether Mother told me and I forgot or if she never told me the details of how Papa got his family back together, but I do remember her telling me that he had 'flipped out'. The stress of losing his wife, working and trying to provide for nine children, had made him suffer a nervous breakdown. Papa established a home again and quickly married, with the idea of providing a mother for his children.

A NEW STEPMOTHER, ONE OF A SERIES!

The new "mother's" name was Ms Gaines. Like so many black people from the south, who were never addressed with any kind of title (Miss, Mrs., Rev. or Mr.) by white people from the south, they chose to bestow the honor upon each other. Good friends, who were on the best of terms, addressed each other by their last names and used titles. So Ms Gains was called Ms Gains by everyone, including her new husband, whom she called Rev. Humphries (Papa was honored with the tittle of, "Rev." even before he was ordained).

The "new mother" didn't last long. She was just the first of a series of women—whom Papa took as wives—and who found themselves being rejected, plotted against, told on, lied on, lied to and undermined by nine children resenting anyone trying to step into their dead mother's role. In all, Papa had seven wives.

At the end of Papa's life, he had to be placed in a nursing home; he was about 84 years old and in very poor health. A woman who worked in the nursing home took him out of the nursing home, married him, and took excellent care of him in her home until she died. I guess he was what is called a ladies' man. Women seemed to love Rev. Humphries. He was probably good-looking in his youth but I don't ever remember seeing any pictures of him as a young man. By the time I noticed him as a distinct human being, his curly hair was already greying at the sides. He was quite short—about five feet, three inches tall, with very erect posture. He wasn't heavy, nor was he skinny. His head was rather square and he gestured with his hands when he talked. Papa's skin was the color of a Brazil nut and he had hair growing out of his ears.

In later years, when I became more interested in knowing my family background, I learned why Papa had moved his family (pregnant wife and eight children) out of Georgia, leaving his farm and other holdings.

Papa and his three brothers had gotten into some kind of altercation where a white man was killed. Papa and one brother (the one they called Pig) had been able to escape. Two other brothers were apprehended by Klu Klux Klan members and put into the "crazy house" (the Georgia insane asylum was located in the same town where they lived) in Milledgeville, Ga., and it was said that they had to be crazy to be involved in a fight where a white man died. The two brothers would probably have been lynched if it had not been for the fact that the white man who owned most of the property in Milledgeville was the biological grandfather to my grandfather, and everyone in the town knew it. The family had enjoyed a level of freedom and prosperity unheard of for "coloreds" in those days. It was because of the un-spoken respect townspeople held for Mr. J.U. Humphries that they were allowed to continue living. If a white person attempted to comment on the behavior of one of the Humphries brothers, he'd be quickly reminded, "That's one of J. U.'s grandchildren!"

But J. U.'s influence could not override the meting-out of punishment to two of my great uncles. They both lived for several more years and the one named Cornelius died in a mental institution in Michigan. The other one, whose name escapes me, is assumed to have died in the mental institution in his home town of Milledgeville, Georgia.

My grandmother, Anna, had hurriedly sold her sewing machine to get travel money for Papa's escape. Anna was pregnant with their ninth, surviving child (three had died in infancy), Solomon was born in Gary, Indiana, which is where the family settled. A few months later, when Anna became so sick that she required the kind of medical care only to be found in a big generous city like Chicago, the family moved there. The year was 1924; Anna Green Humphries was thirty-three years old.

MY MOTHER'S PARENTS' BACKGROUNDS

(Researched and written by Cousin Kathleen Humphries—Rick's Daughter—for The Humphries' Family Reunion, in 1982)

THE GREENS

Anna Green was born in 1890, the daughter of Lizzie Thomas and Joseph Green. Sometimes Joseph was referred to as Sidney Green Jr. because he was the son of a wealthy, white, Irish slave-owner named Sidney Green, who raised him in the tradition of the "young master". Joseph was frequently taken on trips with his father, Sidney, and taught the business of trapping, buying and selling furs from trappers, and introduced to the commercial side of slave-ownership. In fact, Sidney devoted as much time as he could to his son, who, it was reported, looked exactly like him. When Joseph was a very young boy, he and Sidney returned home from one of their trips to find Joseph's mother lynched and hanging on the plantation gate.

Years earlier, Sidney had bought Joseph's mother at a slave market in Virginia. He had fallen in love with this beautiful African girl, and made no secret of his feelings. Sidney moved his love out of the fields and into his home. There, he out-fitted her with servants, clothes and the respect befitting the mistress of the plantation.

Needless to say, Sidney's peers were less enthusiastic about this "unholy union". Recognition was reserved for their own kind, and Sidney was breaking the rules; upsetting the "divine order" of life in South Georgia, which Joseph's birth and Sidney's pride in his son, had made even worse. Sidney learned the kind of wrath his "sin" of loving a black woman could incur when, there; on the gate to his own plantation hung the lynched body of his "wife". The "divine order" once again reigned!"

Joseph, (or Sidney Jr. my great grandfather) some years later; after emancipation, met and married Lizzie Thomas; a light-skinned 'colored' girl. They had seven or eight children, one of them was my grandmother; Anna. Another was my great aunt; Mae Lizzie, (who could pass for my mother's twin if they had been in the same generation). Great Aunt Ellen was tall and stately and owned a barber shop in Detroit when I was growing up. Aunt Hattie (my favorite) was the youngest of the Greens. They were so miscegenated that most of them could pass for white but none of them did. In fact, they all seemed to try to recapture their missing color by marrying spouses who were dark-skinned.

Bouge and Judy (great uncles to me) were my grandmother's two brothers who were alcoholics and always in trouble with the law. One of them had been married and had a son. That son became the most well-thought-of male in this family of hard-drinking frivolous "good-time" people. Ernest Green was an Olympic swimming and diving champion during the 1930s.

Joseph Jr. also settled in Detroit, Michigan, and married a beautiful, petite brown-skinned girl named Rose. And even though Joseph Jr. was my mother's uncle, he and Rose had two children who were the ages of my brother, Theodore, and me. Joseph Jr. died very early and didn't see either of his children grow up. His daughter, Helen (my second cousin) and I became great friends, even though we lived in different cities.

When Anna died, on November 15, 1925 (of acute anemia) the Greens attempted to take the children away from Walter. Mother Lizzie, (whom everyone called "Pet") arrived from Georgia with the thought that she and her husband, Joseph (who was, by then, called "Pa") would return to Georgia after the funeral with some of the older children who could work on their farm, and thus make up for the loss of their own children who had moved to the big cities of Chicago and Detroit during the period of the "Great Migration".

Pa and Pet never anticipated taking all nine of the children under their care. Walter was vehemently opposed to the idea of the Greens, whom his family considered "common yellow trash", having any hand in raising his children, and he was adamant about the children not being separated.

Walter and Anna had fallen in love despite the long-standing animosity between the Greens and the Humphries. During the early part of the twentieth century, both families prospered. The Greens were known to spend their money on drink and having a good time. To them, life was a party to be enjoyed;

THE HUMPHRIES

The Humphries had been raised with pride, culture, and a reverence for religion and education. All three of Walter's sisters became school teachers, one of the noblest careers of that era. They were the children of a pseudo-aristocratic French Creole father (the son of J.U. Humphries) and a newly-freed African bondwoman.

The Greens, for the most part, felt uncomfortable with the Humphries' family lineage of light and dark-skinned people out of the same family, with an odd mix of features and hair textures. They resented their snobbish penchant to instruct and pass judgement on the behavior of those who were not as churchgoing or Bible-reading as they were.

LISTENING

I eagerly learned my mother's history as I worked beside her; snapping string beans or washing greens, or mixing the orange-colored, pea-sized food coloring packet into the white gelatinous matter to make yellow margarine. I was a very good listener and did not much miss jumping rope. I also listened to all the things Mother would rather I not hear. When I should have been sleeping, I listened to my parents' arguments. I listened to conversations between Mother and her visiting friends as well as her side of the talks on the telephone. From these listenings, I learned things I probably should not have. I learned about Manta's husband's accident with another woman in the car. I found out how Mother's pretty friend, Gwen (who was very fat) died. She couldn't stop eating the holiday ham she had prepared for company. She kept sitting there at her table, cutting chunks off the ham and eating it, until almost nothing was left but the bone. Gwen became so stuffed with ham that it killed her.

I learned that my father's brother, Edward, who had come up from the south, and did not stay with us, had sat me on a hot stove when I was a toddler. I still had the burn mark on back of my right thigh, and that's why mother was especially watchful of her children when Uncle Edward, the uncle with no toes, was near.

I was also very generous with any knowledge I garnered by listening, and I became the object of my big brother's hatred as I told on him whenever I got the chance. He would call me 'Nosey' as if that were my name. Of course, I'd tell on him for calling me a name. Sometimes my parents responded to my tattling and sometimes they ignored me. I often felt abandoned when my tattlings were not heeded and Theodore would increase the name-calling, insults, and even physical blows. I disliked his bossiness and I was becoming more afraid of him. My response to him was to become more sassy, critical and disdainful of his break-all-rules behavior. He would say, "You always wanna do what you're supposed to do, but I DO what I wanna do!" In fact, he punched me so often, he must have thought I was his own personal punching bag!

The apartment at 6503 Rhodes was not cherished by our family and almost as soon as we moved in, Mother was trying to move us out. There were always vacant apartments in our neighborhood which we visited regularly. We might be returning from the store when Mother would say, "Let's go down this alley on our way home. I want to stop in some place." No key or agent was necessary to see the apartment, we'd just walk in.

The place was often several blocks out of our way and it's a good thing there were no frozen foods in those days, or they would have melted. Ice cream was not a staple. It was a luxury we got on rare occasions. Even at birthday parties; we couldn't be sure there would be more than a dab of ice cream on top of a lot of 'Jell-o' and some heavy, grandmother-made, cornbread-textured cake. The measure of a good party was in how generous a portion the ice cream was served.

ON RELIEF

One time, apartment searching became an alibi. Theodore, his little red wagon and I, had gone with Mother to pick up some relief goods. Relief goods were surplus food supplies and clothes that were given to poor people who were on the United States' Government's dole through an applied-for-program, commonly referred to as 'Relief'. There was a lot of stigma associated with being 'on relief' and nobody I knew ever admitted to being 'on relief'. There were ways to identify relief clothes; they were, literally, cut from the same cloth.

The relief-goods dispensing station was about seven long Chicago Blocks from our house, and pickups were timed so that each family had just a few hours on a certain day of the month to get supplied. As we approached the station (with red wagon for hauling) there were two families that we knew—also trailing red wagons and children—they were neighbors who would surely disclose our business! Mother spoke and chatted with both, then went right past the relief station without looking in, announcing; "We were just on our way up the street to look at a vacant apartment." When questioned about the address, Mother was indeed able to rattle one off. I remember feeling very disappointed thinking that we weren't going to be able to get any nuts or dried fruit from the relief station that day. The reason I didn't blurt out, "No, we're going to the relief station to get our supply for the month!" is because I, too, felt the stigma of being on relief.

The address Mother quoted to our neighbor was many blocks away and I was very glad that we didn't have to walk that distance when I caught on to Mom's fib. We had walked only about half a block past the station, then stopped to stare at some new nylon stockings displayed in a shop window as we read the information about the new miracle fabric; made out of 'coal, air and water'. Then we doubled back to the relief station and picked up our goods before our time ran out. Our neighbors were nowhere in sight, on the long line of 'reliefers'.

I learned to 'play along' (denying we were 'on relief') without being told by Mom to lie. The very day that it was my turn to come up to my teacher's desk to answer a bunch of questions that included, "Are you and your family on relief?" I was wearing one of the dresses which had been issued from relief, and which was cut from that same cloth. I answered a much-too-quick, "No!" with my heart pounding like drumbeats because I knew it was a lie!

It was a blue plaid cotton, puff-sleeved dress with tiny buttons on the bodice, and several of the poorest girls in our school could be seen on the playground wearing the same frock. My dress had a row of red rick rack sewn on the round collar and around the cuffs of the puff sleeves. Other 'relief' dresses that Daphne and I wore, Mom trimmed with lace or ruffles. Mother was so determined to distinguish us out of the 'relief' cookie-cutter that it wasn't long before she learned to sew. Eventually she was able to make all of our significant clothes. Along with each new sewing technique Mom learned, came a teaching lesson for me. Daphne wasn't interested in sewing but I was. In fact, I was interested in everything Mom found interesting. When she took a course in cosmetology to become a licensed beautician I learned about facial and cranial muscles, Mom's study group consisted of herself and me.

LOOKING AT VACANT APARTMENTS

Going out to look at apartments didn't necessarily mean we were about to move. It was an accepted practice in those days. Lots of people traipsed in and out of the empty or almost empty flats. Some of the apartments had pianos. I suppose pianos were left because they were too heavy to move without incurring heavy expenses. Most of the pianos were upright, large, out of tune, and had some broken ivory keys. People who owned grand pianos took them with them when they moved. They were strapped to pulleys that swung them out of windows and lowered them onto moving vans waiting below. We were never lucky enough to move into a place that had a piano of any kind but Mom and Dad managed to buy a used upright by the time I was eight years old. No decent household was complete without a piano.

PREPARING TO RELOCATE

One day, a white woman was in our apartment talking with my mother when Theodore, Daphne and I got home from school. Theodore and Daphne got busy doing whatever children do upon arriving home. I was so curious that I sat right up under their noses and found out that the white woman was questioning Mother about our living conditions.

"And are there any other problems?" asked the soft-voiced woman. "And the toilet doesn't work right. I reported it but no one has been here to see about it." My mother lied.

"Oh no it's working fine, Daddy fixed it last week!" I chimed in, thinking I was being helpful and wondering how Mother could not know.

The look my mother's face gave me a warning and a promise. I knew that it was time for me to slink out of her presence with my mouth shut. It was time to remember some of her favorite sayings; "A closed mouth gathers no foot." Or, "It's better to be quiet and thought to be a fool, than to speak and remove all doubt."

Later, I found out that the white woman was from some place people called, 'the project', and if we fit what they were looking for, we could move into a brand new home that had an upstairs and a downstairs for our family alone. I envisioned what our new home would look like. It would have a beautiful wooden staircase, with a long rug on it, leading up to the second floor, just like Mrs. Allen's house at 4444 Vincennes Ave. (Margaret's mother's house). I loved Margaret. She was my godmother and my mother's best friend. Margaret and her family had given my mother and her sister a home many years ago when they were homeless.

Our new home would have glass doors separating the living room from the dining room just like Mrs. Allen's house. Only, in our house, no one would make us stop swinging the doors back and forth, like at Mrs. Allen's, or caution us about running in the house, like at Mrs. Allen's, whom we hardly ever went to visit any more. Margaret and her husband and their 3 boys were still living with Mrs. Allen, and almost the only time we'd see them is when they'd come to our house. I envisioned three spacious bedrooms on the upper floor with a wonderful hallway with large windows, just like at Mrs. Allen's house.

The promise of moving into the project's duplex (a new word for me) apartment filled me with joy. Soon, that joy began to diminish when I heard Mother on the phone in conversation after conversation, take a defensive posture when she would say, "The neighborhood's not so bad there are good people everywhere!" I also heard her say, ". . . but they check out their people very carefully. They don't accept any scum!" On another conversation, she said, "I know it's what you call moving backward, I realize it's the heart of the black belt but it's what we can afford!"

And move we did! First to Mrs. Allen's house, where we were so cramped that Theodore had to sleep in the same bed with Earl Jr. (Googie). I suppose we had been evicted from the apartment with the strange windows, the 'clomp, clomp' of the upstairs folks on the one-and-only-staircase, the empty window box, the cement yard and the sound of Ronnell playing 'Flight of the Bumble Bee' on the piano next door.

It was back to hearing Mrs. Allen cautioning us about running in the house, putting our hands on the glass doors, and other 'no, nos'. It couldn't have been long that we lived in the house with Margaret and her family because there were seven of us, five in Margaret's family, Mrs. Allen, one roomer, and the un-married son and daughter who still lived at home. With sixteen people in one house, it was a wonder nobody went stark raving mad!

Whenever I remember how many times Mrs. Allen and her lovely home came to our rescue, I think that she must have been some kind of saint.

WE MOVE INTO THE IDA B. WELLS HOUSING PROJECT

Moving day always seemed to be set for the first day of May (which was my dad's birthday), and so we were to move in then. We had an agreement with McCosh School that Theodore and I would ride the street car to school every day to finish out the term without transferring to our new neighborhood's school, a distance of about seven unsupervised miles each way.

Moving gave me the shock of disappointment. The apartment was a duplex all right, but instead of being on the first and second floors it was on the second and third floors. Smaller, one-bedroom apartments for old people were on the first floor. Next to every other one-bedroomer was a flight of steep stairs which was shared by two, three-bedroom apartments. There were four one-bedroom and four three-bedroom apartments all housed in the same building. The staircase inside our duplex had a solid wall on the right side. It was straight with 14 stairs that were made of concrete. It had a thin, cheap rubberized tile on top of the concrete that was supposed to look like marble. Each step had a metal strip at its tip. Instead of the space, the wood and the carpeting I had imagined, there was metal, concrete, cramped space and black tile. There were no windows in the hallway because there was no hallway to speak of. Each bedroom seemed smaller than the next and when the beds were put up that night by our tired parents, there wasn't space to walk around in any of the rooms

Mom and Dad's room was particularly cramped with the only matching set of furniture; a dresser, double bed, and a chest of drawers. There was very little space between the foot of the bed and the dresser. This was not the largest or master bedroom, the largest bedroom was where my three brothers would be, so that two twin beds and a crib could fit in it. The bathroom was a small box-like cubbyhole where I could sit on the toilet, stretch out my leg and reach the tub with my foot. The ceilings were low and there was dark brown or black artificial marble tile on every floor.

Downstairs (the second floor, our first floor) had no glass doors, it didn't even have a dining room; there was a living

81

room and a kitchen. A kitchen door led out to a common, narrow porch-like walkway that connected all four of the three-bedroom apartments together in the back. The walkway was concrete, the railing was steel and the common staircase was both concrete and steel. There was no rubberized tile to soften the effect on this back stairwell that went from the ground level to the second floor.

The thing that I did like about my new home was the double sink in the kitchen where the drain board could be removed from the kitchen sink and a deep second sink for washing clothes was underneath. I also liked the fact that everything was new.

Theodore and I made the trip to and from McCosh Elementary School for about one month. At first it was exciting but we soon got bored with the long, slow ride from our new home at 702 East 38ᵗʰ Street in The Ida B. Wells Housing Project to our school in Woodlawn. We also got a look at the slums that slowly built up along the path of the street car trolley. Here the spaces between buildings narrowed to the point of squeezing out trees, sunlight, grass and flowers and the buildings grew taller, more ragged, dirtier and crowded. There were stores of every kind along the way with smells and sounds coming out of some of them that would make my mouth water and my ears rejoice: barbecue smoking on the pit, Ella Fitzgerald singing: "A tisket a tasket, I found my yellow basket . . .", louder than a lion roaring at Brookfield Zoo.

We had about three weeks left in the school term, when my brother was called down to the principal's office about some money missing from his class. I think that he was often blamed for stuff that he didn't do because he had a history of being in trouble from St. Anslem. I don't know what really happened but

I do know that we were no longer McCosh School Pupils, we had been thrown out!

I ATTEND MY FIRST GHETTO SCHOOL

With only a few weeks left in the school year, we were enrolled in Doolittle Elementary School on 35th Street, in the heart of the black belt. I was in the fourth grade and the difference between the new school and the school I'd left behind was as different as the tropics are from the North Pole.

Doolittle School was a large, drafty, old red brick building which was so over-crowded that grades four through eight attended only part time. I went to school from eight o'clock in the morning to one in the afternoon. We had a twenty minute break mid-morning where we sat on benches that lined the walls of a basement, ate the dry sandwiches we'd brought from home, and drank the half-pint bottles of no-longer-cold milk which was passed out.

During class, little learning could take place because there was a shortage of paper. We had to share some text books. There were more students than there were seats, and the teacher was always busy dealing with the bad children (always boys) in the class. During most of the day, on my very first day of class, the teacher was trying to get a note to the office about a really bad boy in the class. The boy ran around the class and prevented the monitor from taking the note to the principal's office. He wouldn't let the teacher catch him and he made all kinds of threats and used foul words.

My other days in class were almost as bad. Everyone seemed to want to fight. Children were always getting up in each other's faces and talking about each other's mothers. I had never seen such behavior. The teacher didn't have the power to stop the bad boys from acting any way they wanted. When school let out at one o'clock, there were fights all along the streets near the school.

I had never had a fight, except the squabbles with my brother; where blows were passed and the whole thing was over in a minute or two. One time, a girl had tried to choke me for some reason I can't recall and my little sister came to my rescue by biting the girl on her leg. Up until then, I had led a pretty non-violent life. All of a sudden, I found myself being challenged and threatened. The fear was unbearable.

I was sitting in class when a girl named Frances, who was supposed to be my friend, whispered that another girl, whom I really didn't know, wanted to fight me. I never even looked hard at that girl. All I knew about her was that she always seemed to have fly-away hair—like her mother either hadn't combed it or it came un-braided—and clumps of short stubby hair stood all over her head. I knew enough about the way fights went to not beg out of it. I was terrified all the rest of my class day. Daily, I walked home with my sister Daphne, and my new best friend, Eleanor Cole, who lived in the duplex apartment next to ours, Eleanor Cole's brother, Bookie and various other children from the project. My brother, Theodore, was on the afternoon schedule. He attended class from twelve, noon, to four o'clock. I had no one older to protect me (and I'm not sure Theodore would have come to my defense if he had been around, since we were often at each other's throats). I had no choice but to go through with the fight.

The crowd of children that surrounded us got louder and louder. They pushed and shoved the two of us together while 'Wild Hair' frowned and rocked back and forth, all the while staring me in my face with the meanest expression she could make and her fists balled in fight position. I remember how I felt. I had a terrible sinking feeling in the pit of my stomach and I felt like a complete coward because I was terrified. 'Wild Hair's' first blow caught me in the neck and ignited a fighting spirit in me. I responded (according to Eleanor and other witnesses) by flailing my arms in windmill fashion and delivering several blows. I did not win the fight but I stood my ground and showed the Doolittle School crowd that I could speak their language.

LIFE IN THE PROJECT

The 'Project' neighborhood was safe enough for Mother to allow us to play outside, but always with the warning "Girl, don't you jump rope!" only to me.

During the day, we played mostly in the back of our home. I was always assigned to watch my baby brother, Arnold, and Arnold loved to dig in the dirt. In the evening, after dinner, we usually gathered with other children—and there were plenty of other children—in the space marked off by wooden horses, in front of our house (a large yard-like area) for light socializing. Sometimes girls would bring out their jump ropes, and oh, how I would envy them!

There were four, three-story buildings, with four families each, and four two-story end buildings, with two families each (not counting the small, sandwiched-in apartments of the old people, below). The end buildings were perpendicular to the three-story buildings. This arrangement formed a quad grouping. The two-story buildings, across from each other, were separated by yard space. The three-story buildings were across from one another also. The backs of the buildings had the same arrangement, except that it was a different set of neighbors because the backs of the apartments formed another quadrangle. The end (2-story) buildings did not have apartments for the elderly.

Ida B. Wells' Housing Project was a planned-living experiment. Tenants were very tightly screened. Families had to be intact. There were very few single-parent families considered for application. In later years, I heard about a widow who had her best friend's husband pose as her husband so that she could get an apartment. She had been told that she didn't have a good chance of getting in as a widow. It is my understanding that her scheme was successful, and the man came to the apartment every evening after work pretending to be father to her two children (for the benefit of their playmates) before going home to his own family. He would sit and read his paper just like my dad and many of the other dads in the area.

In our front window, we proudly displayed a small, blue and gold-fringed banner with four gold stars on it to show that we had family in the armed services fighting the war. My Uncle Sidney was in Italy with the army quartermasters Corps. My Uncle Robert was a mess (food) sailor in the U.S. Navy. It was the only job a colored man could have in the navy. The two uncles closest to us, who were more like big brothers than uncles—Rick and and Sol—were both in the Ninety-Second, Buffalo Soldier Infantry, fighting in Europe.

Daddy was able to replace a fighting man who had left a job behind, so he landed a good job where he could be home with us evenings and week-ends. He worked only one job, at The Argo Corn Starch Plant. Mother said that no army would take a man with so many children because they would have to send such a big allotment check every month that there wouldn't be money to put on the war. That is why Daddy didn't get called to serve in the army. Daddy rode to work with a man from his job who picked him up at home and charged him more money than he would have paid on the street car, if the street car went that far. I thought that was terribly unfair, because the man would have to drive himself to work even if Daddy didn't ride with him.

Mother went to work too. She did domestic work for the Harris Family. The Harris' owned a large share of stock in a black-owned insurance company. They were rich African Americans. It wasn't easy to adjust to my mother not always being around, and to her giving me more chores to do around the house, but I adjusted. Our whole family adjusted. We had no other choice.

Mother brought home stories about the Harris Family that were pretty intriguing. Hilda, the lady of the house, practiced some kind of strange religion where she read ether waves and planned her life and the life of her family around the readings from the waves. Hilda was very generous because periodically she gathered clothes from her daughter, Norvell's closet and gave them to my mother for my sister and me. Even though Norvell was a year or two older than I, her clothes were too tight across my chest, and her shoes were too long and too narrow for either of us but I was greatly impressed by the quality and style of those exquisite clothes which were always neatly packed in up-scale clothing store boxes imprinted with the name "Rothchild's" or "Carson Pirie Scott and Company".

Buddy was the name by which Hilda and Tommy Harris' son was known, and in my adult life I met Gregg Harris, Journalist, (the same Buddy Harris, from Chicago) through a close friend of mine, who was also a journalist. Talking with him made me know that my mother probably didn't work for the Harris family very long because Buddy's memory of her was not clear. He said that his mother had many hired help to come and go over the years when he and his sister were growing up.

Even though Mother had the part-time job as maid in the Harris household, she still did hair in our kitchen. She had quite a few customers and I guess she felt a responsibility to them. She also continued to take in sewing—mostly alterations—from friends and sometimes from the cleaner/tailor where Uncle Clyde worked. She also did a big business in turning shirt collars, and taught me how to slit the collar seam with a razor blade, lift the collar off of the shirt, pick all loose threads off of it, turn it over and pin it for stitching. Mother did all stitching on her new sewing machine. Then she'd iron the shirt collar, fold the shirt to look like it was new and collect her fee. The process took about fifteen minutes per shirt.

I LEARN TO SEW

By the time I was twelve years old, I was using the Singer Sewing Machine with Mother's blessings. While she was at work one day, I found some fabric in my parents' bedroom that I liked. I fashioned a dress out of it and I didn't have to work so hard on it because sleeves were already in the fabric. I measured and cut and stitched and trimmed—just as I had practiced under Mom's guidance—I'd surprise Mom when she got home. She'd be so very pleased with me, I thought. If I finish in time, I could put it on and be wearing it when she walked in the door!

I did finish the dress in time but when I tried it on, I decided I would not surprise Mother by having it on when she arrived. The reason was; I had cut the skirt too narrow.

Making aprons or clothes for Daphne's dolls was one thing. They didn't have to move around in them or bend over in them. I had allowed no room for walking. I quickly bunched up my failed project and hid it.

Three days later, Mother confronted me with my "dress" that she found in back of the linen closet.

"What were you thinking! This material wasn't yours, Betty Anne! Why didn't you ask me? This was a robe a lady gave to me to fix for her. Now, instead of making money on it, I'll have to take money from our household and buy her a new robe!"

Oddly enough, Mother didn't hit me. She was very angry with me but she didn't fly off the handle and strike me in the face as she'd done at other times. She spoke sharply, but calmly, and the effect it had on me, was that I developed a huge case of "the guilts".

DISCIPLINE

Before this episode, whenever I did something Mom didn't like, she yelled at me or slapped me. Punishment was usually swift and hurtful. I would seethe with anger, sulk and feel sorry for myself, and I could always make the case, in my mind, that I didn't deserve the punishment. I'm glad to say, these occasions were few and far between but not far enough to save me from the overall feeling that I was being treated like a step child. I developed a fixation on committing suicide and would imagine I'd retaliate against my Mother by causing her great grief from losing me. I had no imaginings about my dad, perhaps that's because he never laid a hand on me or my sister. We were Mother's to discipline.

Daddy had his hands filled trying to keep the boys straight. He spanked Theodore so often that Theodore developed an immunity to pain. It's my belief that those spankings gave Theodore a problem later in life, because he wasn't always able to tell when something was really getting to him. When he was on the high school football team, his nickname was 'Ironhead' because of his very high pain threshold.

The entire household shook with terror when Daddy had to 'chastise' Theodore (and sometimes Bubby, too). Daddy's huge bulk could be seen chasing Theodore all over the apartment, his belt wrapped around his right hand, grasping the belt buckle and administering belt blows—when close enough—with his left hand holding up his pants. Daddy's voice screaming, "Stop!" or "Hold still!" And his favorite, "Boy, I brought you into this world and I'll take you out!"

These declarations were accompanied by recitations of the rules infracted, "Didn't I tell you NOT to go up to that playground!" Or, "How many times have I told you to obey your mother!" The beatings usually ended with a plea from Mother, "Ted, that's enough!"

MAKING 'WELLSTOWN' WORK

People who ran Ida B. Wells Housing Project tried to provide for tenants' social needs as well as dwelling needs. Everyone belonged to a group. Adults had their groups and met in the basement recreation area provided for each housing quadrangle. Children were grouped according to age into clubs and teams. Some clubs focused on planting flowers, some on replacing missing gravel by sweeping or shovelling it back to our play area. Some clubs reported on the condition of the swings in the playground. The duties were designed to give us a sense of pride, caring and ownership in our project long before the very term, 'project,' became synonymous with high-rise warehousing of poor people. And, for a few years, this social engineering worked. "Wellstown", as it came to be called, was beautiful, with well-constructed buildings, none of which were over three stories tall, and with lots of open spaces; areas with plants and flowers and a few trees. Each building had a lawn that was raised to form a low-rise grassy knoll.

In those early years of 'the project experiment' there were many groups of important-looking white people traipsing around 'Wellstown' with a photographer among them, led by a man with a clipboard. There were also reports of many magazine and newspaper articles being written about "us", but I never read any.

Tenants were grouped together to identify and solve problems on their own. Attendance at the adult meetings was mandatory. One of the problems that my dad worked on (with a group of men) was providing window guards for the second and third floors of the project's windows so that young children would be safe and break-ins could be prevented. For years, my father made and sold the guards to our neighbors. I don't think he was well paid, I think it was mainly a service with just enough return to cover expenses. Dad was also enlisted to coach one of the many baseball teams for boys and it was a good thing he was a fast learner, because he knew almost nothing about baseball.

The famous composer and jazz singer Oscar Brown Jr. and his family, briefly lived a few blocks from us. The family didn't qualify to live there because they were poor; they lived in Wellstown because Oscar Brown Sr. was the manager of the project. When things started to change and gangs started taking over the project, the Brown family re-located. Oscar Jr. was older than my big brother, and leadership of the group was bestowed on him because his dad was a big shot. As a result, there were many boys who tried to hang out with him and his crowd, or join the 'Wildcats' baseball team since Oscar was on it. My brother was included in the wannabes, but all the guys were older and he couldn't get in.

PAYING THE RENT

Paying the rent at the beginning of the month was usually the job of the oldest boy in the family. He was given the cash and he walked to the office where the manager, Oscar Brown Sr. might greet him in person and write out the receipt, which he brought back to his parents. This custom was practiced by most of the families in our quad. I thought it was unfair that my brother got to do all the interesting errands. I wanted to pay the rent sometimes. When I begged or complained, I was usually ignored.

One super cold day, (of which, Chicago had many) my brother, Theodore, was given the rent money. Mother made him put the money in his glove, though he wanted to carry it in his pocket. Mother had to insist he carry the rent money in his glove! He did as she instructed, and he was gone a long time. Mother began to worry about him; after all, the office was a distance of nearly one mile, and there had been a few reports about big boys beating up younger boys. That is why Mother had insisted on the glove as a hiding place for our hard-earned rent money. Everybody knew rent was due the first part of the month.

Theodore finally arrived home just before darkness set in. He was dressed in corduroy knickers, long woolen socks, his warm sweater and his long thick wool overcoat. He was wearing his leather hat with the upturned sheepskin visor ear flaps and chin strap, and he was still wearing his leather gloves. He was very cold, very disheveled and very excited.

"There were some boys near the street where the office is. They attacked me and started beating me up. They said to give them the rent money but I said I didn't have no rent money. They went through my pockets trying to find it but I held on to it in my glove. They wanted to know what I was doing over here if I wasn't going to the office to pay the rent." My brother explained. "I told 'em I was going to my friend, Darrell's house, he live up that way!" "One of 'em pushed me down, an' the other one had a knife. He showed it to me an' shoved me in my back!" When I got up, I ran the other way away from the office, up toward South Park!"

Mother was horrified, she hugged Theodore and rubbed his hands. He was freezing cold all over. He reached in his overcoat pocket and presented her with the receipt. Mother helped him out of his overcoat and that's when she gasped!

"Oh my God! Your coat's been cut, right in the middle of the back. That boy stabbed you! Are you hurt? Are you bleeding?"

Theodore was not cut his heavy overcoat had protected him. He explained that he had to wait out his time to go to the office until after the two boys were gone. He had gone by Darrell's house but no one was home. He had lingered in Darrell's hallway and then doubled back to the office using a different route.

I never begged my parents to go to the office and pay the rent again.

ROPE-JUMPING ENVY

Mother continued to warn me about jumping rope and I continued to envy the girls who had no restrictions on jumping. And, sure, I'd sometimes sneak and jump a little, when I could but more often, I'd be a rope-turner. I didn't tell the other girls that I was forbidden to jump rope. I'd just say, "Oh, I don't feel like jumping today." Or "I'd rather just turn the rope." It didn't take long for me to get the reputation as, "The girl who don't like to jump rope."

As a result, I never got any good at jumping rope because nobody jumped rope at school, It was against the rules to bring a rope to school, which is where I would have practiced, far away from my mother's eyes.

It wasn't only the echo of my mother's voice saying, "Girl, don't you jump rope!" that made me feel like I was Cinderella, I was also overwhelmed with household chores. When I got home from school each day, I had to clean the entire upstairs. That consisted of straightening up my parent's room, making sure that the room I shared with my sister was presentable, cleaning the bathroom, and the worst job of all, was cleaning the boy's room. I had to take the sheets off of their beds, go down to the double sink in the kitchen, lift off the lid, and—grabbing the 'sunburst' in the middle—wash the pee stain out and rinse it well so that it wouldn't smell as it dried on the radiator. When dry, I'd make up the beds with the same sheets. There were no extra sheets I could use. We had just enough of those hand sewn sheets, made from the Argo Corn Starch sacks that Daddy brought home from work which Mother bleached, split and hemmed to provide linen for our beds.

After cleaning the bathroom and the three bedrooms on my knees, I had to wash down the steps with a rag. We didn't own a mop until I was in my teens. And Although we constantly begged for them, my sister and I didn't get separate beds until we were in our early teens. My chores did not end with upstairs cleanings I was also responsible for doing dishes some nights.

And later on, I was expected to not just be a cook's helper but to provide entire meals. Making the Sunday biscuits was also one of the things I was taught to produce. My father made a big deal about making the Sunday biscuits, since no one could buy them in a paper tube, (that hadn't been invented yet) they had to be made by hand, and as the oldest girl in my family I was designated to do it.

MAKING THE SUNDAY BISCUITS

After making the Sunday biscuits for the family several times, I thought I would surprise everybody with green biscuits in honor of St. Patrick's Day. Working alone in the kitchen, I looked in the cupboard for some green food coloring, there was none. Determined to exercise my idea, I seized upon the notion of adding green Cool Aid to the biscuit dough. I reasoned, "Didn't it do a good job of turning water green enough to stain our teeth, lips and gums?"

Without first liquefying the granules, I plunked the entire packet of Cool Aid down into the biscuit dough mixture, kneaded, rolled and cut. The baking process didn't turn the biscuits green as I expected they just got to be a dirty grey-greenish color and refused to rise to full puff. By then, the family was converging on the kitchen and serving up those strange-colored biscuits which tasted awful. No one could eat them! For as long as my Dad had his right mind, he swore and be-darned that I tried to poison the family in order to get out of making biscuits on Sunday mornings.

YOU DON'T GO TO CHURCH; YOU DON'T GO TO THE MOVIES!

Sunday morning was a time for negotiation. My Dad would announce that every one of us children had to go to Sunday school; otherwise we couldn't go to the show to see a double feature movie that afternoon. We would dutifully march off to church and leave my parents at home with the baby. These 'church-movies' agreements were faithfully honored until at about age fifteen, I told my Dad, "Well, I just won't go to the movies today. I worked all day Saturday" (I had a job at the local 'dime store') "and I have a lot of homework to do, I don't feel well and I'm gonna sleep late. I am not going to church!" Dad fumed and threatened that there would be no show that day but I stuck to my decision to sleep late.

Later that afternoon; my father, very sheepishly, said to me, "Betty Anne, here's the money for the show for you and Daphne and the boys. Ya'll go on and enjoy the movies."

What a shock this was to me. Dad had always linked movie-going with church attendance and here he was, almost begging me to take my siblings to the local show! That was when it dawned on me, Dad wanted to get us out of the house so that he could be alone with Mother! Until then, I had thought very little about the motives of adults. I was too focused on complying with their wishes. I was always trying to please, trying to make a good impression, trying to boost my image in the eyes of my parents—especially my mother—who awarded few compliments, but many scoldings and warning, so that I was late coming to the awareness that they could have motives other than the ones for which I monitored them earlier, like fighting, which had subsided considerably.

Mother's warnings seemed like they were issued several times a day. She would tell Daphne and me, "Don't ever let NO man make you pregnant when you don't want to be. Don't ever have no house full of children. A boy will tell you every sweet thing you like to hear and not mean a word he says!"

One time, she even warned us against crossing the street with men. We asked if that would make us pregnant or would the men try to "get" us. She laughed and simply said,

"No. Cross the street with a lady because men take too many chances. They are very daring, and you could get hit by a car."

Mom also thought that she might die, like her mother, before her children grew up, so she told me the story of menstruation and ovulation when I was much too young to fully understand the implications and ramifications of such grown up functions.

In January of my tenth year, I had completely forgotten about "menstruating", but it hadn't forgotten about me. When mother confronted me about evidence that she had found in the linen closet where we stashed dirty clothes, my first reaction was guilt. I think Mom handled it well. She instructed me on how to protect myself, and assisted me in putting on the belt and pinning on some soft clean rags. I wore this uncomfortable contraption for a little while and then I must have taken it off to use the bathroom and failed to put it back on.

THE MISS GRACE DALEY
SCHOOL OF FINE ARTS

Miss Grace Daley, of The Grace Daley School of Fine Arts, taught Piano lessons to my sister and me, at our home. She came once a week, and would sit next to me on our piano bench, facing away from the keys and look in her compact mirror and powder her nose with face powder that was, at least, two shades too light for her skin color.

Her hair was thinning and she wore it in a semi-page-boy style even though it was so thin that it barely covered her head. It may have been the original 'comb-over'. She always wore cotton stockings that were in constant need of adjustment. They, too, seemed to be a couple of shades too pale for her. She had unusually large feet, and very skinny legs. The trapezoid-shaped green plaid coat she wore emphasized her thin angularity. In other words, Miss Grace Daley was a character! My friends laughed at her imitated her and teased me about her.

Miss Grace Daley smelled of old perfume and spoke in the most proper way that anyone could speak; enunciating each syllable with the greatest of care. She chose words that would sometimes send us to the dictionary, and one time she asked Daphne, "Daphne, did you dine in your chapeau?" Daphne had just left the dinner table, (to take her lesson) still wearing her hat. I don't think Mother knew the French word for hat but figured it out, and told Daphne to take off her hat before she took her piano lesson.

Later, we attended Saturday ballet classes taught by Miss Daley which were held in a ragged, dilapidated building where the plumbing in the bathroom did not work right, and there was only a one-bulb light fixture hanging from the high ceiling in the entire place. Miss Daley had no 'School' of fine arts. She rented space as needed, but she managed to have enough performing pupils to put on her annual, four-hour recital of music, recitation and dance in the spring of each year, in which we studied with her.

I sat down on the piano bench to take my lesson, and, nature took its course. Miss Daley, quoting Paul Laurence Dunbar, remarked:

> "Break me my bounds, and let me fly
> To regions vast of boundless sky"

My mother was horrified at seeing her not-turning-eleven-for-two-months-old daughter with a great big crimson spot on the back of her dress with the music teacher looking right at it, and reciting poetry. Mom said, (in an unconvincing voice) "Betty Anne, you must have sat in something!"

We continued studying with Miss Grace Daley—learning just enough music to perform our solo piano pieces at her recitals—then, a few months after joining her ballet class, she had us jete'ing all over the stage, so it was ballet and piano for a few years. And, when she discovered Daphne had dramatic talent, she concentrated on grooming her to be a star.

With coaching from Miss Daley, Daphne memorized several poems (mostly written by Paul Laurence Dunbar). She became well known and in demand by local groups for her dramatic presentation of "In The Morning", though I don't think there was ever any payment associated with the demand.

WORKING AFTER SCHOOL

By the time I entered high school at thirteen years old, ours was a family of six children. Theodore, who was fifteen, had a regular job before school as a paper boy. He ran errands for neighbors and swept and mopped the floor of a local business. I had been working for a year for my mother's friend, who was our neighbor. I baby-sat with her two girls while she worked evenings. The older girl was only about three years younger than I, she was about nine years old when I started. She was large for her age; standing almost as tall as I. It was my job to put the girls to bed at eight o' clock, close their bedroom door, go downstairs and sit in their living room until they went to sleep. Then I could go home, which was just two doors away, via the common back porch. Their father came home around nine. I went through this ritual five nights a week and it worked well.

One night, I heard a noise coming from the girls' room. I tiptoed back upstairs, opened the door, and to my utter horror, there was a boy in bed with the older girl. He was on top of her, frantically moving around. When he saw me, he jumped up, all the while pulling up his pants. He dashed out of the already open window. My charge didn't seem the worst for wear, she had not screamed or fought him off. In fact, her spread-eagle position, when I walked in, gave me the impression she was willingly participating in the experience. Perhaps she had opened the window to let him in, because the window guard was unfastened and it could only be opened from inside. The younger sister was in her bed on the other side of the room, apparently asleep. I knew the boy! He was a neighborhood kid! He lived just two doors away on our common porch! He was my brother! The girl said nothing to me. She just lowered her head and avoided eye contact. I never told her mother. I told my own mother, but didn't reveal that the boy was Theodore, but I think she knew because she didn't ask his name.

MY BROTHER, MY NEMESIS

My brother and I, always at each other's throats, didn't even speak after that. I was too horrified to put words to the incident. I also felt guilty that I had not protected the girls more. I felt that after this, my brother would probably leave me alone, stop teasing me, stop taking my stuff, stop signifying on me—and I was right—Theodore walked a wide circle around me and I enjoyed the respect, but I had a hard time regaining any respect for him. He had violated the ultimate taboo! It would be almost a year before I could regard him as anything better than a monster. It took a little growing up on my part to realize that his behavior was not a-typical of teen-aged, hormone-soaked boys.

While I was still in a state of extreme hate for my brother, I returned home from the movies with my younger siblings to find Theodore and two friends sitting on the indoor steps in our home listening to a new kind of music called be-bop. When the musicians hit a certain note, these guys would get so excited, they'd bolt up the stairs and scream, run down the stairs and imitate the be-bop sounds, before settling down to listen again. This went on for several minutes, and, annoyed, I asked them to stop. Theodore, emboldened by the presence of his friends, made the mistake of giving me some smart-alecky reply. I had just seen sword fights, killings and shootings in the double feature movie I'd just left, so it was a small change for me to become an avenger! I didn't have a sword or a gun, so I picked up the scissors and stabbed my brother in his right thigh!

I guess everyone lives with some regrets. For me, this ranks right at the top of my regrets list.

Theodore had many, many friends, and by the time he was 16, he had joined the army, and been honorably discharged because he was underage, (The truth is, he had asked Mom and Dad to send his birth certificate when he found out that he might be shipped overseas where fighting was still raging). He had been sent to Tennessee to live with our father's parents on their farm. He had wrecked the tractor, milked cows dry, and made a reputation for himself as a total nuisance. He had landed in the criminal justice system as an incorrigible juvenile delinquent for his participation in street gangs, yet he was as popular as he could be, and some of his friends were truly nice guys.

One of his friends, called Bubba, who lived in the next grouping of project houses, had a reputation as a good boy. He was often in our house and I suspected he had somewhat of a crush on me. I really didn't like Bubba, but he was safe. I could be in his company and not be afraid he'd say anything fresh or use any curse words. Bubba stuttered a bit, but that was the only thing that the girls could criticize about him. Another thing in Bubba's favor was that his mother and my mother were friends.

PART II
MY TEEN YEARS

THE TROLLEY HOP

A Trolley Hop was a big deal to us teens. Most trolley lines had converted to buses so the Chicago Transit Authority rented out its large supply of electric trolleys (streetcars) for recreational events, we called them Trolley Hops. A single car could carry about forty-eight people. Running by electricity overhead, trolleys delivered passengers to Dan Ryan Woods, where, after a short walk, they could have a picnic with a bonfire for roasting marshmallows and hot dogs. There were a few restrictions for building fires, and since our planned Trolley Hop was being held on a holiday (what was called Armistice Day, now called Veterans Day) and it was sure to be cold, we gathered plenty of wood to burn.

The boy that I had a crush on wasn't able to be my date on the Trolley Hop. After I had gathered all of my courage to ask him to go with me, he said he had been selected to go to New York as a student participant in the opening session of the newly established United Nations. I invited Bubba to be my substitute date.

All went well, the trip out to the woods was fun, we shared the prepared food we'd brought, and then the stuff we cooked on our great big bonfire. We played some games and when it was time to leave, it was my date, Bubba, who took charge, reminding all that we would have to douse the fire. He organized the boys, laughing and whispering to and with them. He polled boy after boy—some were with him, but some were not—the ones with him laughed to show they shared his joke. Bubba shouted instructions that the girls should get on the trolley, and we did. More than half of the boys got on the trolley as well. They were the ones Bubba had not recruited to assist in dousing the flames. Then the remaining boys turned their backs to us as they encircled the fire, and I could hear my date leading the count, "One, two, three, GO!" I never spoke to Bubba again!

I was just 13 years old when I started attending Wendell Phillips High School. A lot of violence took place inside of the school, and security was almost non-existent. Gang members regularly entered the building and beat up boys who'd been targeted. The police were often in the building attempting to catch some of the troublemakers. The most notorious gang was The Thirteen Cats, a group that tried to keep its membership secret but everybody knew who they were. Between the time my brother returned from the south and the time he went into the army, I learned that he was not only a member, but the president of The Thirteen Cats! I held such disdain for him that one day I saw him in the hall with some boy that I didn't know and he approached me to introduce to the guy, but I wouldn't speak to him. The boy laughed at Theodore and shouted, "That ain't yo' sister, that girl don't even know you!"

I think that of all the hateful things I did to my brother, this hurt him the most. For years, he complained about the time I snubbed him at school.

I was turning 14 when Theodore was in the army. He sent money home and asked Mom to get a birthday gift for me. Mom bought me an Eisenhower jacket. It was one of very few times that I got something new to wear that I didn't make.

The daily grind at home was really a lot to bear. With three young boys always messing up the house, peeing on the toilet seat and needing watching when Mother was away or busy, I always had a feeling that I was being treated unfairly. My friend, Eleanor Cole, who lived in the apartment next to ours also had three younger brothers. But they didn't bug her like mine bugged me. Eleanor's brothers were younger, but closer to her age than mine to me. I had liked my brother, Bubby, until he started playing with some of the ruffians in the neighborhood. The other two (Arnold and Kenneth) were just too young to relate to. Mother had her children over a nineteen year period. Theodore was my sworn enemy until the Eisenhower jacket, but that didn't last long. As soon as he was back on the scene, he resumed annoying me.

HOME ATMOSPHERE AND ATTEDING HIGH SCHOOL

The dominant tone inside our apartment was loud. We talked to each other from room to room in very loud voices. We were constantly up and down the un-cushioned concrete stairs, closing a door meant almost slamming it, kitchen tools rattled when they were used, and slamming things down was the only way to place them. We were all 'heavy-handed' and, by example, taught by Dad (who was the heaviest handed of all) we had learned well.

The home atmosphere had to make a drastic change when Dad got a good job with Reynolds Aluminum Company (the job he would keep until he retired) because he worked the swing shift. For two weeks, his working hours were 8:A.M. to 4:P.M., then he'd shift to 4:P.M. to 12 Midnight. These two shifts didn't require much lifestyle change, but when he worked nights, (midnight to 8:A.M.) and had to get his sleep in the daytime—in our loud home—everyone was miserable! Mother would often wake him up trying to keep us quiet. Then Mom and Dad would get into an argument over the fact that she awakened him.

I was very happy to be attending high school. It gave me a place to express some of my creativity, and a place to meet new people, socialize and tell jokes. I had enough talent to join the advanced art class at school and attend classes at The Art Institute of Chicago, downtown (in the loop). It was a special, Saturday class where our weekly paintings were rated. Honorable Mentions were the highest ratings. Students who got 3 Honorable Mentions were kept in the program and could continue to attend, I got two Honorable Mentions.

School lunches cost 35 cents, and that is exactly the amount I was given each day. I bought the lunch a few times, but when I learned that I could go out to the school store and buy what I liked, it was 'good-bye good nutrition, hello candy bars! I ate seven candy bars a day, for several weeks, maybe a few months (in those days candy bars cost five cents each). I developed such bad tooth decay that I had to have 2 molars extracted before I was 15 years old.

CULTIVATING A LOVE AND RESPECT FOR AFRICA

High school was such a joy that I joined every club or association that I could. The modern dance class (which substituted for gym) met every day and had a dynamic young 'Negro' teacher; Mrs Rosella Laws Smith, who told us about Africa and taught us African dance steps. She was an admirer of Kathryn Dunham's work and she imparted a positive image of Africa and all things African, so at an early age I wanted to go there and learn more about our African heritage. This was rare, because almost everything which was presented in media about Africa was negative. When Africans were shown in movie newsreels, the audiences (all black) would whoop and holler, whistle, laugh, stomp their feet and jeer in embarrassment until the Africans were off the screen. The reaction was pretty much the same when 'Negroes' were shown, too.

When Etta Moten, the famous singer—who had traveled to some African colonies (prior to the countries gaining nationhood)—needed models to exhibit the clothes she brought back, I was selected by Mrs Laws-Smith to be one of the models. I learned about the lapa (skirt) the buba (blouse), and the galee (headwrap) long before they became popular during the sixties. This experience led to my thirst to know more about this fascinating continent. I sought out and read all that I could find on the subject. Curiosity about, and love for Africa have been constants in my life ever since.

MY FACTORY JOB AT AGE FOURTEEN

Shortly after turning 14 years old, I heard about a job where the people who ran the place didn't require birth certificates as proof of age. Eleanor (who was a few months younger than I, wouldn't have her fourteenth birthday until August) and I applied, as soon as school recessed for the summer. I was claiming to be 16, and I could probably pass for that, but I didn't think Eleanor could. To me, she looked like she was 12. Her mother cut her arrow-straight hair in the Dutch Boy style and I thought the hairstyle made her look even younger. To my surprise, both of us were hired.

We traveled by street car every day, carrying our lunches in brown paper sacks. We had an awful time trying to be on time, since we had never traveled so far by ourselves. After the first week, we got the hang of it and fell into a routine that required us to wake up earlier. We hadn't thought of that. We would make about twenty-five dollars a week each! We had never even imagined making that kind of money. It was a full time job, eight hours a day, five days a week. Many jobs were available because so many workers were still devoted to the war efforts. The work was very boring. It was a factory that made those new ball point pens, about which we knew nothing. We were still dipping our fountain pens in wet ink.

Eleanor and I had the same duty; we each sat on a stool near a small motorized spindle with sand at its base. Our job was to place a little plastic cylinder on the rotating spindle, hold a small amount of sand against it with a tiny cloth until it was buffed smooth. Periodically, these cylinders were collected and taken to another section of the factory where they were filled with ink, and writing points were attached. Because we had never seen anything like them before, we had no appreciation for them. We didn't even have a name for them; they were just things that gave us a job.

After a couple of weeks working in the factory—chatting and laughing all day with Eleanor—I started to get playful with the cylinders. I discovered that I could squeeze the little cloth squares very hard to make designs on the cylinders, or I could hold the cylinders themselves tightly to make them pop on the spindle. This was far more fun than just plain buffing and smoothing. The worker assigned to collecting our work and checking on quality, warned me many times about the poor quality of my finished product but I was enjoying my new creative outlet. I would perform correctly when being observed but the rest of the time it was whirr, whirr, and pop!

Almost all of us workers were female, and our co-workers really treated us well. When Eleanor's birthday rolled around in early August, they had a birthday celebration at lunch time with individual gifts and a cake. Eleanor claimed to be turning seventeen, but she was just making her 14th birthday. I had the feeling that the women knew she couldn't be seventeen, but just went along with the lie. She and I talked and giggled all day every day, and many times we had to be told to cut out the visiting. We were typical, goofy, young, teen-agers. I wanted to keep the job until school started because it brought me such joy to bring that much money home to my parents every week. But alas, my youthful ways were so apparent that the boss called us into his office, about a week after the birthday party, and citing our excess visiting and the poor quality of our finished product, he fired both of us.

Before school started back again in the fall, I applied for a job at my local five and dime store. I, again, lied about my age and told the interviewer I was 16, when I was only 14 and a-half. She asked for my birth certificate, and I told her the standard lie that most of my friends shared; "I was born in The South, in a small county where Negroes were not given birth certificates. The only record of my birth is an entry in the family bible; do you want me to bring in our family bible?" I had rehearsed this so often that I didn't feel nervous telling the lie, it rolled off my tongue with ease. No one ever wanted us to bring in the family bible!

In truth, I had been born in Chicago and I had two birth certificates. The first was for 'Maudell Hennings'. The second was for 'Betty Anne Hennings', because my mother changed my name a few days after I was born. Mom attempted to name me after Maudell Bousfield, a woman she greatly admired, but my Godmother, Margaret Allen Taylor and her sisters; Helen and Estelle, talked her into naming me Betty (after her) and Anne (after her sister, Anna Mae and her mother, Anna). They thought Maudell was too country-sounding for a girl in Chicago. I would meet Maudell Bousfield later on. She was the principal of my high school.

My mother's health started declining when I was a young teen-ager. She had birthed six children by the time I was 13, and she had suffered mis-carriages as well. She developed a heart condition that eventually put dark circles around her eyes. She continued to work outside as well as inside of the home, she did alterations for the clothing chain called Grayson's, where she worked flexible hours for many years.

Mom was still convinced that she wouldn't live to see her children grow up, so she counseled me about everything all of the time. She started telling me about birth control long before I even knew what she was talking about. At the same time that she was emphasizing, "Don't let a boy touch you!" she was telling me that when I wanted to, she'd take me to the birth control clinic up at Lincoln Center (a few blocks from our house) and have me fitted for a diaphragm. I suppose she was trying to do what her mother never had a chance to do for her—give guidance in life issues—but the greatest teacher was her life style. I didn't need her words to know that I certainly didn't want a house full of hard-headed boys, peeing all over the toilet seat, keeping me up late at night, looking out the window, always worried about where they were and would they get themselves killed before they could get themselves home. I knew what activity would get me in the kind of predicament that would make me live like my mother; with sacrifices, responsibilities and regrets and I vowed to have none of it!

DATING, BEFORE THE SEXUAL REVOLUTION

I started to date, at age 16, before the 'sexual revolution', when we didn't dare to ever even talk about sex. If a boy got 'fresh' with me, I didn't have anything else to do with him again. Getting 'fresh' could be anything from holding my hand when I didn't want him to, to copping a feel. But never anything as blatant as the sex act itself! I remained a virgin until I was 21, and the man I married was a bigamist with a whole lifetime of experiences more than I had, but he was only six years older.

I always had a boyfriend (whether the guy knew he was my boyfriend or not) boys pretty much knew where I stood and seemed to accept it. So I did O.K. in the dating department. The thing I wasn't prepared for was the number of boys who would pay attention to me, with the hope of getting to know my sister. Daphne had become quite a beauty by this time. She was very quiet and studious, and she had a pleasant and sweet disposition in spite of Theodore's teasing. He called her skinny, and she had been, but she had filled out since he last looked. He could still upset her by pressing the nail of his index finger into the nail of his thumb to indicate that her upper arm could fit into the space this gesture provided. No matter how he teased, beat on, bothered or nagged the other siblings—and he really laid it on all of us—I was, by far, his number one nemesis!

I was sixteen years old and still eavesdropping on my mother's conversations. Mother was visiting with a neighbor, when I heard the neighbor say to Mom, "Girl, you look like you're gaining a little weight, could you be expecting?"

Mother answered, "I've got my quota, the next babies in this family will be grandbabies!"

That neighbor couldn't wait to go all around the neighborhood telling everybody that I was pregnant. When it got back to Mom, she confronted the woman, the woman said to her face that Mom had told her that I was pregnant, by saying that she was expecting a grandchild. Mom had to do some heavy teaching to make the busybody understand what she had actually said; that she, herself, was not going to have any more children, and that only when she becomes a grandmother, would there be additional children in the family.

Mom's words proved false when she came up pregnant during my senior year of high school. I was so embarrassed I didn't know what to do. Mom had swelling of the feet, nausea and cravings for ice, and frost off of the refrigerator. She would actually bite the frost off of the freezer compartment, that's how she chipped her front tooth. She was a miserable pregnant woman; she was in her late thirties.

Daddy had become vice-president of his union at Reynolds Aluminium so he was often away from home. The level of support that Daddy had always shown to Mom wasn't there for her during her hardest pregnancy. Theodore was working and living at home only part time. I was attending high school and working three hours a day after school at the dime store. Daphne had just started a part time job after school at the library. Mom was still trying to work at Grayson's, even though she was sick very often.

Everybody was tired when we would finally get together at home, but every evening I would take my mother for a walk around the neighborhood—just the two of us—so that the gossipy neighbors could see which one of us was pregnant! I didn't want anybody to accuse me of the worst thing in my world that could happen to me. I was determined that I would not become another Quentella. Quentella was a playmate of ours who became pregnant at about age fourteen. She was an only child to a single working mother. It was as if Quentella had the plague when local mothers found out about her pregnancy. None of us were allowed, nor did we want, to associate with her again.

SYLVIA

My Uncle Clyde, the consummate businessman, married a wonderful woman when I was about 13 years old. I say wonderful because she had the good taste to choose me as her favorite niece. I had never had the privilege of being anybody's favorite before then. Sylvia took me to events such as church programs, meetings, an occasional movie, but mostly to church. We both loved to hear Rev. Archibald Carey preach. All week, we would discuss what went on in church. Most of the time, when I went around with Sylvia, Daphne would go too, but when we went to church, it always seemed to be just the two of us. Sylvia became my confidant. She would actually listen to me. She always had time for me.

One day, my brother Theodore teased me so badly, called me 'Big Nose', again, (his favorite way to upset me) that I said to Sylvia, "Theodore says that I have a big nose! He's always calling me, 'Big Nose' like that's my name! I don't have a big nose, do I?"

Sylvia took a good look at my face, like she was seeing me for the first time. She took my chin between her thumb and index finger and moved my face up and down and then from right to left.

"Yeah", she said, "Your nose is too big for your face."

I was devastated! Here was my mentor, my favorite aunt, my buddy (siding with my worst enemy) not cushioning the blow with perhaps a small statement to the effect that my face may, in time, fill out and all my features, especially my nose, would be in proportion as I grew older. No, she just answered the question put to her as honestly as she could, without regard for what I wanted to hear. And that pretty much sums up Sylvia's personality. She was an attractive woman, but she had no frills about her, she said what she thought, without regard for listeners' feelings. Sylvia was good for my uncle, she worked hard in the cleaner side by side with him. They added tailoring to the business and prospered. When Clyde and Sylvia joined my other uncles in the grocery business, that store prospered, too.

MOTHER RUINS MY CHANCE TO HAVE A RADIO CAREER

One Sunday, when Sylvia and I were in attendance at Woodlawn A.M.E. Church, Rev, Carey introduced a man who invited everyone to attend a demonstration of a revolutionary device to record voices. The demonstration took place immediately after service, in the rear of the church. I was very excited to see how this brand new technology worked. It was a reel to reel tape recorder, spooling our voices back to us as we talked into it in normal conversational tones. The only other time that I had witnessed, and been a small part of, a recording session; was when my friend Mona's little brother, Boogie, had a wonderful birthday party to which all of the children in the neighborhood were invited. Their parents had hired a man to set up a small booth with phonograph recording equipment in it and each child was given the chance to speak for a few seconds. The cumbersome gramophone cylinder that recorded our scratchy voices during the party bore no resemblance to the neat suitcase-sized, clear-voiced, reel to reel.

The gentleman operating the reel to reel in back of the church had attracted only a few people, so I was able to speak as much as I wanted into the machine. He had some affiliation with a radio show called 'You Are There!' (a show that reported historical events as if they were happening at that moment) or so he claimed. He turned his full attention on me, telling me that I had a beautiful voice, and that I spoke really well and should be on radio. I lapped up the flattery like a starving puppy dog. Soon, Sylvia wanted to leave, but I didn't want to go yet. The man was telling me that he could get me, (this fifteen-year-old, inexperienced girl) on a radio show! Radio was the primary media of the day! All I'd have to do was meet him at the restaurant named 'Army and Lou's' on Tuesday, at 7:p.m. because he would be having dinner with the guy in charge of the show and he would love for me to meet him, but he was sure that he, himself, could get me on the air in a part-time job.

When my mother heard the news, she developed a smirk on her face that I had never seen before, and when Tuesday came, I was prepared to go to 'Army and Lou's (which was a well-established business, and a straight-shoot bus ride from our apartment) to meet up with Mr. tape-recorder-man. Since it was winter, darkness surrounded me like the gloom of having my mother go with me to the restaurant. She would surely spoil my chances of having a career on the radio, I thought.

For many years, I had to endure Mother telling and re-telling the story of, "How Betty Anne Almost Became A Great Radio Star!"

"Betty Anne didn't want me to go with her. She wanted to go to the restaurant alone, at night, to meet up with some man who said he could put her on the radio. She had her mouth stuck out so far she could almost trip on it when I told her that I would go with her, or she couldn't go!"

"When we got to the restaurant, the man was eating his dinner—chicken gizzards—the cheapest thing on the menu! He was all alone, wasn't no big boss with him, and he didn't even offer us no dinner, not even a coca cola. He was surprised as heck to see that she has her mother with her. He almost choked on those cheap chicken gizzards. He jumps outta his booth, with his run-over shoes that needed new heels, and his shiny suit that looked like he just had it polished that afternoon, and offers us a seat, but doesn't call the waiter over to order anything for us. And then, when he finds out I'm the mother, he starts in on flattering me! Telling me how young I look and talking about he knows where Betty Anne gets her good looks from."

Of course, we never heard from that little man again, and it took several re-tellings of the story before I could get over my embarrassment and several more, before I could see the humor in the story. There had also been several telephone conversations between Mother and Sylvia regarding how I had met the man, which I was not told about until I matured.

WHO NEEDS ANOTHER HIGH SCHOOL PROM?

It was Aunt Sylvia who led the charge to get me to go to my own high school graduation prom. By the time I was ready to graduate from high school; I had already been to two of Wendell Phillips' Proms, as dates of graduating seniors. I decided that I didn't need to attend my own prom. I told my mother that I didn't need another prom, it was too expensive and I didn't feel like making another dress. I had just finished a green taffeta fishtail suit for my own senior luncheon. By the time I was seventeen, I was making most of my clothes. Mother just said, "Well, Betty Anne, if that's what you wanna do, I have no objections."

About a month before the event, I secretly felt a little shaky about the decision I had made. When my friend, Kennie, whose parents were of a religious persuasion that made them prohibit her from having a boyfriend, asked me to loan my boyfriend, Jimmy, to her as her date for the prom, I thought it would be a fitting way to allow my guy to be able to attend the prom—since

I had declined—and it would be a way to help my friend out, who had never had a date. I had been on many dates by that time and reasoned that I wouldn't miss one little ol' date.

As time grew nearer to the prom, and there was talk and arrangements were being made, I began to feel that I had made a big mistake, but I wasn't about to admit it to anyone.

Four days before the prom, I got a call from Sylvia, "What's this I hear, that you're not going to your own prom?"

"Yeah, that's what I decided. I was prom date to two fellas, that's enough. I don't need to attend any more." I said, probably unconvincingly, because she retorted,

"Oh, Betty Anne, you'll regret it the rest of your life if you don't go! Why would you NOT go?"

My argument about it being just another dance, I'd loaned away my date, I had no prom dress; fell on determined ears, and by the end of the conversation, I'd agreed to go by Sylvia's apartment the next day to pick up a dress.

It was a beautiful dress, one of Sylvia's best. It was red velvet, v-necklined with a circular skirt and long sleeves and a full size too big for me. It was the kind of dress for which I couldn't afford to even buy the fabric, if I had the skill to make it, which I hadn't. Now it was a case of my family forcing me to do what I secretly wanted to do. This allowed me to save face and to wear a terrific gown that I didn't have to struggle to make.

Two days before the prom, the arrangement was that I would be escorted by my big brother, Theodore, who would be dressed in my father's tuxedo, and I would be wearing Sylvia's dress. The only thing new that I had to buy was a pair of nylon stockings.

On the day of the prom, in the afternoon, Theodore says to me, "Hey Sis, you know that good-looking light-skinned boy,

Calvin, from up the street?" "No, I have no idea who you're talking about." I replied, "You know him, he's sweet on you, crazy about you, always asking me about you!"

At this point, I knew something was brewing because my brother did not want to ever go out with his sisters. I remembered the way he had acted when he had been forced to take me and Daphne to a party in the neighborhood, a party which he wanted to attend. He walked along beside us, but stayed on the side by the curb so that if any of his buddies saw us, he could say we weren't together. He had harked and spat every three or four minutes to show his disgust at having to be with his sisters. When we got to the party, he didn't go in with us and we didn't see him again until it was time to return home. So why wouldn't I be suspicious, he certainly didn't volunteer to be my escort; his arm was being twisted by Mom, Dad and Sylvia.

"Well, you know, I ran into Calvin, he asked about you and I tole him you was going to your prom. An' he said he wish he could take you—he has a tuxedo and everything—he gonna come by and take you in a cab, wif a corsage and everything. So, how about it, you go wif him, instead a me?"

Somehow I agreed to this plan, even though I thought it was stupid, and I certainly couldn't identify this Calvin in my mind.

I got all dressed up in borrowed clothes; I even wore my mother's coat with the fur collar. It was January in Chicago, and my winter coat didn't provide enough warmth over a scooped-out neckline.

Calvin arrived late, without a cab, much too late for us to join my friend Kennie and her date (my Jimmy) or any of my other friends in the neighborhood, most of whom had joined forces (two couples to a cab) to get to the affair. Limousines for us kids were unheard of in those days. A few kids had fathers who had cars, this was another way a few got there, but many arrived by bus even though by bus was considered totally unsophisticated.

I had never laid eyes on Calvin before in my life. He was a total disappointment. He was several inches shorter than I was in my high heels. He had a bad case of acne, his tuxedo made him resemble a cartoon character and he brought me an artificial corsage. We rode to the Parkway Ballroom on the bus.

When we got to the prom, we met up with Kennie and Jimmy. Jimmy made it a point to befriend Calvin, and during the course of the evening Jimmy quizzed him about himself and about how he knew me, because the last Jimmy had heard was that I was not going to be there. Calvin told Jimmy, "I didn't know Betty Anne before today. I know her brother, Ted, from the pool hall, an' I owed him some money. He said I didn't haffa pay him if I took his sister to her prom. I axed him, how ugly is this chick that you haffa pay somebody to take her out? Don't she got a boyfriend that can take her, a prom is a special thing? He say she ain't ugly, she attractive, an' she got a boyfriend, but you know how it is, her boyfriend be expecting her to put out if she goes to the prom wit' him."

Jimmy was so hurt that he almost cried when he told me what Calvin had said. We both knew that he had never pressured me in that way.

This was as close to a discussion about sex at that time, as I ever got with a boy. As one of the girls who was determined to not become intimate with any boy, I knew that when a guy started telling me how much he loved me, it was probably over. Guys would take you out for about three months before asking the question. After that time, I would become non-communicative.

I wouldn't talk to him on the phone, and he'd better not come by my house!

I don't think I was that much different from a lot of the girls I knew, many of us treated boys in this harsh manner. It wasn't a case of not liking the guy. I had as much libido as any other girl, I was just more determined than a lot of them to avoid the trap of falling for some guy and ending up like my mother. I was strengthened in my determination, perhaps, by the fact that I was more experienced than my friends at suppressing my feelings. My friends didn't have a bunch of little brothers and sisters they had to always take care of, so maybe they would take chances—I couldn't—I knew, first hand, the frustrations and hardships of too many children, too soon in not enough space, with not enough income

MY FIRST MARRIAGE PROPOSAL

When I was a high school junior, I came into my late afternoon Spanish class, and there on my desk, in the front of the class, was a neatly folded note. The note started off with the words, "Baby look . . ."

I don't remember the rest of the wording, although, I saved it for years and had it almost memorized. It was a proposal of marriage from one of the guys in the class that I couldn't even remember ever speaking to. He claimed to be a veteran, and he said that he had rings for me and we could go downtown and get married that very day! I didn't even know his name! In the note, he had to tell me which seat he sat in. I looked back at him, and he nodded and tapped the breast pocket of his suit jacket. I suppose that was to indicate that he really did have a wedding ring set. As silly as I was, and as much as I wanted to whoop and laugh, I looked at him, in his blue suit, looking very serious, and I became uncharacteristically cool. I had the whole class time to think about what I would say to him.

When the class ended, I told him that I was too young to get married and that I planned to finish high school and go on to college. He accepted this without much comment. Then I sought out my good buddies, Bootsie, Kennie, Gwen and Mary Katherine, read them the note in the girls' bathroom and we all fell out laughing! I never saw that boy in class again. I kept the note for years, then lost track of it among my things.

WORK HARD, ACHIEVE GOAL, SLACK OFF!

My high school years were pretty happy. I was so glad to join the many organizations available to students that I over did it and participated in much more than I should. My favorite was working on the school newspaper, and then—in my senior year—working on the graduation journal. I even had a short stint of serving as mayor of the school (that title was given to the president of the student council). In addition to all of the school activities, I worked three hours a day at Neisner's Ten Cent Store, weekdays, and all day on Saturdays. I rarely studied, except when there was a specific goal that I wanted to achieve; like the time I wanted get my picture in the school newspaper and the journal as a member of the honor society. I worked hard to qualify for inclusion, and then lost interest when I had obtained that goal. I let my grades slip and did just enough to get by in most classes.

There was a lot of sharing of answers to homework amongst my peers, and a lot of lazy teachers who didn't seem to care that I wasn't in class due to a school activity meeting. Many times they'd excuse me from doing the work. But, in the second half of my junior year, Miss Alpert flunked me in Spanish. This was a rude awakening, but oddly enough, my respect for Miss Alpert increased ten-fold. I knew I didn't deserve to pass this hard-working, organized teacher's class. She was one of a few who had high expectations of her pupils, whereas many of the teachers let me slide because I was one of the 'nice girls'.

Wendell Phillips was one of only two completely 'Negro' academic high schools in Chicago at that time. The other was DuSable, and there was fierce rivalry between the two schools in sports and in expressive arts. There was little competition in academics, because it was not stressed, and just barely taught. Nat King Cole had attended my school, years before I arrived and left his influence, for decades, over performing groups trying out for the annual Spring Festival Variety Show. Girls were never part of these trios, but our modern dance group, which was all girls, got a chance to interpret their music in movement. We also danced to other popular recordings of the time. Our choreography of Billie Holiday's 'Strange Fruit' was said to beat anything DuSable had ever produced. I felt like a star after our performance, knowing that I had helped to create the dance.

'BUNYON BETTY'

The only regret I had about attending my modern dance class was the nickname that my friends gave me. They called me

'Bunion Betty'. We always danced barefoot, so I was unable to hide my deformed feet. I pretended that the name didn't bother me, but it did—a whole lot. I had developed bunions when I was eight years old, and I've been ashamed of them all my life. I think that a combination of two practices caused these ugly knobs to grow on my feet; the x-ray machine in the shoe department at Sears Roebucks and wearing shoes that I had outgrown.

People are very surprised when I tell them about what I recall; a neat self-operating x-ray machine where customers could check to see if the fit of a shoe was correct. It stood prominently, with no restrictions, in the children's section of the shoe department in downtown Chicago's Sears and Roebucks. Every time my siblings and I visited the store, we'd go up to the shoe department and play in the x-ray machine. This was when I was a girl of five to eight years old. For a couple of hours, we'd stick our feet (and sometimes our hands, too) in the machine, press the button and watch; with great amusement, as our phalanges transformed into greenish, murky movies on the small screen inside the cabinet. Mother encouraged us to spend time in the shoe department so that she could shop in peace. My bunions are the most prominent among my siblings, but all of us who 'played in' the x-ray machine have them, as well as other problems with our feet. I refer to them, and to my replaced teeth as my 'scars of poverty'!

SURE STOP!

Just about everything I did, during my high school years, was in groups of about five or more kids. We knew there was safety in numbers, so when we walked the two miles to the Y.M.C.A. for our Hi Y (boys) and Tri Hi Y (girls) meetings and recreation sessions, we were always with neighborhood friends.

Most of the time, the weather was not in our favor on those dark winter nights in Chicago; with the wind whistling through our outerwear and the tears freezing on our cheeks. We would sometimes shorten our trip home by hitching a ride. We perfected a method we called 'sure stop'.

One of the girls (sometimes I was the one) would stand on the curb near the street and thumb for a ride. That was after checking to make sure there was plenty of space in the car that was being thumbed. In those days, most cars were big six-seaters, the compact cars we know today hadn't been invented. We would look for a lone driver with no passengers (almost always a middle-aged man). When he pulled over to the curb and stopped, the girl would grab the door handle with her left hand and step back so that the driver wouldn't be able to pull her into the car. Then she'd gesture with her right hand and shout, "Come on gang, we got a ride!"

The other kids would appear from behind trees or doorways or wherever else we were crouching, and fill up the man's car. Drivers were almost always good natured about giving us lifts but a few demanded that we shut their door, and then sped off.

'Getting Over' was something we did for fun. The teacher who taught U.S. History was a woman who had elephantiasis. Her legs resembled mobile tree trunks, the class was on the third floor. She was always late. We organized ourselves into a homework group whereby each student would have to answer only one homework question. Since the teacher assigned about 30 questions per night, out of a workbook, we always knew what the assignment would be. We'd take one question each per day, get to class before the teacher could make it up the stairs, and simply fill in the answers supplied by the other students. This smart-alex-y attitude did not serve me well when I got to junior college and found that I didn't even know the parts of speech and that I knew almost nothing about history. Most of us didn't think about the missed opportunity for learning.

The history of Abraham Lincoln was taught at even the poorest of ghetto schools. Every senior class was required to take the trip to Lincoln's home; (our state's capitol) Springfield, Illinois. We arrived by bus for this day trip and almost immediately found out about formal segregation. When some of our group tried to buy malted milk and soda pop from the near-by Walgreens, they were refused service and told that 'coloreds' were not allowed to be served at the counter, we'd have to buy it at the fountain and take it out.

HOW AMERICA WORKS!

It was around this same time that I got another lesson in how America works. I had been promoted on my job at the ten-cent store; from sales clerk to floor-walker and office clerk. As floor-walker, some of my duties were to supply change to sales clerks and to help secure the many small items from theft by placing glass over them. I learned how to measure and cut one-quarter-inch thick glass and put it over the designated items. As office clerk, I was exposed to the books of this dime store chain. Each store had a number; our store was number thirty-eight. The other store in the 'colored' neighborhood was forty-seven.

When new items were delivered to the stores, a document was sent from headquarters that listed, by store number, how much was to be charged for each item. Store numbers 38 and 47 always had items marked up at least 10 cents above the other stores. When I asked my boss about this (she was a former sales clerk who worked full time in the office and was rumored to be the girlfriend of our married, German manager who was rumored to be an escaped Nazi prisoner of war) she told me that it was because the theft rate was so high. With this answer, I wondered why I was cutting so much glass and messing up my hands since the store was recouping those theft expenses. I practiced what I was learning to do; suppress my need to blurt out my outrage, keep my mouth closed, and continued to cut glass.

I had worked at the dime store for only a few weeks when the promotion was made. I still made only fifty cents an hour and I still had to cut glass.

BACK AT HOME IN THE PROJECTS

With each new baby, our family shifted from poor to poorer, and by the time my baby sister, Sandra, was born we were so poor that we couldn't even afford to replace the area rug in the living room. We had always had a nine by twelve foot rug to cover up that ghastly black, fake, marbleized tile that masqueraded as flooring in our housing project home. When the rug had gotten so ragged that we were constantly tripping, it had been thrown away.

Because of shifting hours, Dad wasn't able to work more than one job, he still made window guards, but that didn't pay off in enough extra cash to make a difference. In fact, it became the subject of many arguments between my parents; with Mother accusing Dad of . . . "liking to go into other women's apartments on the pretense of installing those damn window guards!" There were other arguments that recurred over and over, like the one about my dad's participation in his labor union. He had been voted in as vice-president of his local, and that meant he had to attend meetings. Dad had always been a real stay-at-home guy. If he wasn't at work he, was at home so this was a new subject in my parents' arguments that I had to monitor. More than three years of loving behavior did not prepare us for a very ugly episode:

Daddy's sister, Wilma, was visiting from Tennessee. She came to Chicago as often as she could get away from her studies because she was dating my uncle Clyde (this was before he married Sylvia). Daphne and I used to speculate about Clyde and Wilma marrying and blessing us with 'double cousins' but Sylvia put an end to that dream.

Wilma had just finished her nurse's training. Mother wanted to show her a good time, and since there was no school, we had all gone to Brookfield Zoo. Daddy came home from work a few minutes before we got back and became upset because no one was home and his dinner wasn't ready. As soon as we got in, he started to argue with Mom. He became so angry that he used curse words, something I almost never heard him do, then he struck her and knocked her down the stairs! Wilma was horrified! In fact, we were all horrified. Every one became silent. It was a good thing Wilma was there, and able to put her nurse's training to use, as she administered cold compresses to Mom who had passed out from the blow. That was the last time I witnessed a physical encounter between my parents. I was about thirteen years old.

YOU HAD THAT BABY, NOT ME!

I was a senior in high school, working every day and visiting the Y for group activities when I could find the time. I had a boyfriend whom I saw mostly during group gatherings. We didn't have many formal dates. It was through group gatherings that we stayed in touch. The one thing I didn't have time for was babysitting! I felt I had certainly done my share with my three brothers from the time I was eight to the time I was seventeen. Yet, here comes my mother one Saturday night, with my new little sister, telling me that I would have to baby sit Sandra because she and Dad were going out. I was so mad that I saw red. I had a date with my boyfriend. I had worked all day, and I had bought a new blouse to wear to the party we planned to attend.

Mom had let me know how unhappy she was with her last pregnancy, she had complained all the time, and had admonished me to, ". . . never let a man keep you pregnant all the time! Get your education, make something outta yourself, be able to earn your own money, don't be beholding to NO man!" She had almost bugged me about going to the birth control clinic to be fitted for a diaphram but I had always refused because the example of her hard life had inoculated me against having pre-marital sex.

As she stood there, demanding that I baby-sit with her baby, her words of warning flooded my memory, and, with passion, I told her,

"You had that baby, I didn't! If you didn't want her, why didn't you take your own advice, why didn't YOU go to the birth control clinic and make SURE YOU didn't get pregnant like you're always telling me about!"

When I got up off the floor, I decided, maybe I would go on and baby-sit my little sister after all since I didn't want to go on a date with bruises all over my face and have to explain to everyone at the party how they got there . . . along with the black eye and busted lip.

THE NEW TELEVISION SET

In the beginning of my sophomore year, someone at school made the announcement that the Hadley Family had a new television set. This was sensational news! Everyone from school was dying to view this new form of entertainment. I don't remember being invited, but I do remember having the feeling that I had to see it, like, it was not as if it were someone's property to which they were entitled to have privacy over, but more like some public spectacle, like a train wreck, that anyone had a right to see. After all, hadn't we all seen pictures in the newspapers of these sets being sold in downtown stores? So, now, one had arrived in our very own neighborhood, and I just HAD to see it!

The details as to how I arrived at the Hadley's house, or with whom I went, have long been forgotten, but the scene at the house is locked in my memory.

Everyone at school knew Inas Marie Hadley, she was the girl who had been caught smoking in the girls' bathroom, and the guidance counselor, Mrs. Mosley, (who was "Negro" like us) had sent for Inas' mother. Inas was a very heavy-set girl, and her mother was about the same size. Inas came to school late the next day, dressed in her mother's clothes, including a hat with a heavy veil which covered her face. During the course of the interview with Mrs. Mosley, while pleading that, ". . . my daughter not be suspended . . ." declaring that, ". . . I will see to it that this never happens again!" Mrs. Mosley peeked up under the veil, pulled it up and declared, "INAS MARIE HADLEY, THAT'S NOT YOUR MOTHER, THAT'S YOU!!"

There were about thirty people sitting shoulder-to-shoulder on chairs and on the living room floor. All were staring at a small, flickering, green-lit screen in a darkened room. Because of the snow-like quality of the screen and the large number of bodies in the room, a picture or a program was impossible to discern but that didn't keep me from talking about the experience for days. I had actually seen this new phenomenon called television!

YMCA; THE CENTER OF MY WORLD

Most of my social needs were expressed and met through the teenage girls' program, Tri-Hi-Y sponsored by the YMCA. My friends and I were members of Alpha, one of several 'clubs' which met at the South Side YMCA. The boys' groups were known as Hi-Y and they were named for the schools they attended, but the girls' groups were named after Greek letters of the alphabet, such as Beta or Gamma; however, we were still separated by schools. All Alpha Tri-Hi-Y members attended Wendell Phillips High School.

Meetings were held every Sunday afternoon, with other activities after school during the week, and dances and other social events on Saturday evenings. I attended something at the Y about three times a week. There would be scores of 'Negro' teenagers attending club meetings on Sundays. The opportunity to meet kids from other schools was wonderful. I soon concluded that the boys from Tilden High School (an integrated, all male school) were the best-looking. Girls from Englewood, the school that I had wanted to attend, had the reputation of being the smartest and the prettiest. It was also the safest school for 'Negroes', and it was integrated. This meant that all of the white people had not as yet moved out of the community.

When I began eighth grade, my mother urged me to tell my teacher that I had moved. She said, "You better tell the teacher, now 'cause if you tell them near the end of the year, they won't believe you. They'll know that you just wanna get a chance to go to Englewood High. If you say so now, they will send your records there. Don't wait, they'll just ask for the gas bill, or phone bill with your uncle Clyde's address on it, if you tell them that now you live with your uncle and aunt." I found it very difficult to go up to my teacher and tell her that bald-faced lie, so I procrastinated until warm weather came, then I went up and told the lie. By then, my records had been sent to our slum school, Wendell Phillips; my neighborhood school.

On my first day of high school, I showed up at Englewood with my mom, and was detained in the office for most of the morning because my records had been sent to Phillips. Mother had left Daphne in charge at home.

There were many cases like mine—students trying to get into a better school than their neighborhoods had to offer—and the shrewd clerks in the offices knew just how to handle them. When the clerk finally got to us, she asked a few questions: "With whom did Betty Anne live? What are the names of all the children in the family?" My mother answered that we all had moved in with Clyde and Sylvia on Sixty-First Street. Then the clerk read the Thirty-Eighth Street phone number," Drexel 0006", aloud, and asked if that was the old number.

Before leaving the apartment, and in preparation for the lies she would tell, Mother had cautioned Daphne (who was left at home with the younger children) to not answer the telephone. She had stressed that command when she emphatically told Daphne, "No matter what, do not answer the phone!"

My mother answered, yes to the clerk's phone number question. The clerk called the number. It rang only twice. She said, "Hello, what is your name?"

We could hear the response on our side of the phone. "Daphne!." I never attended one class at Englewood. It was off to Wendell Phillips for four years!

HI-Y, TRI-HI-Y

Phillips Hi-Y and Alpha Tri-Hi-Y had the largest number of teenagers in their clubs because the YMCA was closest to our school. We could see Gordon Parks out in an adjacent lot filming tin cans and bricks with his woolly hair, as long as mine (now that my hair had decided to grow) bending with the wind. He resided at the South Side YMCA, and we thought of him as kind of crazy by the way he'd look at us and by the huge 'natural' hair he sported, long before it became stylish. I suppose he was using his artistic eye when he'd look AT us and PAST us at the same time.

We would linger in the halls and visit with some of the young men who lived at the Y. One guy, from West Virginia, was particularly attractive to me. He was kind of weird, because he brushed his thick bushy eyebrows up to give himself an Orson Wells look. He was attending mortuary school, and he joked that he could give us a lift home in his hearse if one sat up front with the driver and if eight lay down in the back. Actually, he didn't have access to a hearse, he rode a motorcycle.

After club meetings we could attend a loosely-structured class, taught by Mr. Dade who was not part of the YMCA staff that supervised our meetings. In fact, Mr. Dade didn't have a meeting room assigned to him, he was just sort of, there. He would show up shortly before our regular meetings adjourned, wait, and gather those of us who wanted to hear his lecture, and march us to wherever he could find an open space. One time, when there were no empty rooms at the Y, he marched us into a near-by school playground and we sat on concrete and in swings listening to him.

Mr. Dade was in his mid-twenties, very well groomed, (except for coarse, bumpy skin where he shaved) always dressed in shirt and tie, and quite good-looking. He did not live at the Y. I looked forward to his talks because they were interesting and made me think, but also because Donald Gist, a boy from Englewood High School usually attended, and I had a crush on Donald, who paid little attention to me and probably had no idea that I liked him.

When I found out That Donald Gist was going to the Halloween Hop, I was determined to make an impression on him, there. I didn't have a costume so I convinced a girl I knew named Lourdes, that she should loan me the costume she wore for her dance performance. It was orange, red and yellow, tight-fitting and full of ruffled flounces on the skirt. She had danced with castanets in a Spanish scene. Lourdes was the daughter of one of my mother's club members who was from the Philippine Islands, she wasn't a close friend of mine and she attended a different school.

At first, I thought Lourdes wasn't going to loan the dress to me. She said she'd have to ask her mother. It took so long for her to get back to me that I started thinking about what other outfit I could wear, but I knew that nothing else would make Donald look up and take notice like that bright, sassy 'Carmen dress'.

I got the dress from Lourdes the day of the Halloween Hop and squeezed into it. I put a dime store fake flower behind my ear and attended the hop. I waited, strained my neck, searched the crowd and peered into every boy's face who had the general configuration of Donald Gist. He was not there. He never showed up!

And it was a good thing I knew how to sew because, before returning the dress to Lourdes, I had to re-enforce all of the seams in the bodice of that dress.

Mr. Dade always started his talks quoting Karl Marx, "From each, according to his ability, to each, according to his need!" Then he would tell us about the wonderful system of government, called Communism, where there was no racial discrimination and everybody was a valued member of society. It was a system with no slums and no suffering. Mr. Dade probed us with hypothetical scenarios; such as, "Let's say you want to become a doctor. You have the brains but you don't have the money. Everybody knows you need money to go to medical school and you can't work your way through medical school. What do you do?" Of course, the answer was always, "The Communist System!"

I attended Mr. Dade's lectures long after Donald stopped coming. Donald had graduated high school and gone away to college. His brother, Gerald, was still in our social circle, that was how we got bits of news about Donald.

Mr. Dade's talks started to get pretty predictable, and then a little boring. I soon stopped going.

One thing I admired about Mr. Dade was that he never got flirty with the girls in the group. He was always polite and respectful. Yet, he operated in a culture of extreme macho male flirtation, where many low-class men would stand on busy street corners ogling females passing by, calling out to them in often obscene language, and even reaching out as if to grab the girls' breasts. Afterwards, they would laugh and touch their crotches when the women cursed them or the young girls dashed out of their way.

This kind of harassment was so common that (even though we hated it) we just accepted it as part of life, even assessing (in an off-hand way) our levels of appeal to the opposite sex by its frequency and intensity. These men did not shout out to unattractive females.

One day, as my friend, Bootsie (who was beautiful) and I passed the 'colored' hotel near 35th and South Park, one of the men standing around ogling the girls, said, (in a very raspy, unmistakably familiar voice), "Hey Baby, how y'all today?" It was Louie Armstrong! Calloused lip, handkerchief and all!

DAPHNE IN BLOOM

My sister, Daphne, was sometimes with me on my trips to the Y, but often she was not. Daphne was becoming quite the beauty. She was petite—about a size six—had great legs and a fine figure. The hair she wore in ringlets as a little girl, when processed, hung down as long silky tresses. She was quiet and shy and studied all the time. She was a member of the honor society for her full four years of high school.

Daphne had her own circle of friends; lovely, college-bound, classy girls who were very much like her. When she turned sixteen, she got a part-time job at our local branch library. Daphne was saving money in a large, pink crockery piggy bank to buy a typewriter. She made regular deposits in the pig. The pig sat imposingly on the dresser we shared, as my extremely neat sister washed and blocked her five sweaters on weekends in preparation for the coming week. It was always five sweaters, one for each day of the week. When they were dry, she folded them and placed them in her drawer. It was on only one occasion that I snuck one of the sweaters out of her drawer and wore it to school. Daphne put up quite a fuss and snatched me by my hair, so I never tried that again! She could FIGHT—with her 'rope-jumping' self!

I, on the other hand, almost never studied and paid little attention to clothes. On a Friday you could tell what I wore on Monday by counting down five outfits slung across my chair in our room. I saved no money, had few plans, many diverse friends, and was a sloppy mess to live with, especially when I was involved in some art project.

Like many big sisters, I took Daphne for granted most of the time. She was a fixture, a steady, reliable presence that neither assisted me in my pursuits nor hindered me. We had a loving relationship because I loved to tell jokes and she loved to laugh at them. But there was an aloofness about her that made me confide in my best friend, Bootsie, before I'd confide in her. For example, after a date with a new boy, if I tried to find out if he attempted to kiss her. She wouldn't talk about it.

Daphne was very talented, she was a member of Mask and Gavel Drama Club at school. She had played the character, Jean Marie from 'The Seagulls', and had won a 'Best Actress in A One-Act Play' certificate when she appeared downstate in Aurora, Illinois' all high school drama competition. Appearing in dramatic productions at school had raised her profile, so everyone knew her and many boys had crushes on her. And wow, could she jump rope!

There were many occasions when boys from school approached me and had me thinking they were interested in me but they were really trying to get to my younger sister. When I caught on to the game, I was generally amused and would encourage the game, especially if he had a car.

Later, I learned to distinguish the Daphne Admirers from those who were interested in me by who made eye-contact. If they made eye-contact with me, I would peg them as Daphne's boys because the boys who were attracted to me would, generally; stare at my chest.

One day, two boys from our Hi-Y club approached me to let me know that their club was having a dance and the guys decided to have a queen. I was very flattered to think that I was going to be queen for their spring dance, otherwise why would they mention this to me? Just about the time I was going to make my acceptance statement they said all the guys had voted for Daphne. They wondered if I, as her big sister, could get her to consent. I don't remember if she was crowned queen or not, I do remember that I told her about the selection, and joked, with mixed emotion, about my mistake.

ARE YOU GOING TO DONALD GIST'S FUNERAL?

As I sat at the lunch table where I usually ate my lunch, a classmate of mine joined the table at the other end, sat down and asked the boy next to him, "Are you going to Donald Gist's funeral?"

I was stunned! I couldn't ask, "What happened to Donald?" I suddenly lost my ability to speak, to move, to cry, to call out with any kind of questions, to swallow the food I was eating! I was incapable of doing anything human. I just sat there until I had to go to class. I don't know how I made it to the end of the school day, but I do remember being at my job and hearing the most popular, and best-selling record of that period being played over and over on the record player at the record counter. The singer on the single disc, 78 RPM record slowly repeated, "What'll I do when you are far away, da dah, da dah, what'll I do?"

For three hours, I had to endure that song, as the clerk on the record counter rang up sale after sale of 'What'll I Do?'

When I got to school the next day, I still couldn't muster the courage to find out what had happened to Donald. Since he wasn't a Wendell Phillips student, not everyone knew him. I couldn't ask my close friends—some knew him, others didn't—for fear of letting my emotions flow all over the school. I had never confessed to anyone how much I cared for him. In my world, a girl would never reveal that she liked a boy before he made some indication that he liked her first.

It was a few days later, at the YMCA that Donald's death was openly discussed. I was not the one who brought up the subject and I was still not able to ask any questions. I was still plunged into emotional lock-down at work every time I heard that song torturing me, by asking, 'What'll I Do?' Finally, I got the full story from the weekly 'Defender' Newspaper (our 'Negro' newspaper that my family read every week).

Donald was attending Howard University and staying off campus with a family in Washington, D. C. He rigged up some creative way to shoot himself with a shot gun at their house. His was a suicide.

'What'll I Do?' remained popular for a very long time, and even today it can occasionally be heard on some jazz stations. I can never hear it without experiencing a small piece of sadness and thinking about Donald Gist.

I think, especially, about the last time I saw him. It was during a Y-sponsored trip to Bahia Temple, in Winnetka, Illinois. It was a place we visited, like going to a museum. I and my friends hardly associated it with religion, although it was a place of worship, with its many-sided, golden, gleaming façade and its expansive beautiful interior. The monks who greeted us always made us feel welcome, no matter how many times we came. And it cost nothing to go there—just the price of the elevated train ride.

We visited Bahia Temple only in the wintertime, though, because we could walk across the lake to get there from the elevated train. Warm weather visits required going a different route that cost an extra fare and it was difficult to find.

I can still remember seeing Donald, walking along with his brother, Gerald, crossing the lake with the rest of the Hi-Y guys and Tri-Hi-Y girls—a party of about 25 kids, headed towards the beautiful dome-shaped temple. I can't remember whether Donald even spoke to me, but I picture him throwing a few snowballs with the rest of the guys on that trip, and I can recall being happy that he was in the group.

One of the boys who liked Daphne, but found me more approachable was a guy from school named Leo. Leo owned a used Hudson car. He wasn't bad-looking, in fact, he could have been good-looking if he hadn't worn a 'fan'. A fan was long hair at the front hairline that got combed back over the very short haircut on the remaining part of a boy's head. The really classy boys wouldn't be caught dead with a fan. My father was the barber in our household, and no matter how my brothers would have pleaded, Dad absolutely would have refused to allow them to wear fans. The 'fan-comb-back' was very popular at our school but not generally among college-bound guys.

Leo offered me many lifts in his car. He was often near when I needed a ride from school to my job. I got so used to Leo's lifts that I began to rely on them and make excuses to my friends about why I wasn't walking home with them. The times that I hoped for lifts from Leo, but he didn't show, were the times I walked the two miles, alone, having missed the opportunity to have company by waiting to see if he'd show.

I GET ARRESTED

Summer vacation was just underway when, one evening, Leo drove up to the wooden horses that blocked our street. I was standing outside, so I saw him arrive. Of course, I recognized the car immediately. He had come to visit Daphne. No one was at home in our apartment so I wouldn't even think to invite him in.

Everyone else had gone to see a movie, but I had been at work until 6:0'clock, when the dime store closed. I greeted Leo and got in his car to chat with him. About two minutes into our visit, the two flunky colored project guards who patrolled our section of the project on foot, came up to the car, and, with very rude language, ordered us to get out of the car! This was observed by many of my neighbors and I was embarrassed. The two 'uncle tom' guards proceeded to search Leo's car. Leo was cool. He just stood there like it had happened before (and maybe it had), but I became furious! When the search was over, Leo jumped back into his car and drove away. With embarrassment fueling my outrage, I went in hot pursuit of the two uniformed project guards who had continued to walk up the street. I caught up to them near our closest business street, Cottage Grove. "Why did you all pull us out of the car?" I demanded. "Why did you search the car?" I screamed. "Go on home, girl. Don't be axing us nothing!" said one of the guards, in his meanest voice. "You don't know who you're messing with, my parents can get both of you fired!" I threatened, with no idea how that would be accomplished. "Didn't we tell you to git on home! You better go on now or we'll lock you up!" The other guard warned. "You can't arrest me. Y'all ain't nothing but guards, them uniforms don't make you no cops, y'all ain't nothing but flunky, project guards!" I screamed at the very top of my voice.

A small crowd of people had gathered, and darkness was descending. I was wearing tight-fitting, cut-off jeans and a tee shirt. Those two burly, middle-aged guards grabbed me by my wrists and held me in an immovable vise. I kicked and screamed, and proved how bi-lingual I was by changing into my other language: profanity! This scene continued for about three minutes before a squad car stopped and two white Chicago cops got out. The guards told them that I was disturbing the peace. One of the cops frisked me even though I was wearing skin tight clothes, and there was no way I could have been carrying a concealed weapon, so it amounted to him getting a free feel. Handcuffs were placed on my wrists, and I was shoved into a squad car, taken to the precinct, put into a holding cell and locked up.

Nothing I had ever experienced in life—no movie, nothing I'd read, no story on radio, no personal recount shared by somebody! Nothing my vivid imagination ever concocted, NOTHING—prepared me for the experience of being locked up, in jail, incarcerated, arrested!!! The feeling of being totally alone, cut off from those who cared about me, at the mercy of hostile white men who had stories told about them abusing defenseless Negro girls, was overwhelming. The feeling that I was no longer in charge of myself caused a pain to seize the lower part of my abdomen and wretch it up in a dry heave of excruciation.

The cell was all concrete and steel, with a cot that hung from the wall and a wall-hung toilet without a seat. The place was about the size of my bedroom at home, but since there was nothing on the floor, there was more move-around space. The cot had a thin mattress covered in blue and white ticking with a gray, itchy-looking army type blanket on it.

At the station, there were a couple of other cops and a woman, who did some swift paper work, and after I was locked up, everyone left. I couldn't scream out to anyone, I was so traumatized that I became quiet.

I rebelled against becoming a real prisoner—as if to say, 'I will not validate this thing that is happening to me as being reality'—I refused to sit down on the grimy little cot. I stood by the bars of my cell, as far away from the toilet as I could, until I was exhausted. Then I hugged the bars and slumped down as far as I could without touching the floor. The smell of Lysol and the clang of the cell gates are the indelible memories of the half hour or so that I spent in lock-up.

I can't understand how anyone could go through that experience and not do everything in his or her power to keep from going through that experience again. The first arrest should inoculate ANYONE against future imprisonment possibilities.

My parents and our precinct captain rushed me out of that cell before I could work up a good cry, and although I didn't even talk about getting the two guards fired, one of them got rotated over to another section of the projects and both were paired with different partners. I went about my business of trying to live down the most embarrassing experience of my life, because absolutely everybody knew about it.

ON TO JUNIOR COLLEGE

Mine was the last class at Wendell Phillips High School to graduate in January. There was no summer in which to acclimate to college. I had to plunge right in to Herzl Junior College the first Monday after graduation. I chose to go to the far-away Herzl because most of my friends would be attending Wilson, which was nearer to my house, and I knew that I would not study if I went with them. Travel to Herzl was over an hour each way and there were no Leo Lifts from there.

My load of college courses was: pre-MED biology, business math, accounting and English. I had avoided being placed in remedial English—where all 'Negro' students were placed—by simply not taking the placement test. However, if there was ever a student who needed remediation in English, I was one. On the first day of class I discovered how I was handicapped by not knowing my parts of speech, which was basic English, taught in lower grades in elementary school. Our ghetto schools were staffed with some teachers who were being punished by being assigned there. These teachers would transfer if their teaching ratings were higher. They did not, for the most part, prepare us for college or for much of anything else academic.

I had no idea that we had to buy all of our books. I had no money saved and I couldn't work because of the long hours I had to spend in class and to travel. Mother gave me the money for books and the whole family had to eat beans all week. It was much later that I learned about purchasing used books or getting them from the library, keeping them for the entire semester and returning them to pay a maximum fine of only about 60 cents per book. The English books, from which I learned the parts of speech on my own, were borrowed from the library.

Our family profile was; POOR! Daddy was the only breadwinner. Mother was home with Baby Sandra. Theodore got married at age 19 and his wife was expecting their first child. Daphne had the after-school job at the library that gave her pocket change but I wasn't able to work at all. Though I had tried to work on Saturdays the demands of college were too great. We were still without a rug to replace the one that had to be discarded. Bubby had grown into his teens with a lot of resentment towards Daddy's methods of discipline and by age 14, he was distancing himself from the rest of the family. Arnold and Kenneth were attending Catholic School because the public school had become unsafe.

We still lived in the project, but many of our old friends and acquaintances, buoyed by the improving post-war economy and spurred by deteriorating neighborhood conditions, had moved. Some families had purchased homes on contract in Lawndale and other far-away parts of the city. The contracts were iron clad documents that allowed 'Negroes' to purchase homes with little or no money down since mortgages were generally not available.

Red-lining was the norm in 'Negro' neighborhoods and restrictive covenance was still on every deed. Red-lining was a property rating system used by banks to withhold mortgages and insurance from neighborhoods considered poor economic risks. The advantage of contract buying was that houses were in a somewhat integrated neighborhood where the schools had higher ratings. The disadvantage of contract buying was that the houses were greatly overpriced, most available housing was inferior, and one missed payment could result in loss of the property with no compensation.

Our neighborhood was becoming more and more dangerous as drugs flooded it and made zombies of some of our young people. Newspaper and magazine articles identified Chicago's 39th Street and South Park Ave. as ". . . the drug capitol of the world . . .", and I lived about seven blocks away from there.

GEORGE

One of the most heartbreaking cases of a young man falling into drugs was a boy in my neighborhood who had everything going for him. He was handsome, he had ambitions of going to college. He was a good student, a good athlete, and he had a supportive family. His name was George McLaughlin. He was a casual friend to my brother, Theodore, and, at one time—before heroin—I had a small crush on him.

George was about 16 when he dropped out of school because of his heroin habit. By then, George wasn't allowed into anybody's home because he'd steal anything not nailed down. Before he left school, he was even suspected of stealing Dolly Ferguson's shoes from her gym locker. That wouldn't be such a big deal if the shoes were just an ordinary pair of shoes, but Dolly had very unusual feet. They were very long and narrow and shaped funny. All of Dolly's shoes had to be custom made, and the stolen shoes were no exception. They were medium brown 'swords' that laced up. They had absolutely no value to anyone but Dolly, so we all concluded that George must have stolen them, 'just to keep in practice'!

George became such a junkie that he would 'shoot up' in the hallways that led to our project apartments, and anyone could watch him through the half-glass door 'cooking' the stuff with a kitchen match and a spoon before tying an old necktie around his arm and then injecting himself with that poison. Sometimes he would be so knocked out by the injection that he'd sleep right there until roused by someone who knew his folks. The person would threaten George into vacating the hallway so that he wouldn't freeze to death.

If George McLaughlin made any contribution to society, it was as a negative role model. Children, as well as adults, knew him as the worst junkie in the neighborhood.

There were other guys in the area who were 'on the stuff', but they weren't as notorious as George. However, some became known through other exploits: Henry Smith was just 16 when he and another boy, influenced by Bogart and George Raft movies, stepped in to rob a diner with the undercover gun they'd bought, only to be blasted away by the owner. Henry had been a very close friend to Theodore. Neighborhood boys Douglass C. and James D. spent most of their youth in prison for the murder of a Chicago policeman. They were both on the 'stuff'.

This was the late 40s and well organized criminal powers were flooding our neighborhoods with narcotics. Our leaders had no experience with this kind of menace and were ill prepared to cope with the consequences of what it was doing to our communities and to our youth. Parents were baffled too. Those who could, got out. There were many problems which arose quite suddenly. There were unsafe streets, house break-ins, business closures, and vandalism from newly-made junkies who stripped every piece of copper and other sellable metal, from every place they could find it.

Even though it was common knowledge that a person could serve ten years in Leavenworth (the harshest prison in the country) for possession of just one marijuana cigarette, marijuana had long been a fact in our communities. Some entertainers were stigmatized by their association with it; nevertheless, smoking it was widespread and much out in the open. Strangely enough, in my day, girls were almost never involved. It was usually only boys who became junkies. It wasn't until the late sixties that drugs offered girls equal opportunities for 'junkie hood'.

There were no drug counselors, re-hab and treatment programs, only the criminal 'justice' system. So every time my friends and I heard about one of the boys we knew going to jail for a crime, we would scan our memories to identify him as one of the marijuana users, and he usually was. Smoking weed had not wrought these visible, devastating changes to our neighborhood, but it had provided a corridor to other drugs which had.

It was the new stuff, heroin, that was plaguing us. The young men who started out as pot-smokers were risk-takers who got caught up in addiction. Risk-takers start businesses. Risk-takers attain higher education, risk-takers pursue elected offices, and risk-takers are always the ones in the vanguard of the changes made in any social order. So heroin was robbing our community of our risk-taking youth, as well as leaving our areas poorer and poorer.

POVERTY HURTS

My life was as routine as it could get, with school, homework and chores. I had never felt the sting of being poor so much. Not having money was 'the pits'! It also made me feel totally guilty! I had been a contributor to the household income when I worked at Neisner's because my father charged me rent, which I was glad to pay. Dad charged rent to everybody who worked and lived in his house. It was usually about half of our take-home pay. Now I was extracting from my folks instead of contributing and I didn't know what to do about it. I was really trying to keep up with my studies, in spite of my poor study habits, but I was having trouble in some courses. Even though Daddy earned a decent wage, he was still the only one working, now that Theodore had moved out completely.

Being poor meant that everything purchased for the house was bought from Sears on credit with high interest rates. Being poor meant that every Christmas Season, Mother would don her snuggies and half of her winter wardrobe and walk to the bus in four—degrees-below-zero weather to go downtown to work in the Post Office as a temporary worker. Being poor meant that the adults in the family were happy when the three month's wait was over, so that they could sell some more blood. Being poor meant that when extra money was needed, mother would go to the pawn shop and pawn her wedding ring. When she was ready to redeem it, she would get into a big argument with the pawnbroker because she'd refuse to pay usury prices. She would cite the Illinois law that allowed her to pay only three percent interest, then the pawnbroker would hurl insults at her and curse and tell her to, "Never set foot in my shop again!"

Being poor also meant that instead of Daddy being remorseful about getting burned on the job, when—as a hot metal pourer—impurities in the alloy liquefied, popped and spewed hot liquid aluminum on him, he was jubilant. He would calculate what percentage of his skin burned, and how much money he would be compensated for his injuries. By the time Dad retired in 1974, with a little more than twenty-five years as a pourer, he had burns that added up to more than one hundred percent of his skin surface. These 'windfalls' would go to satisfy those overdue bills (there were always overdue bills) which were about to go into garnishment, or to quell the endless phone calls from people at collection agencies.

PANGS OF GUILT

There were two major pains I endured during this period of my life. One was the pain of guilt. Here I was—a high school graduate struggling with college courses, not bringing any money into the house—I did better when I was just a sophomore in high school. And I just didn't have it, when it came to my studies. I was always tired. My courses offered little joy (except for biology) and I had more than a two hour per-day commute. The other pain was physical, monthly and severe; sometimes lasting two days! The first day of my monthly menses put me in bed for at least the whole day with cramps so severe that I would scream and cry. Nothing I took would relieve the pain for long. 'Midol' would give me about an hour's worth of relief. Then the sharp, grasping, debilitating pain would overtake me again, long before the directions on the package allowed me to take another dose. I suffered with menstrual cramps for over twenty years. In addition to cramps, I developed a heavy case of pre-menstrual symptoms (PMS). PMS produced: shortness of breath, bloating, depression, ravenous appetite, cravings, phobias, mood swings, headaches and crying spells.

PMS would start ten to seven days before actual menstruation began, and grow worse until flow-time. Then the cramps and all of their pains began. After the cramps, I was a new person; jolly, good-natured, humorous and fun to be with. I was told that I had a hormone imbalance, but no one seemed to know what to do about it. For many years, this disorder gave me a real 'Jekyll and Hyde' personality. It interfered with my relationships and, would—later on—add to the souring of my marriage.

THE END OF MY FIRST COLLEGE TERM

Spring staggered in against a background of my not feeling very good about myself, and when it was time for final exams, I caught the worst case of the flu I had ever had. Except for English, I missed all of my finals. I obtained the necessary note from the clinic where I was treated, but I didn't know where to present it, or to whom. In spite of all the hard work I had done during my first semester in college, I accepted my fate: I was a college drop-out.

I left Herzl Junior College with only three semester hours of credit and a C in English. All of the other courses yielded no credit, only a mark indicating incomplete.

This was long before affirmative action, there were no counselors assigned to potential drop-out cases. There were no deans or peer advisors to help me. I had fulfilled the predicted statistic regarding freshmen (which was; over fifty percent of the freshman class would drop out during the first semester). Many Negro students were openly refused admission, some were pushed out, or Negroes were admitted under a quota system. I was totally baffled about advocating for myself. In my own community, where I knew the rules, I could argue with the best of them, but in this large institution, where almost everybody was white, where, (according to my limited experiences) white almost always equalled hostility. There were no friendly hands held out to me. I was just a lost, timid soul.

Finding a job for the summer was a must! I wasn't able to go back to the dime store, all of those jobs were filled. I traced down every lead I could, but it was the same old story everywhere. I was becoming desperate, it seemed all summer jobs were taken. My friends were no longer a cohesive unit, so I didn't have my buddies to rely on as buttresses for my flagging ego. My best friend, Bootsie, was married, expecting a baby and living on the West Side of Chicago; which was like another part of the world! My second best friend, Barbara, was away doing nurses' training with residency requirements. I didn't even have a boyfriend since Jimmy and I had drifted apart shortly after prom night. It was a time when I suffered from low self-esteem in all areas of my life. I had always been accustomed to having spending money, now I was completely broke. I was also trying hard to conceal from my family; the fact that I had flunked out of college.

THAT OL' PINK PIG!

One day, I was in the bedroom. Daphne was at work. I looked at that big old pink pig sitting on the dresser like it owned it. I picked up that pink pig and shook it. It was not as heavy as I thought it would be. I shook it again, and concluded that what I was hearing was a muffled, sliding noise—the bills—and some muted jingles—the coins—but mostly bills, otherwise the coins would jingle much louder, and it would be heavier. I thought, "Of course there would be more bills than coins. Hasn't Daphne been saving for months to buy her typewriter? She puts money in there every time she gets paid."

I returned the pig to the dresser and tried to stop thinking about all the cash sitting right there, inside that painted pig with that big upturned smile painted on his pink face, mocking me, while I was as broke as broke could be.

Several days later, I learned about some possible job openings at the hospital. Michael Reese Hospital was within walking distance of our apartment, but it was a mighty long walk and that summer was very hot. I would have to take the bus to go apply for a job. The day before, mother had told me about some hardship she was facing, so I knew not to ask her for any money.

Daphne was working extended hours for the summer. She had already gone to work when I lifted her pig and turned it over to see if any coins would drop out—just enough for carfare—which, of course, I'd pay back as soon as I got the job. Well, surprise! The coin tried to come through the slot, but a bill was blocking its way, so the edge of the bill protruded about three fourths of an inch. My nail file just happened to be on the dresser. Anchoring the upside-down pig between the side of the dresser and my bosom, I gingerly slid the nail file half way into the slot, flipped my wrist and extracted the five dollar bill, which was quite enough for bus fare and whatever else I needed for the day, and for a few days to come. 'Of course, I would put the five dollars back as soon as possible! If I don't get a job at the hospital, I might get a job doing something else, but I would definitely pay the money back. After all, I was no thief. I had never stolen anything in my life and I wasn't about to start being a thief at this age,' I reasoned.

1a) FAMILY MEMBERS CAME TO SEE ME ACCEPT' EXCELLENCE IN INTERNATIONAL EDUCATION AWARD' AT THE UNITED NATIONS IN 2013

1b) FAMILY MEMBERS WERE WITH ME IN 1980 FOR MY AWARD AS OUTSTANDING ETHNIC HERITAGE COORDINATOR

2a) MY LIGHTHOUSE HAT CREATION LIT UP NO WINS

2b) I SAT AT THE CONTROLS AND FLEW THIS PLANE FROM TRINADAD TO TOBAGO

2c) THREE TIMES A WEEK; "AQUACIZE" AT THE YMCA

3a) I INTRODUCED KWANZAA TO OUR SCHOOL DISTRICT

3b) I WAS LIBRARY TEACHER FOR TEN YEARS

3c) MASTER'S DEGREE 1987

4a) MY MOTHER . . . . AGE 14

4b) MY FIRST PROM

4c) I'M THE 3RD 'ELF' (FROM L.), 2ND ROW

5a) I AM THE BIG SISTER

5b) MANUE L AND I TOAST OUR WEDDING

5c) OUR FIRST CRUISE

6a) MOM (WEARING THE DRESS WITH NO BACK) AND DAD; DRESSED FOR A BALL

6b) MOM/DAD (FRONT AND CENTER) AND OUR EXPANDING FAMILY (I'M SITTING TO THE RIGHT OF DAD)

7a) I'M WITH ACTRESS/WRITER RUBY DEE AT THE GUILD'S ANNUAL PICNIC IN MY YARD

7b) I'M WITH GRACE F. EDWARDS, DIRECTOR, HARLEM WRITERS GUILD, AUTHOR OF 7 BOOKS

8a) I'M WITH IRVING BURGIE, AUTHOR/SONGWRITER; "DAY-O!!!"

8b) I'M WITH DR. MAE JAMISON, FIRST AFRICAN-AMERICAN FEMALE ASTRONAUT

9a) JAMAICA, 2003

9b) SAN FRANCISCO, 1992

9c) SWIMMING WITH DOLPHINS IN MEXICO, 2013

10a) HAWAII, 2004

10b) CUBA,2011

10c) ATLANTA, 1997

10d) ALASKA, 1995

10e) COPPER CANYON, MEXICO, 2000

11a) EGYPT, 2009

11b) EGYPT, 2009

11c) SOUTH AFRICA, 2009

12a) DISNEY CRUISE, 1987

12b) NEW ORLEANS, 1991

13a) CANCUN, 1994

13b) JAZZ CRUISE, 1997(ONE OF MANY)

14a) JEFF AT 8 MONTHS

14B) SIX-YEAR-OLD JEFF

14c) JEFF'S H.S. 'GRADUATION'

14d) JEFF AND HIS DAD, 2007

15a) OUR FAMILY; WHEN I WAS SIX-YEARS OLD

15b) I WAS 13, JUST GRADUATED 8TH GRADE

15c) NEWLYWEDS; WINSTON AND SANDRA (WITH BIG
BROTHER KENNETH, LATE 70'S)

16a) GAME PRESERVE HOTEL; ZAMBIA, AFRICA 2009

16b) BOOK SIGNING, 1985

16c) GIANT "RUBIK'S CUBE" (1992?) WON 2ND PRIZE

17) MOM/DAD'S GOLDEN WEDDING ANNIVERSARY
CELEBRATION, 1979 (STANDING L TO R) DAPHNE,
KENNETH, SANDRA, ARNOLD, TED JR., BETTY ANNE,
ROBERT (BUBBY)

I WORK WITH POLIO PATIENTS

I applied for the job at Michael Reese Hospital one day during the week and reported to work the very next day. The job wasn't what I was hoping for and the pay wasn't much, but it was full time. I could keep it for the rest of the summer then make my decision about school.

My duties were to wheel patients from their hospital rooms to the physical therapy department for treatment. Some of the patients would be in wheelchairs, but most would be polio patients from pediatrics who had to be transferred from their beds to big, heavy hospital carts that were hard to steer and took a lot of energy and strength to push. These children were pitiful victims of poliomyelitis who had twisted limbs, or torsos, or other disfigurements. They would scream and cry in the physical therapy lab as the therapists kneaded and twisted, trying to coax their disfigurements away.

After I had been on the job for a few days, I, along with a co-worker, was assigned the task of treating the children's limbs with the 'Sister Kenney Method'. This consisted of applying very hot, wet, steam-soaked woolen cloths to the children's arms and, or legs, and leaving them on until the heat penetrated their muscles. Most of the children were not able to move or jump around because the polio had rendered their limbs useless but their howls and screeches let us know that they felt the pain of the burning cloths on their skin. I don't remember the treatment causing blistering, the temperature of the cloths was well regulated, but the reddening of their white skin indicated the level of pain the youngsters endured.

I felt very conflicted as I applied the burning cloths and saw the suffering of the young patients. On the other hand, I felt I was helping them to get better.

I also felt conflicted as I applied my nail file to Daphne's pig's slot and extracted paper money to cover my expenses (and a few luxuries). It was so easy! I had to always make sure no one heard me because sometimes coins would fall out—having been up-ended by my patient twists of the nail file. I had learned to place a towel on the dresser to avoid the 'cha-ching' of the coins falling on the dresser top, and then, I would always replace the coins in the slot. I certainly didn't want to reduce the weight of the pig and upset my sister. After all, these were loans I would most certainly pay back all that I had borrowed . . . when I figured out how much it was, and when I got my first paycheck.

By the time my first payday came, I had taken two days off (I wasn't able to wheel hospital carts around as I suffered with my monthly cramps). Then there were deductions for some kind of union, and deductions for some kind of old age benefit, then another deduction for some kind of insurance. And, I had borrowed money from a friend. This left me with very little money to put in the pig. "Well, piggy-pay-back would just have to wait until my next payday", I thought.

When the next payday dawned; I had to pay rent to Daddy. That took half my money. Paying the pig slipped down my list of things I must do. By the time I was paid again, some kind of emergency claimed my money.

The summer was fading fast and I had to make a decision about what I would do with my life. I had grown to hate the job at the hospital, the work was much too hard and the children showed fear when they saw me. The fear bothered me more than the hard work.

I really struggled over the decision to quit college. My aunts and two uncles on my father's side were being college educated and two were teaching (or, in Aunt Wilma's case, nursing). I wanted to be the first in my immediate family to carry on the example set by my aunts and uncles. So, partly driven by finances, and partly driven by shame at having flunked out, I decided I would enroll in Peter's Business College, attend at night, and get a full time job at Montgomery Ward's Mail Order House, filling orders.

I GO TO WORK AT 'MONKEY WARD'S'

You were really considered a loser if you had to resort to working at Montgomery Ward's. It was the pits but they were always hiring. The commute was almost as long as the Herzl Jr. College commute, the work was repetitious, and the pay was minimal. I prevailed by telling myself that it was temporary.

At Peter's Business College, it took little time for me to discover that I had very little aptitude for learning secretarial work. My typing was dismal and my shorthand was abysmal. I had taken courses in bookkeeping in high school and done well, but Peter's Business College, on Chicago's South Side, was all about training secretaries and I was just not the secretary type! I lasted three weeks!

Meanwhile, the daily grind at 'Monkey Ward' had one advantage; I worked with all kinds of people, and got to experience the differences in people. There were Poles, Mexican and Czech on our team of eight. I got a chance to really know them, learn about their lives, their problems, their families. I genuinely liked them and felt a bond with them.

My self-esteem was still flailing when, as a challenge to myself, I decided to see if I could double or triple my work output. One day, instead of visiting and exchanging pleasantries with my team of co-workers, I furiously finished more orders than the whole team combined. It was a self-imposed test to give me a good feeling about myself.

Our supervisor acknowledged my accomplishment in front of the team, and admonished them for not turning in the same, or similar, amounts of work. This was certainly not the outcome I was looking for, and my co-workers turned their backs on me. They accused me of upping the required quota of orders that they were expected to finish. I was ostracized from then on. The friends who had been my rock, were now my enemies. I had to eat my lunch alone, sit at my work station alone, and take my ten-minute afternoon break all by myself. The pain was almost unbearable for sociable me.

DAPHNE SMASHES PINK PIG

Two days after my 'super-order' stunt, I arrived home to face two graven-faced parents, and a hysterical sister, standing in front of pink ceramic pig-fragments mixed with coins! There was not one paper bill of any denomination in the mess on the dresser. The pig and my nail file had brought great comfort to me, Now it was reversed.

Daphne had decided to break open her pig because she thought she had saved enough money to get the typewriter way ahead of the date of her original goal. She was a good typist, and hoped to do her last year of high school work using her new typewriter.

Daphne's words to me, fortunately, are lost to my memory, but I do remember Mother telling me how disappointed she was in me, and I remember how badly she made me feel by using the word 'disappointed' because I had always tried to please Mother and make her proud of me.

Daphne had kept a running tally of the amount she deposited in the pink ceramic pig, and that was good because I had not counted how much I 'borrowed' since the first five dollars. The total, she said, was sixty-eight dollars. Paying back sixty-eight dollars on my measly salary from 'Monkey Ward' would take a very long time. I was still paying tuition to Peter's Business College for the two secretarial courses I had abandoned in October.

Daphne, still in high school, would start saving in another pig. The new one wasn't as big as the pink ceramic pig, and it was made of see-inside glass with an amber tint. I had to re-pay the money in equal amounts each week, by giving it to Daphne, and she would deposit it in the pig's slot. Her re-shaped goal was to try to get the typewriter before she graduated and started college in a year. To no one's surprise, the new pig did not rest on our dresser, but it resided somewhere in my parent's bedroom. I only got to glimpse it once; when it was brand new, being filled with coins which were being transferred from the remains of the pink ceramic pig.

OAKLAND BRANCH LIBRARY

I was about to start my fourth month of working at Monkey Wards' and dreading being there for the Christmas Season. Daphne was working until nine, I had been home for a couple of hours. The Oakland Branch of the Chicago Public Library was about one quarter of a mile from our home. Someone, or two, or three members of our family always walked up the street to Lincoln Center on Oakland Blvd. and accompanied Daphne home after dark. It was in the building where the library occupied the first floor of this historic Frank Lloyd Wright structure. Built in 1898, it had a magnificent cage elevator (as big as a living room) with built-in, hand—carved benches.

My two youngest brothers and I got to the library well before closing time in order for the boys, ages six and ten, to pick out books. It was the same library where I had read every book in the fairy-tale section when I was much younger. It was quite familiar and very much loved. I was also fond of the building. Lincoln Center had an enormous vestibule that gave me a feeling of grandeur. There were apartments on some of the upper floors above the library where some very prominent people lived. Most of the people were white, and there were some 'Negroes' living there, who were in the arts. Later, I was to learn that the tenants, who were living an integrated experiment, were labeled 'communists' by the police. The building had six, high-ceilinged floors and a large, wonderful parlor on the top floor where teas and other events had been held. I imagine that the building was extremely fashionable at one time, but now it showed signs of wear and was always dusty. The neighborhood had once been a boulevard showplace, but now Lincoln Center anchored over-crowded slum buildings on one side and the Ida B. Wells Housing Project on the other. It also housed the local Planned Parenthood Clinic that Mother mentioned so often.

I had been in the library so often that I knew just about everyone who worked there. The whole staff was 'Negro'. Mrs. Brown and Mrs. Metzler were lovely women who were about the same age (late twenties). Both were married with one child each. Their toddlers were about the age of my baby sister. Mrs Hill, the head librarian, was one of the nicest people I had ever met. Miss Allen was single and from a large family, and Mrs. Willis headed the children's section. They all just loved Daphne. They said Daphne was the best library page they'd ever had.

"Where are you going to school, Betty Anne?" asked Mrs. Hill, as she walked into the adult section of the library. I was bending down looking for books on the 'astrology' shelf, trying to find some I hadn't read. "Oh, I'm not in school now Mrs Hill. I'm taking a little time off." I was reluctant to answer her, because I didn't want to let my own ears hear me say that I wasn't in school, and bring back the dreaded feeling of self-loathing I'd been experiencing of late.

As Arnold and Kenneth came out of the children's section to have their books stamped at the circulation desk, I eased myself out of the adult reading room, (which opened into the circulation room) because I was afraid Mrs. Hill would ask more questions about college. Instead, to my surprise, she said, "Betty Anne, how would you like to work here at the library, full time?" "Oh, Mrs. Hill, I would love to work here at Oakland Branch Library!" I gasped. I couldn't think of a better place I'd rather spend my time than in the building I loved, working with books that I loved even more!

Mrs. Hill told me that Mrs. Willis needed an assistant in the children's room, and that she could hire me, but I'd have to take the library clerk examination and pass it to become civil-service certified. A high school diploma was all that was needed as education.

With our two brothers, Daphne and I walked home excited about the possibility of working together, I would be full-time, she would continue to be part-time.

EXAM STRATEGY

When I found out that Mrs. Brown and Mrs. Metzler were also scheduled to take the exam, we got together to plan some strategy because 'Negroes' had a hard time getting past some of the questions on the exam. There were questions that asked: (supposedly, for identification purposes, only) "COLOR OF YOUR COMPLECTION?, HAIR COLOR?, EYE COLOR?" They were the questions which had been the focus of the complaints from groups like the NAACP that the tests were discriminatory. What we agreed to write was: "COMPLECTION; MEDIUM, Hair; BRUNETTE, EYES; HAZEL", so that we wouldn't help the examiners single us out to fail the exam. There were just two chances to take the exam, and we didn't want to blow it.

Our strategy may or may not have been what helped us pass the library clerk's exam, but we were sure thankful for whatever went right, when we found out that we all had passed.

Working in the children's room of Oakland Branch Library was a great pleasure. It provided an opportunity for me to exercise my creativity by producing wonderfully decorated bulletin boards, paper mache' characters from children's stories, and posters urging children to read. I consulted style books and taught myself to do the lettering for the posters I created.

The only drawback to the job was having to endure Mrs. Willis' gossiping and bragging. She had been a children's librarian from the time that the only 'literature' the shelves provided for our Negro children had been 'LITTLE BLACK SAMBO'. And Mrs. Willis loved to tell about her successful fight to purge that '... prejudiced African Tale from our colored libraries!'

It had been a noble fight, one worth waging, and it took a lot of courage to buck the establishment during the late 1930's and 40's, a time when literature was replete with overt racism, disdain for, and lack of respect for Negroes. This included such celebrated author's work as none other than Booth Tarkington's PENROD AND SAM (required reading on school reading lists) where the author points out that Sam's dog, ". . . looked like a nigger's dog, with almost no hair on his chest . . ."

Not many people knew that the "jungle" in LITTLE BLACK SAMBO was originally in India, not Africa, and that the 'tigers' who turned to butter were also Indian, since there are no tigers in Africa, except in zoos. But these details aren't important enough to negate the fine work which Mrs. Willis and others had done; attempting to shield our children from racial stereotypes.

Mrs. Willis was in her-mid-to-late fifties, a stately, handsome, woman with a milk-toast of a husband—to whom she didn't even bother to utter simple, polite, courtesies like 'please' or 'thank-you' when she ordered him around. She had come to Motherhood late by continuing the raising of a relative's daughter.

Mrs. Willis talked about her daughter, unceasingly! The girl, a college student—a little older than I—was engaged to one of the 'best catches' in Chicago. He was a rookie cop on the Chicago Police Force, but his parents were the proud owners of a Negro detective agency. His name was Doug. Mrs. Willis' daughter's name was Ginny. They were, indeed, a gorgeous pair. Ginny was a beautiful girl. She seemed to be very nice, too.

On days when Mrs. Willis and I worked together (which, because of scheduling, were few) I was bombarded with every detail of Ginny's wedding, an analysis of everyone connected to it, and all the inside gossip and family secrets that our working hours could provide. Mrs. Willis demanded that I be a participatory listener; she wouldn't settle for passive listening. I had to face her, nod, shake my head, assume the correct facial expressions and even offer an occasional verbal comment. I was fed up with all the details of Ginny's marriage, especially because I knew I would never be able to afford the kind of wedding that was being planned for her.

DePAUL UNIVERSITY: ON THE RIGHT TRACK

I started working at the library in the fall. By early December I was enrolled (on probation) at DePaul University's downtown campus (just a big office building). It had a beautiful campus with several buildings on Chicago's all white North Side. DePaul (A Catholic School) had dropped its quota system and was allowing 'colored' students to enroll freely in its so-called 'University College'. I was a part-time student, just one among the hundreds who worked full time and pursued a degree at night. And since

DePaul was on the quarter system, hard-working students could amass credits much faster than students in traditional semester schools. I became a hard-working student. My school schedule was aligned with my working schedule which was adjusted to insure that I could stay in school. Our boss, Mrs. Hill, led the entire staff in this way of thinking about scheduling for those of us who were students. Mrs. Willis seemed not to like the idea because it meant that she had to work until nine p.m. one or two times a week—just like the rest of us—and she had more seniority than anyone else but she, too, went along with the plan.

Home life improved in direct proportion to the money I brought in. My check was seventy dollars. I gave half to Dad for 'rent'. Dad charged me no rent when I had tuition to pay. After working at the library for a while, I was able, with my dad as co-signer, to open an account at Mad Man Muntz so that I could buy a Muntz Television set. It was the latest model: a radio, record-player, and twelve-inch television console all in one.

I didn't like the idea of paying finance charges on my purchase, so I decided that I would pay the entire balance in ninety days. That way, no finance charges were assessed. Anyone could figure out that the savings would be quite substantial since finance charges were between twenty-five and thirty percent of the purchase price.

AVOIDING ENTRENCHED POVERTY

I gave the money I had saved up to my dad so that he could pay-one third of the price, and that way we'd have no interest charges. Dad was in arrears on some other bills, and used the money on them instead. He paid just the minimum on my bill. I was very disillusioned. I consider this my first lesson on how poverty becomes entrenched in people's lives and I was dead-set against that happening to me! I didn't know much about financing, hadn't heard about compound interest—how money could increase by just leaving it in a savings account—nor did I have a good, close, role-model to follow since my parents were always financially hard-pressed. But I did know that I should save some money and I did. I joined the credit union for civil servants, made payday deposits, and watched my meager dollars become a little less meager.

This period in my life provided a series of boyfriends, but no one serious, and they wouldn't last too long after the going-over they had to endure at home. Our house rule required that the first date be in our apartment with everyone present (which sometimes included aunts and uncles, and always included siblings) before going out alone with some guy. Very often, a huge mass of us attended a dance together.

On one such occasion, my family made up a party of about twelve; Mom and Dad, my brother and his wife, a couple of uncles and their wives, Daphne and her date, and my date and me. We were having a grand time, dancing and drinking Four Roses Bourbon. As the evening wore on (or out) I noticed that Mom wasn't dancing, and Mom and Dad usually loved to dance together.

When they were courting and first married, they used to make the rounds of the dance halls and win prizes in the competitions dance halls set up to stimulate business. Many of the furnishings in our home, such as lamps, cookware and clocks, had been won in this way. Sometimes the awarded prize wasn't what was advertised, but only a fraction of the stated value. Because Mom and Dad were so well known in the dance halls, it was often arranged in advance that they would win. By rigging the contest this way, a club owner didn't have to come up with as expensive a prize as advertised and could stay in competition with all of the other dancehall owners.

Since they were great dancers there were no complaints., as long as it didn't happen too often. It hadn't happened for a long time because Mother started having children and Daddy started putting in more hours at work. So their dance hall days ended, but they remained fond of dancing with each other for as long as they lived.

Dad was out on the floor dancing several dances with a strange woman. The woman was demonstrating how much she enjoyed dancing with my father by hugging him, laughing, shaking herself, and just out-and-out flirting with him. He was enjoying the attention to the utmost, and was also very clearly under the influence of the alcohol he had been drinking!

At the end of the dance, Dad brought the woman over to our table to meet his family. He introduced the few of us who were at the table at the time, and I heard the woman say to my Mom," You mean y'all got seven children?" I could smell Mom's burning fury as the woman continued with, "How can you hang on to such a fine man with all them other women out there?" And Mom said, in a very loud clear voice, "I can hang on to him because he knows, ain't nothing out there but whores like you!"

As we were all leaving the dance hall, we gathered around Mom to shield her in case the woman wanted to start something physical. Later, my sister and I discussed the fact that perhaps shielding Mom made sure that she didn't attack the woman, because Mother was clearly the more aggressive.

DATING

Dating was the way we got to know the boys and young men we met at group affairs such as meetings or dances and the routine of meeting and spending time with the family wasn't always so strictly adhered to if the guy was exciting enough. I had one occasion where I sneaked out with a guy before 'the examination', but I didn't feel right about it and didn't make it a habit. I never wanted a boy to meet my family, I wasn't proud of the fact that there were so many of us children, or that some of the children were so young, or that I lived in the project, or that the project was located in the middle of the slums.

PART III
MY YOUNG ADULT YEARS

DATING ALEX

Alex was an exciting guy I met at a dance when I was still in high school. He had big brown eyes, a nice smile, a very open demeanor and he seemed to really like me. He had graduated high school and had been working at a woodworking factory for three years. He was an only child of divorced parents. His father had been re-married since Alex was quite young and I didn't have to talk with him long to find out that he spent a lot of emotional energy hating his step-mother and resenting his father for having married her.

I immediately took Alex on as my project; to restore him to 'right thinking'. We talked on the phone for hours at a time. I had seen a psychological movie or two so I became his analyst. I told him he was wasting himself, he should enroll in college and make something of himself, and if he was as interested in me as he claimed to be, he would have to measure up because I was going to get my degree, and I certainly wouldn't be interested in somebody who made table legs all day.

Alex's mom was a homeowner. He wasn't from the project, but he didn't live far away. On Alex's birthday, he was to come to my house and we'd go out together. He had already passed scrutiny.

A couple of hours before date time, Alex called to tell me that his "play sister, Barbara" had called to tell him that his mom was giving him a surprise birthday party. Barbara had said that, ordinarily she wouldn't divulge the secret, but since he had told her so much about me, she was sure that he'd want me to be at the surprise party and could we maybe skip whatever else we'd planned and go over to his house on thirty-six and South Park—the house where he lived with his mother—for the surprise.

I agreed to go to his party on condition that we stop by my friend Ernestine's party for a little while. This would give us plenty of time to arrive at his party and, (for his mom's sake) pretend we didn't know about the surprise.

When I introduced this amended plan to my parents, to my surprise, they said, yes. Before leaving with Alex, I had copied down his phone number and address for my folks. What I hadn't told my parents, after finding out about the surprise, is that we would stop by Walgreen's to buy a gift because we were still planning to go by Ernestine's party before going to Alex's.

I was looking at selections at the perfume counter in Walgreen's, when I looked up and saw my father and my brother, Bubby! Dad was in a big huff as he rushed over to Alex, grabbed him by his coat lapels and demanded, "Who are you trying to fool, Boy? This ain't your Mama's telephone number! You're just trying to pull a fast one!"

Bubby was a few steps behind Daddy slinging his fists and calling, "Sock him, Daddy, sock him!"

Daddy practically dragged Alex over to the public pay phone and had him call his mother to verify the surprise birthday party story. Alex was, literally, shaking in his boots.

I had made a mistake when I copied Alex's number to give to my folks, I had transposed two numbers. It really was an honest mistake. In the ten or so minutes it took us to walk up the street to Walgreen Drug Store, Daddy had attempted to call Alex's mother, but gotten a wrong number. He told my mother that he was going out for pipe tobacco and he took Bubby with him. They had walked up the same street (perhaps Dad was thinking he might see us) but was not expecting to see us in Walgreen's. Dad ruined Alex's mother's surprise by making Alex call her to verify his word.

In later years, Mom told me that Dad was so cautious about Alex because Dad said, "He looked just like one of those 3-F guys; find 'em, f—'em, and forget 'em!

Alex became a regular visitor around our home. He loved to hang out at my house and soak up the family that was missing in his own life. One day, he even walked with me when I took my little sister, Sandra, out for a stroll in her buggy. And, of course, a neighbor saw us, and later called Mother to tell her, "I saw your daughter out with her husband and the baby. The baby looks just like her husband!" The truth was Sandra looked nothing like Alex! The old witch was just groping for Mother to explain why I was seen with a man, pushing a baby stroller.

Alex enrolled at Wilberforce University and majored in sociology (now Central State University in Ohio) and went away to live on campus. I like to think that it was because of the advice I gave him to make something of himself.

It was kind of a relief to have Alex away at school. He had pestered me to agree to marry him, which I had agreed to do, and he had a way of putting his business in the street and mine, too. He would tell people, "Betty Anne is my fiancée, we're gonna get married when we both finish college, but we don't have sex. She's a virgin."

The people he told weren't people I wanted in my business. Alex didn't seem to have much discretion. The openness in his personality, which had attracted me to him, was becoming annoying.

Another reason I was glad to see him go was that now I could go out with other guys. I wasn't taking this engagement thing seriously, I was just seventeen. There was no ring on my finger but Alex was very possessive and my father was totally suspicious of him. While Alex was away at school, my father read the mail he sent me. I found this out when Dad confronted me with a quote from one of his letters. Dad wanted to know what he meant by, ". . . Baby I need you . . ."! Alex was away for over a year before he invited me down to the big deal of a homecoming weekend. I was nineteen, attending DePaul University and pledging Sigma Gamma Rho Sorority. It was the only time I'd been on a college campus so I was anxious to experience the 'campus life' that many of my friends talked about. My best friend, Mary Butler, went with me and we had a grand time in spite of Alex's "play-sister, Skip" acting more like his girlfriend than a 'play-sister, Though Alex had invited us, we saw little of him that weekend.

A couple of weeks before Alex graduated, he and Skip came to Chicago for a funeral. I was surprised that he called me because we had had little contact since the homecoming week-end two years earlier. We had stopped writing and he had not invited me to his graduation. Nevertheless I went to meet with him at his relative's house. Skip had an attractive, older-looking man with her. He was not handsome, he had a receding hairline, he didn't have deep set-eyes, but he had a magnetic presence about him and a physique that was extremely appealing. He had a very charming, assured manner, and he worked with Jesse Owens as executive director of the South Side Boys Club. He was quick to announce that he earned a whopping seven thousand dollars a year! The average living-wage salary in the early fifties was about twenty-five hundred dollars. I was very impressed with him and all evening he kept sending signals to me. Jim and Skip had just met that evening so theirs was a tag-a-long date and Skip made it clear that there was no romance between the two of them.

Alex, in his usual indiscreet manner, mouthed off about our so-called engagement in front of Skip's date, Jim, and the other people at the gathering. He included the part about me being a virgin. Even though Alex had been away for almost four years and hadn't asked me to verify that I was still a virgin, I was. I had done some dating and some petting during the last year or so, since I had been maturing and trying to experience some life, but it was still within the parameters I had set for my healthy-libido self. Working at the library and going to night school didn't take up all of my time.

Jesse Owens, the great Olympian runner who had defied Hitler's "master race theory", was an approachable fixture on Chicago's South Side. His daughter was engaged to a classmate friend of mine, named Malcolm, so Jim's story was easy to check. The only part that wasn't accurate was that he was acting executive director instead of the full-fledged director he claimed to be. He had recently moved to Chicago from Washington, D.C.

DATING JIM

On our first date, Jim admitted to having been married before. He said he was divorced and that there were no children. He claimed to be twenty-seven years old (to my twenty-one) but he looked five or six years older than he claimed. I just knew he was lying about his age. I told him that I'd have to see his divorce decree before I'd continue to date him.

On our next date, Jim showed me something that looked like a certificate. I had never seen a divorce decree before. Since I guess I was subconsciously willing to suspend some credulity, I really didn't read the thing well. I was a little embarrassed that I had shown my distrust by asking to see the document, which he had produced with great speed. Without further scrutiny, I happily accepted the document as proof that Jim was divorced.

With each date I was becoming more and more enamored with Jim, and I knew that he was falling for me. The 'bid to bed' came up long before the traditional time period of three months that I had experienced with younger boys. I was dealing with a confident, grown man! But I was still unwilling to 'put out'.

At about the third or fourth date, as Jim held me close, I felt something in his breast pocket and like the old joke goes: "Is that a gun or are you just glad to see me?" It truly was a gun! Jim surprised me by telling me that he worked part time with a Negro detective agency on Chicago's South Side so he was sometimes armed. He knew Mrs. Willis' son in-law, Doug, and his parents because he worked for them. Doug and Ginny had married in a lavish, high-society type wedding (to which I was not invited) and produced a daughter by the time they celebrated their first anniversary. They were now separated and I was still having to listen to Mrs. Willis' talk about her son-in-law, except now, it was about what a no-good person he was.

WE ELOPE!

By the time Jim and I had been dating six weeks, he had proposed, surprising me with a ring. We started planning our wedding. It was becoming almost impossible to hold on to my virginity, but I was still refusing his advances. Then, one day, he laid out several reasons why we should elope: it would save my folks a lot of money (which they didn't have), It was summer and we could use vacation time to travel to Minneapolis, get married and have a honeymoon. The money he was planning to give me towards the wedding could be used to buy our furniture. His parents would be spared from making the trip from D.C. to Chicago at this time, since his dad wasn't in the best of health.

The more Jim talked, the more his plan became my plan. I had never imagined myself as the bride at a big, expensive, wedding, so I didn't have a dream that I had to revise, however I always thought that I'd be married in church. The idea of eloping became more exciting, the more I thought about it. We agreed that we would have the reception later (with maybe a small ceremony repeating our vows, I thought).

We traveled by bus to Minneapolis, I had told only my sister, Daphne, about the elopement She had seemed almost as excited about the plan as I. We checked into the hotel with no problem. There were very few 'Negroes' in the liberal state of Minnesota in the 50's, so we weren't subjected to any kind of discrimination. We arrived too late in the afternoon to file for a marriage license. We had to spend the night together, unmarried. It was magical, Jim was wonderful, very tender and delighted at the proof of my 'first time' status.

I had caught Jim in a few lies early in our courtship. He had a tendency to exaggerate things, and he had told me, "Baby, I'm not going to tell you that I'll never lie to you, but I want you to know that I really do love you with all my heart!"

We got to the courthouse early the next morning, filled out the marriage license, and found out that there was a five day wait before we could be married. I've mulled it over in my mind for many years—whether Jim knew about the waiting period or not—I'll never know the answer to that question.

For the waiting period, we toured the town and did all the things honeymooners do. On the fourth day, my period started, and I spent the entire day in bed, writhing in pain. We were married on the fifth day, in judge's chamber, and we returned home that evening by bus.

Jim convinced me that I should go on home to my parents' house for the night, that he would come for me in the morning and help me move out, and into his apartment. He said that Mom and Dad had to get used to the idea that I was married now, and the best way to handle it was to go on back to their home and break it to them in person. This didn't make a lot of sense to me because I knew that Daphne had told them that I'd eloped. They were probably greatly relieved that they didn't have to go through the bother and expense of a wedding, and since the whole family had fallen in love with Jim, there was no problem about my choice. I felt that Jim had other reasons why he wanted me to go home and return to my single life of sharing the room with my sister. I thought that he probably needed time to fix up his apartment, or that he wanted to surprise me in some way, so it wasn't a problem to go along with his directive.

JIM ANNOUNCES, "MY FATHER DIED!"

Jim arrived, graven-faced, the next morning and told me that he had to rush off to D.C. because his father had died. I pleaded to go with him, telling him that his loss was my loss too, but he wouldn't hear of it. I was to stay here with my folks and when he made the funeral arrangements he'd send for me.

Calling long distance in 1952 was a rare thing. It was very expensive and rarely done by ordinary people. Jim called to tell me that his father's estate was tied up, and that he wouldn't be able to send for me because he had used all of his own funds to cover the funeral and to transport relatives to D.C.

I returned to my regular routine, and told as few people as possible about getting married. Something was fishy, but I didn't know what. Jim called me every week, with another reason why we couldn't be together: 'his father's estate' excuse was good for a few weeks. His mother's bereavement was good for another couple of weeks, then he, himself, had developed a 'lesion on his jejunum' and had to have an operation. When I asked how they had gotten to it—local or by incision?—he said it was a local operation. When I pressed him as to which orifice, he said the doctor had operated through his mouth. I looked up the jejunum in the dictionary and found out that it was part of the intestines.

In sharing this with Mom and Dad, we concluded that the doctor must have had some mighty long scalpels to reach into Jim's mouth and remove something from his intestines! Humor was the way we dealt with our problems. The more serious the problem, the more humor we applied.

It had been several weeks since Jim had been gone, when I got a call on my job from the jewelry store where Jim had bought my rings. He had not kept up payments on the ring set, could I tell them how to reach him? They had made several attempts, but he didn't answer at work or at home. I admitted to knowing him, but lied by saying, "I know him slightly, not as someone who'd buy me a ring." I felt very grateful that I did not, like some couples, go with him to pick out my rings, but I wasn't about to release my wedding rings. And, if all it took was a lie to maintain them, I felt justified in telling the lie.

A few years later, I pawned the engagement ring, under an assumed name, lost the ticket, then forgot what name I had used, and never got it back. I don't remember what I did with the wedding ring.

After that blatant lie about the operation I figured it was time to get a lawyer. Daddy worked with one through his union. I wasn't impressed with him, but I could afford his retainer. He did do one small part of his job, he checked to see if Jim's father had died. No one by that name had died during that period in D.C.

I continued to work with Mrs. Willis, and listen to her woes about her daughter and that 'immature bastard she'd married and had a baby for.' She told me all about Doug's home life, all his family's secrets and how he'd messed up in the marriage, and had moved out and gotten a bachelor apartment. I took it all in—along with many other things she told me—not knowing that it was information I would need in the future.

After the extreme shock of finding out that Jim had not lost his father, I went into revenge mode. We had met in May, married in August, and now it was the end of October. I was still talking to Jim every week as if I didn't know about him not losing his dad. I still sympathized with him and pretended to go along with whatever he said.

Mr. Sheeie, the lawyer, advised me to file for annulment, but I wanted to make Jim pay! I wanted money for legal expenses, for my bruised reputation, my suffering and my extreme embarrassment. I wanted to make him suffer! I had no idea how to proceed in my revenge. Mr. Sheeie wasn't much help in finding information about Jim. The main thing I wanted to know was whether he was married to someone else, too. I was convinced that he loved me, and the only reason he would be away from me was that he had another wife! He had taken something from me that I valued, my virginity, and I wanted to witness his suffering.

DOUG TO THE RESCUE

I had met Doug, Mrs. Willis' son-in-law, through her. He had driven her to work on occasion, had stopped in the library in his uniform at another time, and had even been there with Ginny and the new baby, when they were still a family, to show the child to the staff. I had also seen his picture in the Defender Newspaper. I decided that Doug might know something about Jim that would be useful to me, but I didn't know how to approach him. Should I just look him up in the phone book and call him? I hadn't had the chance, nor was I inclined to tell my co-workers about my marriage before it became a non-marriage. I suspected they probably knew and were too polite or concerned for my feelings to broach the subject. Even when they noticed me wearing my wedding ring for a brief time, they said nothing. The library staff was very supportive, very much like family.

Should I confide in Mrs. Willis and become the subject of her gossiping? She probably couldn't get Doug to tell me anything about Jim now. Since the separation, there were very bad feelings between them. I didn't know where else to turn for information about him, it was Doug's family business for which Jim worked part time.

Skip, Alex's 'play sister' had found out about Jim and me when we had first started dating. She had told a friend of hers, who knew Mary Butler (my best friend whom she had met when we visited Wilberforce for Homecoming and had stayed in the same dorm room with her) that she didn't care if we were dating, that Jim meant nothing to her, she had just met him when she took him to that party, and, He wasn't her type, anyhow!' I'm sure the message was meant for my ears, as they had undoubtedly also fallen on Alex's ears, since he no longer called me or tried to contact me in any way. So, trying to find out about Jim through Skip was out of the question. The only other person I knew who knew him was Mr. Jesse Owens. I couldn't just go up to him and ask him about Jim, even though I probably could find him at The South Side Boys' Club. I didn't know his daughter very well, I only knew her through her fiancé, Malcolm. No, I didn't have enough nerve to approach them, nor did I want to tell my business. Embarrassment was the emotion I felt all the time. The only thing I did was call the boys' club (prepared to use an assumed name, if asked who's calling) and ask to speak with Jim. That's how I found out he didn't work there anymore. "No", they couldn't tell me what his new number was, he did not leave a forwarding number.

Harry's Lounge was the leading 'hang out' place for my age group, or for any age group, for that matter. I had been visiting there since I had to sneak in when I was in high school. In fact, Harry's had become a little passé' to me, but I found myself drawn to Harry's very often during this time of disillusionment over my marriage. I would go in, generally with a girlfriend or two, usually sit at the bar, order something like a Tom Collins, and test my ability to attract the guys to flirt with me. And flirt they did, for I had gained some confidence in myself. Whereas, before I had been full of complexes—my bunions were so ugly, my nose was so big, my hands were too rough, my legs were too thin, my hairline was so low that it met my eyebrows, and my breasts were so heavy that my mom wouldn't let me jump rope—now, I had more self-assurance.

HOLLYWOOD GODDESSES TO THE RESCUE

With maturity I had learned to wear shoes with bows or flaps so that the bunions didn't show. I had learned to shave or pluck the hairs off of my face to make me appear less fierce, and to lotion my hands constantly. As for the breasts—the bain of my existence when I was in elementary and high school (where dressing and showering in front of the other girls made me desperate to cover up my 'deformity')—they now were assets.

In my late teens, I learned that there sometimes was a fine line between looking matronly and looking glamorously provocative;

or 'sexy' (the new 'in' word). A heavy-chested-woman will look matronly in almost anything that's closed up over the chest or neck. I got over my shyness about revealing some skin and became a glamour gal by dressing to flatter instead of settling for the matronly look. Who wouldn't want to be known as sexy, rather than matronly, when these were the two choices?

I owe thanks to Playboy Magazine and Clubs, Jane Mansfield, Jane Russell, Marilyn Monroe and all the other heavy-chested Hollywood Goddesses. They snuffed out the flat-chested, flapper-era style, and brought a new status to us bosomy gals. The popularity of the flapper flat-chest-ness style had persisted throughout the forties' and into the fifties' in minds of people like my mom. I felt that Mom equated bosom with sin and worldliness, and it's opposite with innocence and purity. Her views left a shadow of their imprint on me. This new found 'sexiness' promised to provide a counterbalance for being raised in a rather restrictive environment, not allowed to jump rope, and adherence to codes of behavior which stifled some freedom of expression.

One evening, while I and a girlfriend were in Harry's, who should walk in but Doug! I was sitting at the bar, on the left side of the lounge, but not at the very front. There were two or three tables in front of the bar. Doug stopped at one of the tables in the front to talk with some people, and he appeared to be alone. I became nervous, and dreaded doing what I had to do, but I knew that this was probably my best chance to make contact with him and maybe find out what he knew about Jim.

Putting on my most casual attitude, I approached the table where Doug sat with some men, and found it a lot easier to start a conversation than I had imagined, they were all in 'flirt mode'.

"Of course, I know you. You work with my Mother-in-Law", began the conversation. Before I left Harry's I had agreed to go out with Doug, and I had his address and phone number. Doug even gave me and my girlfriend a lift home that night.

Getting picked up from work by Doug for our first meeting was tricky business because all of the staff knew him, but we think we managed to avoid being discovered. It was like an adventure to dodge the usual questions about what's doing after work and then to get out of the building and into his car without being seen.

The first thing we did was to drop by a store that sold cigarettes, liquor and other things, because Doug had to pick up a couple of cartons of cigarettes from a guy who worked there.

We parked in the alley behind the store and just waited for a few minutes, until the guy brought the unwrapped cigarettes, concealed under his jacket, to the car. Doug proudly explained to me that he had caught this guy trying to break into a place and had threatened to run him in. When he found out where the guy worked, he bargained with him, saying that he wouldn't arrest him if the guy would supply Doug, every week, with cigarettes that he stole from his job. The thing that shocked me about this revelation was that Doug was so assured in assuming that I thought this a clever arrangement, whereas I thought it was despicable! It told me a lot about Doug. I could see why he and Ginny weren't making it, even though it was quite evident, from just a brief conversation; he was still very much in love with her.

The second time that I saw Doug it was to pick his brain about Jim, but I found myself talking more than he did. He proved to be a very compassionate listener, and I needed to unburden. I found myself crying and releasing some of the pent-up emotions I'd been holding in for months and, Doug seemed genuinely moved. The next time I saw him, he had all of the information I needed and then some! He had acquired Jim's army record. The only thing Jim hadn't lied about was his age—the one thing I was convinced he was lying about—almost everything else was fabricated. Jim had no father. His mother had raised him, an only child, working as a scrubwoman in the Capitol building, instead of as the shrewd businesswoman he claimed. He had been a juvenile delinquent and had a long history with the juvenile justice system as an incorrigible youth. He had only gone to junior college, so he hadn't graduated from McGill University in Canada, as he had said. His army record was unblemished, but he had only achieved the rank of private-first-class, not lieutenant as he had told me.

The devastating blow was that he was very much married and had two children, when his wife had gone back to Washington in May (the month I met him) to await the birth of their third child. The report Doug gave me told me everything I needed to know about Jim. It was a triumph to get the facts, but the veracity of the information was bitter, indeed!

MY TURN TO ROLE-PLAY

I gave the information to my lawyer and he was amazed at what I had found. He asked me more than once how I'd come by it, but I wouldn't tell him. My thinking was, he should have been able to get this information he's the one I was paying!

I filed a lawsuit as plaintiff in a bigamy case with a warrant to have Jim arrested. Since I was in Chicago and he was in Washington, D.C., Jim would have to be lured back to stand trial and I knew just what lure I would use.

Jim was crazy about dressing up in formal wear to attend big formal balls. He looked fabulous in formal wear because he was so well built. He didn't just go for tuxedos, he always wore tails. With the holidays approaching, I had an invitation to the formal ball that was the most prestigious event of the fall season. When Jim called that Friday, I talked the formal up, big time! I told him that I simply had to attend, that it would be the way he could redeem himself with my Mom and Dad since they suspected him of not intending to come back. I threw every bit of reasoning I could think of into the argument—along with a very private personal appeal—and he said, yes.

The plan meant that he would send money for me to rent a hotel room for the week-end, rent his full dress suit and we'd go to the ball that Saturday but he'd have to start back to D.C on Sunday evening because he had some important business to take care of that concerned his father's estate and he had to be in court on Monday.

True to his word, (that time) he sent the money. I reserved a room at the Negro hotel on 61st. Street. I think it was called 'The Southside Hotel'. This would give the bailiff an address where Jim could be served with the warrant. I didn't bother with the suit of clothes. He wouldn't need it since the arrest was scheduled to take place early Saturday afternoon.

In the meantime, I wasn't about to miss one of the best dances of the season so I put the finishing touches on the gown

I had designed, and made arrangements to go with my girlfriend and her fiancé.

Jim and I met up at the hotel, and in spite of the hurt I felt, I was genuinely excited to see him and he was even more excited to see me. I began to have pangs of regret and feelings of compassion but those pangs were neutralized by my feelings of outrage and jealousy. It was very difficult to keep Jim in the lobby and then in the small café (with me eating a lunch for which I had absolutely no appetite) because he was anxious for us to go up to the hotel room. We finally headed upstairs when I started to think he caught on to the fact that I was stalling.

In our hotel room, it did not take much acting talent for me to burst out crying, but it took a whole lot of reserve to forgo the apologies, regrets, promises and embraces Jim supplied to quell my tears.

The designated time for the arrest had come and gone, with no one showing up. On the excuse that I had to pick up his suit before the rental store closed, I left him in the hotel room and went to check on what went wrong. My lawyer had found out that the bailiff had gone fishing, and would, in all likelihood, not be back that day. He put on a show of being furious, but later on, I suspected that the lawyer had not done his own homework, and that was the real cause of the delay.

A few hours later, when I called Jim at the hotel, I told him that I was being held captive by my parents and that they had forbidden me to come back to a man who had deserted me for three months. In the meantime, we kept calling the bailiff with the arrest warrant, but to no avail. We would have to try again on Sunday.

That evening, I got dressed in the blue satin and chiffon dress I'd made for the occasion, stepped into the car with my girlfriend and her date and I was off to the Parkway Ballroom, leaving strict instructions that only Dad was to talk to Jim, should he call. For it was Dad who'd tell him that he, ". . . wouldn't allow Betty Anne to see you since you have caused her so much grief!" (or words to that effect), as cover for the fact that I wasn't home. But Jim didn't call all evening.

Sunday was spent on 'pins and needles' because I didn't hear from the bailiff until quite late in the afternoon. I had made one (supposedly 'sneak') call to Jim with the true purpose of checking to see if he was still in the hotel. I sweet-talked him and told him that I still loved him, but my parents were the barrier to my being able to be there with him. And, oddly enough, much of what I said was true. In spite of the hurt and embarrassment he'd caused me, I still had a lot of feeling for him. This seemed to make sense to him, but he said that he would still have to take the six-o-clock Greyhound bus back to D.C. on Sunday evening.

It was almost five-o-clock when I, the bailiff (who had finally arrived), a deputy and my lawyer started downtown to the Greyhound bus station. It was necessary that I go with them because I had to make the identification. It must have been a few minutes after six in the evening before we got to the departure lanes inside the bus terminal.

Just like a scene from a movie, we rushed into the station, frantically searched for the bus with the D.C. destination, and found it, as it slowly starting to roll out of its berth.

With the four of us screaming and shouting for the driver to halt, the bus came to an abrupt stop. The bailiff showed the driver his credentials and ushered me ahead of him. I boarded the bus and searched the faces of the passengers until I found Jim. He was seated in the back, almost at the very last aisle seat on the right side of that packed vehicle. All of the tensions and emotions of the week-end burst out of me as I threw my arms around Jim's neck and sobbed. The bailiff held Jim's hands behind his back and handcuffed them. And in a very rough and forceful manner, he led Jim off the bus and pushed him into the car in which we had arrived. My lawyer and I had to make it home on the bus.

LEGAL ACTION

The hearing was before a judge who scolded Jim in a very dramatic manner. I remember him saying, "How dare you, a married man, take this young woman's virginity!" And I remember thinking, "How does he know? I never told him that." But I guess the circumstances in the case could lead only to that conclusion, which was true, but made me feel all the more embarrassed.

Seeing Jim in court, under restricted conditions gave me no pleasure at all. The feeling of regret was overwhelming. I regretted doing this to him, I regretted marrying him so hastily, I regretted eloping, and the most regret I had was for dragging his mother into this. I was told that she had to supply the money, and I know it must have been very difficult for her.

Jim remained in Cook County Jail for about ten days. That's how long it took for his Mother in Washington, D. C. to raise and send the money to cover the cost of my annulment and to supply me with a few hundred dollars for my pain and suffering.

I used to kid around and talk about my "First husband, my second husband, or even my third husband". It was a silly, made-up game we single girls played. It had started after seeing some movie where a much-married character made reference to her former husbands, and this showed how sophisticated she was. Now, I really did have an ex-husband and I was only twenty-one years old. However it didn't make me feel sophisticated, it made me feel embarrassed. The thing I also felt was; lucky. I was very lucky that I had not gotten pregnant!

After the trial I never saw Jim again, I suppose he went back to Washington and remained there. I had talked with his mother during the time he was in Cook County Jail, and I had told her about Jim marrying me, and all she said was "Why would he do that?"

For years I pondered her question . . . why WOULD he do that? And the best answer I could ever come up with is that he must have loved me beyond reason.

DAPHNE JOINS ME AT DePAUL

Life for me had not really changed. I still lived in the project with my parents. I still worked in the library up the street, I was still slogging to DePaul University at night and accumulating about eighteen semester credits a year. My social life had been put on hold for a short while but was now back in full swing. I saw Doug a few more times, and tried to convince him that he should try harder to win his wife back but he resented me trying to butt into his business and refused to discuss it with me. I had enough good sense not to pursue the subject any further. He did get back with her, but it was much later.

My sister Daphne was attending Chicago Teachers' College full time and, if I had thought about it, I would figure she had amassed enough credits to make application to graduate. I have forgotten (or perhaps I never knew) what the circumstances were that brought her to DePaul, but she enrolled there with me. In fact, we were in the same Psychology class. She still worked part-time at the library and whenever time permitted; she performed with the 'Windy City Thespians', a South Side acting group. How she found time to go to class at DePaul was a mystery to me. I do know that she attended for only a couple of terms and it was a pleasure for us to be going to the same school, even though she was there briefly.

DePaul was sponsoring a contest to see who would be chosen for its homecoming queen, and each branch, or school, would be represented. There would be only one overall queen, chosen from among the winners of their particular schools.

There were many Negro students attending DePaul's University College School of Liberal Arts and some of the students thought that one of our Negro girls might get enough votes to have a chance to represent University College as homecoming queen. It was the school which had recently gone off the quota system. I was delighted that my sister was chosen to run. I helped with Daphne's campaign by making and mounting posters, and standing in the hallway to talk about her to anyone who would listen. The Negro students were surprised and thrilled that one of our own was competing, and to me, she was the prettiest candidate in the running. White students mostly ignored the contest, but Negro students took time out of their busy schedules to vote for her and she won. It was the first time that DePaul had one of us representing anything that they sponsored.

Daphne's very glamorous picture was in the Chicago Tribune where she posed with four other girls from other branches, or schools, of the University. She attended a press conference and a pre-homecoming luncheon. It was a big deal in the black community, and boosted DePaul's image among Negroes. This was early 50's, and it was unheard of for a 'colored girl' to compete for anything in a white institution, least of all, on the basis of her looks! The white media had given us Lena Horne and Dorothy Dandridge and we were supposed to be satisfied!

Unfortunately, Daphne did not win the overall contest so she could wear the crown and ride around the stadium in the queen's car. She was able to attend the homecoming as a runner-up; with the honor of having been the first 'Negro' to compete in a major contest sponsored by the mighty DePaul University. I was very proud of her!

A LITTLE PSYCHOLOGY IS A DANGEROUS THING

The saying that 'A little learning is a dangerous thing' was proven by Daphne and me as we advised and criticized mother in her upbringing of our little sister, Sandra. Whatever we learned in our psychology class, we'd pass on to Mother. Sometimes we'd try correcting Mom in front of Sandra. Although Mom would sometimes resist, telling us to, "Keep your book learning to yourselves. This is my baby and I'll raise her like I want to!"

There were other times when she'd actually seek our advice, asking, "What does your psychology book say about this?"

We interfered so much that Sandra, (who has always been very bright) probably did experience some confusion. While attending an assembly program at Holy Angels Catholic School (Arnold and Kenneth's school), Sandra was suddenly missing from her seat next to Mother. She appeared up on stage and just stood there in front of the audience. People started laughing, some started clapping. The Nun who was leading the assembly bent down and said, "Here's a pretty little girl, what is your name?" She put the microphone in front of Sandra's face, and Sandra replied, "I'm Daphne Hennings, I'm nineteen years old and I go to Chicago Teachers College, and I am going to sing 'Tennessee Waltz'."

The Nun held the microphone in front of Sandra until she finished singing. By then, Mother had made her way down the aisle and collected her baby. Sandra was only four years old. Mother accused Daphne and me of, ". . . confusing the child so much that she don't even know her own name!" Mom rejected all advice after that and we were convinced that Mom and Dad were bringing Sandra up wrong. We also thought the same about our younger brothers, but for some reason we didn't make as much fuss about them. Perhaps it was because we had hoped each one of them would be a girl.

With their grown children moving away, Mom and Dad had to vacate Ida B. Wells' housing project. Policy had changed, and a different kind of tenant was taking over. Welfare mothers; gaming the system, seemed to be the dominant type replacing the 'intact families' of previous years. Lumped together, these people seemed to compound their own problems. One such family moved in next door (into Eleanor Cole's old apartment). The young mother had four children—one of which was disabled—but she didn't seem to seek any help for the child, who was probably deaf because she didn't speak.

This mother would lounge around the apartment all day looking unkempt and stinky. Then she would doll herself up, go out in the evenings, and sometimes return with a man. I think she left her young children alone most nights.

SANDRA HAD A LITTLE LAMB

Mom and Dad were not in a position to buy their own home so they rented a second floor apartment from Czechoslovakian refugees, Mr. and Mrs. Pavlov. The Pavlov's backyard was Sandra's play area and one day, in early spring, Sandra came home from school to find a beautiful white spring lamb cavorting about in her yard.

Sandra was delighted, She had not lived there long, and had made few friends, so she was more than happy to have a 'pet' to play with. She gave the lamb a name, chased it around the yard, fed it, hugged it, tied colored ribbons around its neck and had a grand old time trying to play ball with it. She looked forward to visiting with the lamb when she returned home from school each day. The lamb was the topic of every one of her conversations with children at school, and two girls wanted to befriend her and come by her house to meet the lamb.

The Easter holiday was approaching and Mrs. Pavlov, with her thick accent, tried to tell Sandra that the lamb was food, that it would be killed for the Easter Feast. Mother also tried to explain that the lamb was to be eaten, not fed. I, also, tried to explain the situation to her.

The slaughter of the lamb was delayed when Sandra's denial turned into hysteria as she finally realized what she was being told, that her pet was The Pavlov's Feast! The pleading and crying that Sandra did changed the Pavlov's tradition that year. They gave the lamb to Sandra, they didn't have the heart to upset her again.

A few weeks later, an agent from the Chicago Board of Health came and took the lamb away, saying that it was against city ordinance to have a farm animal within city limits. Sandra was told that the lamb was taken to a farm. She accepted it.

DAPHNE GRADUATES BEFORE I DO

Daphne was no longer attending Chicago Teachers College (CTC) or DePaul University. She had enrolled in a private college that had a reputation for graduating students who could come up with the sky-high tuition they charged, even when the student's academic standing was questionable.

Along with the few credits she had earned at DePaul, her CTC credits and this new enrollment, she applied for graduation. This was before student loans were available, so Daddy had to borrow money and Mother had to go back to work to come up with enough cash to see Daphne through her college graduation.

Mom didn't share everything with me about Daphne. She may have thought I'd be envious that Daphne, a full-time student (working part-time) got so much support from them, while I, a part-time student (working full-time) was left entirely on my own, and even paid them half my salary in 'rent'. Mom would have been right. I might have been envious, when I was paying attention, when I wasn't wrapped up in my own life and my super-busy schedule of working, attending school, sewing, dating, and going to meetings. The meetings I attended were of the various clubs and groups, including my sorority (Sigma Gamma Rho) in which I was active. On occasion, I did wonder why Daphne was so fortunate. But I was so self-focused that I didn't wonder often, or for long.

It was many years later when I learned, from one of her long-term friends, that Daphne had suffered an 'episode' while attending CTC, and Mother knew it. It was the kind of episode that is a precursor of illness to come. It answered the question; why hadn't Daphne stayed at CTC until graduation?

Daphne and I still shared the same bedroom and I knew that she was a little strange, but I had no indication that mental illness was at play!

MANUEL TALKED WITH HIS HANDS

I had been off the dating scene for months, really hunkering down to my studies and taking my courses seriously, when I met a nice guy. He was clean-cut-looking. nice-looking, not handsome, and certainly not smooth like Jim. He waved his hands around a lot when he talked and he had a strange-looking widow's peak to his hairline. He seemed to have some trouble getting his words out but he was kind of attractive with his thick-rimmed glasses and tall, slim, stature. His overall appearance was one of strength and reliability.

Much later, I learned that he had been a stutterer, and had learned to speak without stuttering by using his hands, sort of how an orchestra leader directs an orchestra. We met at The Pershing Lounge Dance Hall, a part of the Pershing Hotel where top name entertainers such as Ahmad Jamal and Miles Davis often played. We met through 'mutual introduction': he asked my name and told me his. He turned out to be a good dancer. When he asked, I was happy to give him my telephone number.

When Emanuel called, I found him very interesting to talk with. He had met me a few years ago when I was still in my teens, and in my very silly state (little did he know that I was still in that silly state, but I had learned to mask it) and he complimented me on my maturity. I felt so comfortable talking with him on the phone that I told him about having been married, and that I was still married because my annulment hadn't been finalized. He shared with me that he had a son. That he had been married for a short time, but was fully divorced, and that he paid child support to the tune of seven dollars a week to his ex-wife who worked at the main library downtown in the Loop. Emanuel was from Georgia. He had made the trek to Chicago with his older sister and his parents, when he was eight-years-old. He, along with his parents, owned their own business; Jackson Food and Liquor. He was a college graduate with a bachelor's degree in business accounting.

I was impressed with this guy because there were so many things about him that I could relate to: his Georgia roots, my mother was from Georgia, he was in business; my family owned businesses. He had been married, I had been married. He had a college degree; I would soon have a college degree. But what impressed me the most was his car: a Chevrolet station wagon, the very fashionable kind with real wood on it and 'Jackson Food and Liquor' printed on the side. It was a very classy ride! The more I found out about him, the more I liked him. I decided that I would just have to learn to have patience with the hand-waving; he seemed to be worth it.

MANUEL RELATES HIS ARMY EXPERIENCES

Manuel (as he was called) had been barely 18-years-old when he was drafted and sent to occupy Germany during the closing days of World War II. The war with Japan had not terminated, but the war in Europe had. He had many stories about his army experiences and I was fascinated to hear his first-hand accounts. The Nuremberg War Criminal Trials were among the things he talked about. He had been able to attend the trials because he was in the Army's Quartermaster Corps and it was his duty to drive officers to the trials, wait for them, and drive them back. There were no restrictions on lowly-ranked service members attending the trials, so he was able to witness most of them.

Years later, when the movie, 'Judgement at Nuremberg' premiered in the United States, Manuel was in a southern city attending one of the many mandatory courses required by his job at the Internal Revenue. He went to the local movie theater and was told that he had to sit in the second balcony—the "colored "section. "I was there! I was in Nuremberg! I was at the trials, and yet I was ordered to the second balcony in the colored section", he bitterly complained, with a few profane words about racial segregation.

I was, happily, allowing Manuel to take up a lot of my dating time and it wasn't long before I was dating him exclusively. When I had first learned about the family business, I had thought of him as some pampered over-privileged guy who had just stepped into his family's business as a career. That impression didn't last long. When I met his parents, I found that he (Manuel) was the boss. It had been his idea and his money that started the business. His Dad was a small man with a handicapped left arm (from falling off of a wagon as a young child). He had been an insurance agent before they opened Jackson Food and Liquor'. His mom had worked as a hairdresser, mostly from her home. The money to invest in starting the business had been made by Manuel, on the black market, during the American Occupation of Germany.

It is said that there's a great crime of theft behind every great fortune. Manuel saw an opportunity and took advantage of it by selling anything he could get his hands on and sending the money back home.

Manuel even sold sandwiches to soldiers aboard the ship traveling to Germany. He said, "Everyone was seasick on the ship. I was too, but I would throw up, feel a little better and when I could stand the sight of food again, I'd go into the mess hall and collect all the leftover bread and meat that the soldiers weren't able to stomach. I'd make sandwiches out of them and sell the sandwiches back to them when they felt O.K. By then, the guys were hungry but the mess hall was closed. If I needed more meat and bread, at mess time, I'd get in line behind a group of guys and as they got served, I'd do a fake heave sound and that would make them automatically recall their seasickness, abandon their trays to run to the 'head'. I'd grab the meat and bread off their trays and stuff it into my fatigue pockets. This would give me more food to work with. I made so much money that I doubled my soldier's salary. I did the same thing on the return trip. By the time I got out of the service I had sent enough money home to start the business."

Manuel was a smart businessman, and he had more nerve than a dozen men. It was the middle of the 50's and things were beginning to open up for our people. Most of the young black men with college degrees were trying to get positions in government or in the corporate world. Not Manuel, that would come later. If he thought a venture would pay off, he was willing to try it. He believed he could make more money on his own, and he was right. The store was providing livelihoods for four people: Manuel, his dad, his mom, and one employee named James. The store also had provided investment capital for the two apartment buildings he had.

WE DON'T SERVE COLORED PEOPLE HERE!

One building was leased, it was a S.R.O. (single room only) type property that came with a lot of headaches. Manuel didn't keep it long, but managed to make some money from it despite the problems he had with some of the occupants.

One tenant from the leased building skipped out owing many months' rent. Manuel got a lead on where he was and went after him by driving to (what was at that time) the forbidden part of our world, Southern Illinois. I went with him on that Sunday afternoon. He wasn't able to locate the guy, but what makes me remember the trip so vividly was that we were about three hours out of Chicago, about 150 miles away, and we faced blatant segregation when a young waitress told us to our faces that, "We don't serve colored people in here." The Dick Gregory joke would have been the perfect retort: "That's O.K., I don't eat colored people." But this was before the humor of the Civil Rights Era, and far too daunting an experience to be anything but humiliating.

Manuel's other building was a six-flat, cut into fourteen apartments. It was in a fairly decent part of the black ghetto. He was buying the building on contract, which was about the only way our people could purchase property, since the FHA (Federal Housing Authority) prohibited issuing mortgages in black-belt neighborhoods. These neighborhoods were identified by the red lines drawn around them on the map of the city. This is how the term, 'redlining' came to mean racial discrimination in housing by a government agency.

The people who lived in the building were mostly decent and hard-working, but a few were the 'get over, any-way-you-can' type. They had their own grudges and resentments to a young 'brother' trying to 'make it'. They knew tenant rules backward and forward: 1.) "How long, from the serving of the five-day-notice, could a tenant occupy an apartment before the bailiff set his things out on the street? 2.) When would a landlord have to get a court order? 3.) What excuses could be used to get an extension on a lease? 4.) What things make a landlord culpable?

One tenant ran the water in his sink at full blast for days because Manuel didn't dash in immediately to fix a problem about which he had complained. He had put special locks on his door, so nobody could get in. Bathrooms were on the left, in the hall and shared by two apartments. Manuel could access all bathrooms by simply entering the front door from the shared hallway. The two apartments had entrances on the right; the one in the front as well as the one in back.

Fully clothed, Manuel bedded himself and his wrench down for the night in the tub. The tenant finally came out of his apartment, at about 3: A. M. to use the bathroom, and was startled, as he opened the bathroom door, to see his landlord dash past him (wrench in hand) declaring; "I am here to fix the problem in your sink!" Manuel headed into the man's apartment, turned his water off, and left by the back door! The tenant moved out several days later, before his water was turned back on.

Another tenant held church all day on Sundays in her apartment. She was 'Bishop' something-or-other, and her congregation of faithful worshippers numbered no more than a dozen, which included a couple of children.

Every week, this large imposing-looking woman donned her robe and preached loud enough for everyone in the building to hear her.

A year or two later, after Manuel and I had married, and I was living in the building, we were all saddened to hear that Bishop 'what's-her-name' had passed away. It was my intention to stop by her apartment to offer condolences to her daughter who lived in the apartment/church with her, but I got busy and it slipped my mind.

A few days later, I was in my apartment when I heard several dull thuds and bumping noises. I walked out to the hallway onto the third floor landing to check out the noise, and to my utter shock, there were pallbearers hauling the Bishop's casket up the stairs to her second floor apartment/church for her funeral.

Manuel did all of the maintenance work on the building. He became a pretty good plumber because he was called upon so often to perform plumbing work. He said that he had always enjoyed working with his hands and building things so owning the building on 56th Street gave him an outlet for what he enjoyed. He could plaster and paint an entire apartment in a day or two. Some things he did well, on other things, he was obviously a beginner. I remember seeing his newly plastered ceiling and thinking that it looked just like icing on a cake. And, of course, everyone knows that icing on a cake is very 'textured', but ceilings are supposed to be smooth.

The third floor rear tenant had not paid rent in months and Manuel was trying, without having to bear the court costs of eviction, to encourage him to move out. The man had previously complained that something was wrong with his back door, but Manuel had not gotten around to fixing it. The tenant had recently argued with Manuel when he was caught stealing electricity from the hall which was on the landlord's bill. The temperature was in the nineties when Manuel took the man's door off of its hinges and carried it down to the basement and locked it up. The guy and his family moved out the next day.

I admired Manuel for his resourcefulness, his daring, his smarts and his tenaciousness. He was one clever guy! My family adored him, except my brother Bubby, who never forgave him for intervening in a street fight while he was smacking his girlfriend around. Manuel used those long, strong arms of his to restrain Bubby from hitting her again. Manuel fit in well with my extended family, too. Since he had been part of the war, my uncles could relate to him. He proved to have the same brand of humor that sustained my family: a silly sense of the ridiculous and an ability to tell a good joke. He became my mother's 'Canasta' partner in the eternal card games played at my home. These two Georgians could tease with the best of them in any cut-throat game that required skill and cunning. As partners, my dad and I opposed them, but we were defeated most of the time.

Sandra developed a crush on Manuel when he brought her a barber-pole sized peppermint stick for Christmas, and she got very upset and cried when she caught me kissing him. She thought he visited our house to see her. She was only five years old when we got married.

TIME TO PERPETUATE THIS RELATIONSHIP

When Manuel proposed to me, he had already bought the ring (having sized it by playfully slipping off the ring that I wore all the time, and trying it on his little finger). He didn't get down on one knee he simply sat behind the steering wheel, waved his hands around in the air and said, "Betty Anne, I'd like to perpetuate this relationship!"

CAREER CHANGES

The Chicago Public Library was opening a new displays department and I was chosen to be assistant to Clara Ream, who headed the department. This would mean working downtown at the main library in the loop. There was no additional pay, but I would be doing art and lettering all day, every day. I jumped at the chance to be able to do what I loved, and it would be close to DePaul University, where I averaged two nights-a-week attendance.

I found out later that Mrs. Willis had been instrumental in my being chosen. She had bragged to colleagues about the wonderful displays her assistant made, not thinking that word would get back to someone who had the power to recommend me, and probably not thinking about the fact that she would be losing me.

My first day on the job found me suffering with the worst (PMS) I'd ever experienced. For no apparent reason, I sat in my new office/studio and cried like a baby. Clara Ream didn't know what to make of her strange assistant in this new two-person department.

Another reason I was anxious to work in The Loop was that I could get to know Manuel's ex-wife. Now that we were engaged to be married, I reasoned, 'I'm going to be step-mother to her son so we should become friends. After all, the boy will probably spend a lot of time in our home.'

We had set the wedding date for Valentine's Day, 1954. My new job started in October, 1953.

Working in The Loop reminded me of working at Montgomery Ward because there were people from different backgrounds. At Oakland Branch Library everyone was 'Negro', all staff, and all of the patrons. When DePaul was on vacation, I could go weeks without seeing anyone other than 'Negroes'. The strange part about this integration in the workplace (which was not apparent to me when I lived it, but is quite clear in retrospect) was that at quitting time, all of the white people stood and waited for their buses on one side of the street, and all of the 'Negroes' stood and waited on the other. The housing segregation pattern was so ensconced in Chicago's culture at that time, that all people of color lived on the South Side, and almost all white people lived on the North Side.

MAKING FRIENDS WITH DOROTHY JACKSON

I deliberately attempted to seek Dorothy Jackson out and make friends with her. I had no idea what she looked like, but by asking a few questions, I was able to spot her in the employee's lounge. I started a conversation with her, and found her to be conservative but friendly. At every chance I got, I would look for her. She had her six-year-old son with her one day but people were crowded around her to admire the boy, and I wasn't able to speak with her or the child. I did get a good look at him, enough to decide that he resembled his dad. I had not told Dorothy who I was, nor had I told Manuel that I was making ovations toward her. I thought the time wasn't right. I wanted to get to know her better. Our friendship was just beginning to bud, I thought.

As my wedding day approached, more people found out about my engagement. An old high school friend, Rosemary Booker, had taken the job of teen reporter at the Chicago Defender Newspaper during high school. It was the job that I had secretly wanted but was too shy to admit it. Rosemary, by then, had a fully-blossomed career as a major reporter for that paper. She got in touch with me about my engagement. She had a photographer take pictures, and Manuel and I were featured on a full page of the newspaper with cupids, roses, ribbons and hearts. The article that accompanied the pictures revealed all of our personal information. It told of plans for our wedding and our reception; including the fact that we would be serving champagne at our reception. This was rare in the early fifties, especially for a girl from the project. That kind of announcement in the paper would have cost a fortune if I had initiated it. I was asked how much I paid to have the announcement put in the paper. It cost nothing except a good lesson in, ". . . it's WHO you know!"

As delighted as I was to have that spread, the other side of it was not so pleasant. Dorothy stopped speaking to me at work. When I was in the lounge and she came in, she would toss her head, pivot around and leave. She called Manuel and cursed him out and said many things that were intended to hurt—including a complaint that we were serving champagne at our reception— and ended by threatening to take him to court to increase the amount of child support he was paying (which I thought was a ridiculously low amount even for those times). Later, she carried out her threat

OUR WEDDING

Our wedding was at Quinn Chapel AME Church, the church to which Rev. Carey had transferred after leaving Woodlawn AME. Woodlawn was the church Sylvia and I attended when I was a girl. I had joined Quinn Chapel because of Rev. Carey, and the fact that the church had a center aisle. This was important to me at the time because I knew that I would get married again and I wanted Rev. Carey to perform the ceremony with me walking down a center aisle.

As it turned out, Rev. Carey would be out of town on Valentine's Day. I had to choose between not having Rev. Carey perform the ceremony or changing the date of the wedding. I chose to be married by the assistant pastor, Rev. Bright, whom I knew from childhood because he lived next door to us in Woodlawn. He was Ronell's grandfather.

Plans for the wedding and reception got underway with full cooperation from both Manuel's family and mine. Manuel's sister, Mildred, designed and made the dress which Daphne wore as maid of honor. I believe she also made Sandra's dress. I designed and made my own ice-blue, satin and lace wedding dress. I also made my own crown by bending some of my mobile wire into a looping shape, covering the wire with satin ribbon and attaching some miniature silk flowers. The bride's veil was simply a piece of matching tulle. The effect may not have been stunning but it was adequate and it was what I could afford. The whole bridal dress, veil, crown, and shoes cost about seventy-five dollars.

The reception was held in the parlor on the top floor of Lincoln Center which cost fifteen dollars to rent. We had to go there the day before and clean up the place and it really needed it! I don't think it had been used in years. The piano was quite a bit out of tune, but I don't think too many people noticed as my mother's long-term friend, Magga Johnson and her husband, Eugene, belted out song after song. Both singing and Eugene playing violin with Magga playing piano. Their performance was my wedding present. Magga and Eugene had been in show business for years, and had even played on Broadway in such

well known productions as THE MACADO! Refreshments
were open-faced and tea sandwiches, prepared by a professional
caterer who charged Mom only a fifty dollar fee. Punch and
champagne were the drinks. Manuel had gotten wholesale
prices on the champagne from one of his liquor salesmen.

Compared to today's ten-course-meal receptions, my
reception would seem pitiful, but in the fifties, this was
considered adequate. I went to many weddings during those
days, and not one of them served full-course dinners.

My flowers cost seventy-five dollars, and included; corsages
for our mothers and my hostesses, the bride's bouquet,
boutonnieres for our fathers, the groom and his two best men,
and even the bouquet for the maid of honor.

Many years before, Daddy had worked for a German baker
who had become quite prominent in the business. Dad called
him, made him remember him, and got a good deal on my
wedding cake. Even with new clothes for family members, I'm
sure my wedding did not cost five hundred dollars. My jewelry
was borrowed, and so was the fur coat I wore to the reception.
Thanks to my God-mother Margaret for her pearls, and Althea
for her Persian lamb coat, this coat was not dry rot and did not
shed hairs when the wind hit it.

Manuel's father had a cousin in Cleveland who was a
number's banker. He needed to be able to assess how much
money he would have to pay out on any week-day's betting
action. The number that 'hit' was the number (published in the
paper) from the 'butter and eggs' Future's Market, which was
listed on the stock market pages of the business and financial
section of the paper.

The 'Chicago Tribune Newspaper' ran these figures daily in its morning edition. For a fee, these figures were supplied by phone to stockholders (who subscribed to receive them) prior to the time that the paper was delivered. Mr. Jackson (Manuel's dad) was a 'subscribing stockholder' (even though he owned no stock). He would call his cousin in Cleveland and give him the 'butter and eggs' numbers early in the morning (before 9:30 A.M.) so that 'Cousin' knew the winning numbers while people were still laying down their bets.

'Cousin', being such a big shot in Cleveland, got a deal from a friend, for us to stay at a 'Negro' hotel for our honeymoon. I just knew we'd also get a wonderful gift from him and his wife. They sent us a lovely salad bowl.

OUR HONEYMOON

The drive to Cleveland took about six hours, with Manuel doing all of the driving, so we were very tired by the time we arrived, which was after midnight on our wedding day. My husband was enrolled in a graduate class at Northwestern University where he had to use a slide rule. He had never used one before, he had brought the slide rule with him to study it on our four-day honeymoon. On the day we returned, he would have to attend class. Manuel had ordered a room with twin beds for our honeymoon, because; he said, "I thought that was what you wanted, since you bought twin beds for our apartment!"

It was true. He had left the shopping for furniture up to me since he was always too busy to attend to such things. I had gone to Marshall Field's Department Store and (greatly influenced by movies and television) purchased twin beds. But the difference between the beds in the hotel and the ones in our apartment, was that the apartment twins could be hooked together to make one king-sized bed, and there was only one headboard for the two. The twin beds in the hotel were so heavy that they couldn't even be moved, forget about hooked together. The other reason that I thought twin beds were for us, was the way I suffered every month during my menses. I was sure that both of us would be happy to have separate beds at these times, and that proved to be the case. We both took a lot of teasing from relatives and friends about our twin beds.

THIRD FLOOR—FRONT, SHARE THE BATH

Married life on the third floor—front apartment, share the bath—in the building owned by my husband was off to a good start. We had decorated the three-room apartment with painted stripes and blocks, and I had painted a huge sunburst in gold on a purple wall in our bedroom. Our apartment became a topic of conversation among our acquaintances for its boldness and many friends came just to take a look. I was happy with my new husband, except that working in the store kept him in a bad mood.

The store was in the heart of the ghetto and many of the people were the kind who'd try anything to 'get over'. Manuel worked long hours every day except on Sundays he'd leave about one in the afternoon. Daily, he'd come home and stretch out on the floor to nap because he was too dirty and too tired to bathe and change. His conversation was often about some customer who got arrested or got murdered and still owed him money.

Many of his customers were alcoholics and it was against the law to sell liquor before twelve, noon, on Sundays. The store's one employee, James, lived in the neighborhood where the store was located so he would go home with a supply of half pint bottles on Saturday nights, and the people who couldn't wait until noon on Sunday knew where to go to purchase their booze until 'Jackson Food and Liquor' started selling it on Sunday afternoons. James had a hustle on the side that we found out about when a customer came in to pay his bill from the books, and there was no entry for him on the books. The customer had dealt with James. There was no way to tell how much of 'Jackson's Food and Liquor' merchandise James had sold and then pocketed the money.

PAT, BUD, GEORGE AND MURDER!

There was an apartment in the back of the store which Manuel rented out to a young woman and her two pre-school children. I'll call her Pat because I don't remember her name. Her common-law husband (Bud) was in jail, and she had taken up with an older man who would spend money in the store buying groceries and milk for her and the children. The older guy (George) might have been married because he was never known to spend the night. During the day, Pat would parcel out her kids to anyone who'd baby sit them and spend several hours behind locked doors with George.

It was Mother's Day, and I had prepared my best meal for my mom and my new mother-in-law. Manuel and his mom were very late, and they hadn't called. My mom and I had been sitting in my apartment wondering why. Manuel was to leave the store early, with his mom and join us. Every time we called the store's number, it was busy.

When they finally arrived, Manuel related, with horror, what had happened and how they had to deal with their customers and the police. "Before we could get out of the store, Bud comes in—back from prison—has a few drinks with some of the people in the store and finds Pat in the back with George. Bud becomes infuriated, the two men argue, Bud whips out his switchblade and stabs George in the heart. The murder takes place right outside of the store on the sidewalk. I was the one who checked George's pulse and declared him dead!"

Bud went to jail for the crime and served about seven years. 'Jackson Food and Liquor' had gone out of business by the time he was released on parole. Bud and Pat, as plaintiffs, sued 'Jackson Food and Liquor' under "The Dramshop Law". Dramshop is the law which makes the owner of an establishment culpable if he sells liquor to an individual and makes that person drunk enough to commit a crime. The plaintiffs; Pat and Bud, claimed that the liquor Bud drank early Sunday afternoon in the store, was enough to cause him to become intoxicated to the point of committing a felony. The store's insurance, which was in effect at the time of the murder, settled out of court for thousands of dollars. So, actually, Bud got paid for killing George.

TELLING JOKES, A FAMILY TRADITION

Manuel and I were very busy newlyweds. In addition to our careers, we were both in school, and we tried to keep up, socially, with our friends. This was difficult because Manuel had quite a few good buddies and I had a whole lot of friends and acquaintances. This meant double-socializing, because we tried to attend every function as a couple, and we both attended the parties that were given by my extended family. Our family tended to celebrate everything; especially birthdays. Ours was a joke-telling family, and it was not unusual for the morning sun to brighten our faces in the living room of an uncle's house, where the party had started the night before, and we had sat up all night telling jokes. Many of us honed our joke-telling skills during these sessions. I still have many jokes in my memory, which I add to as often as I can, and which I am more than willing to share at any time. Today, I obtain most of my jokes from the internet.

My new husband was a natural, he became a great joke-teller, his hand movements diminished and eventually stopped and he was able to hold his own in any group.

Joke-telling is from a legacy of 'self-entertainment' practiced by many of us descendants of slaves. Teasing, partying, food-sharing, and joke-telling substituted for the clubs we couldn't join, the fancy restaurants we weren't welcome in, and the resort and vacation spots from which we were excluded, and couldn't afford anyway.

JOIN THE DISPLAY-WORKERS UNION? I DON'T THINK SO!

I enjoyed working in the displays department so much that I made inquiries about joining the union for people who did that kind of work. Every project was different and a challenge. Each completed project was there for all to see, whether it was a sign that I lettered, or a bulletin board that I decorated, or a mobile (they were very popular in the 50's) that dangled and moved above our heads. Perhaps it was a poster that was silk-screened, or the Civil War artifacts that we re-labeled and encased in the museum section of the library.

The union for display workers and window trimmers, "... did not accept applications from colored people." I was told. The advice that went with it, was, "... get with an interior decorator to continue display work." But everyone knew that there was only one interior decorator (meaning, only one 'Negro') on the South Side of Chicago, and everyone also knew that there just wasn't enough demand for more. So, I didn't frustrate myself by trying to buck the status quo. I wasn't of that mind-set yet, nor was the climate ripe for that kind of action. The Civil Rights Movement was years away. The prevailing thinking was that 'Negroes' were making progress if now we could go to another restaurant downtown, where we could spend our money, which served us without insulting our dignity by seating us next to the kitchen or the bathroom. Discussions about removing the restrictions that prevented Negroes from owning those restaurants were for future activists.

And progress was being made! Jobs were opening up for our people that had previously been reserved for whites only, and the Trianon Ballroom (a whites only dance hall, located on the South Side) was a site that had pickets and marchers swarming around it for many months. 'The Great Migration' had swelled Chicago's 'Negro' population to the point that something had to give in jobs and in housing.

Manuel's sister (Mildred) and her husband (Calvin) occupied one of the apartments in the building on the first floor. They had four children and Mildred was pregnant with their fifth. Her husband was working as a Chicago Transit bus driver, and It had been only a few years in which 'Negro' men were working in that capacity. My uncle, Rick, was one of Chicago's first Negro bread truck drivers, and it was a big deal that he, as a veteran, had been hired.

STARTING OUR FAMILY

Manuel must have had a keener sense of competition toward his sister than I realized because he started in shortly after our honeymoon talking about 'catching up' with Mildred and Calvin in producing babies. This was talk I didn't want to hear for at least a couple of years. I had other goals before I wanted to be called 'Mommy', and I certainly never wanted to be called that by more than two small voices.

Manuel kept up the pressure to start a family, he was more than ready. We hadn't discussed 'when', but we had established that we 'would'. I dodged for almost a year. Then, when he dared me, even though I didn't have strong commitment for it, I got pregnant! I had only been married eleven months. I still hadn't amassed enough college credits to apply for graduation. Jeffrey was born the next October. I had been married only one year and eight months, and I was a Mommy. My life, dramatically changed, my husband, dramatically changed.

The pregnant months seemed like years. I started out with the best doctor attending to my needs and then my mother-in-law had an operation on her varicose veins. When I was about four months pregnant, my husband had closed the store and was just starting to work for the Internal Revenue Service.

My mother-in-law developed a blood clot that was heading for her heart. For weeks, she had to have private nursing service around the clock. My husband was the only working member of the family since Calvin had lost his job and Mildred couldn't work with five children. I had vacated the job I loved in my fourth month of pregnancy due to morning fatigue. I had very little morning sickness but I was seized with morning tiredness. We were all living in the same apartment building and joint savings were diminishing fast. No one had health insurance in those days.

My brother's wife, Marjorie, said, "I don't know why you want to keep going to Dr. Johnson, spending all that money, when you can come on out to Illinois Research Hospital where I work and have that baby for a fifteen dollar registration fee." And that is what I did. It is the decision that I consider the worst I've ever made. The one decision that I'll regret until the day I die!

Marjorie had all four of her children at Illinois Research. When she delivered Karen (her first-born), there was no problem of which I am aware. Eleven months later she had twins, one (Celeste) died of something congenital. When (and if) I thought about the loss of Celeste, it should have been a warning signal for me. I should have dashed back to Dr. Johnson! I suppose this teaching hospital wasn't staffed to take care of special needs.

Prenatal care was O.K., even fun, because of all the new women I met who had not heard my jokes. As we sat in the clinic, waiting to be seen by the interns (whom we didn't distinguish from full-fledged doctors) I would practice my joke-telling ability and laugh along with my new audience.

Delivery was difficult because labor started with pains that were five-minutes-apart. These pains had to be tolerated until we could make it from the South Side to where the hospital was located; on the West Side. The decision to allow me to deliver was not my decision. By the time it should have been decided that caesarean birth was required, Jeffrey was almost here. I was cut so deeply that the stitching-up process lasted longer than the painkillers, and the last seven or eight stitches were made with nothing to dull the pain. In addition to the misery of childbirth, I had caught the worst cold I'd ever had, and it was in the coughing stage.

The size of my baby had been improperly calculated because weight gain was the main way to prenatally measure him. I had stuck to the suggested diet so closely that the baby's weight gain was offset by my overall weight loss. Jeffrey's birth weight was eight pounds, two-and-a-half ounces, which was a lot of baby for a hundred twenty-two pound, me. After delivery, I weighed seven pounds less than I did before I got pregnant.

In the delivery room, after delivery, I felt a protuberance like the baby's knee was still in me. That's when I was told that I had a fibroid tumor. I didn't find out until later that I also had prolapse of the uterus, a condition that can occur when a baby is delivered, but should have been taken.

Apart from my misery, the worst thing about the delivery was that forceps were used and this gave my baby brain damage, which deprived him of the life he could be living if my decision had been different.

PROBLEMS WITH BIRTH; AND BEYOND

We were not aware, right away, that our baby had been damaged. To this day, the hospital has never owned-up to its role in creating this nightmare. All that I knew, in the eight days I spent in the hospital, was that my baby didn't nurse properly. At feeding time, he would suckle for a minute or two, then fall asleep as if he were too tired to ingest enough nourishment to sustain life. The nurses directed me to thump his little fingers to wake him up. I hated doing that; I could see that it hurt him! It did little to help the situation, anyway. He would simply fall back to sleep. Then, when he was returned to the nursery, he would cry because he was hungry. This did not endear him to the staff of nurses and nurses' aides working in the nursery. I could detect a negative tone in their attitudes, as they'd bring my red-faced, screaming, feed-me-on-demand baby (at all hours of the day and night) to me.

When he was exactly fourteen days old, my baby began projectile vomiting (vomiting that juts out like a fountain) from every feeding he was given. This meant that he was getting no nourishment. The diagnosis was dire, he had pyloric stenosis. To save his life, he would have to have an operation!

The pylorus is the opening from the stomach into the intestines. It had constricted, or narrowed to the point that no milk could pass this gristle-like part of his anatomy. He was exactly four weeks old when he had the operation. No one could explain to us, why this had occurred, but we did find out that it was not an uncommon disorder, and it usually happened to boys.

From being a woman with breasts that were much above average size, as a nursing mother; I was enormous! Milk dripped all down my legs when I first stood up from my delivery. Now, with my baby in the hospital, I had excess milk which I pumped out every day, refrigerated and took to the hospital for Jeff's feedings. This was a painful ordeal because I had to travel by bus, and I had not healed from my delivery cuts.

Life settled down to normal when we were able to bring our baby home, but little did we expect that life would not be normal for us, ever! In the long run, life, along with the joys, would also be full of pain, disappointment, and frustration.

We were just as enamored with our beautiful little newborn as any couple. Manuel would sit and hold Jeffrey for hours, just staring at him with a look of amazement on his face. Jeffrey was a precious prize; he looked just like his mommy and his daddy. He was the perfect blend of his parents, he had his mother's hairline and shoulders, but everything else was like his father.

Cracks started appearing in our marriage during Jeffrey's infancy. My husband showed what a controller he was when he required me to keep a record of every dime I spent. If I bought a loaf of bread, I had to record it in our budget book. I wasn't accustomed to such stringent control. We weren't even poor. Manuel made an above-average salary, was a property owner, and was buying United States Treasury Bonds through payroll deductions. He provided well for us but allowed me no freedom with money.

In reaction to my husband's stringent controls, I developed a new goal in my life. This made me determined to finish my bachelor's degree in order to become employed and have money of my own that I could control. Finishing my degree required tuition money, and in his wisdom, Manuel recognized that if he invested in me, a good return was assured. We used some of those treasury bonds to pay the rest of my way through college.

I RETURN TO SCHOOL

Jeff was ten months old when I went back to school. I was so very lucky to have a mother-in-law who adored my baby, and who also lived in the same building. She was always willing to baby-sit. I enrolled, as usual, in the University College for nine credits of night school, and, during the summer session, enrolled in the uptown campus (day school) carrying six credits, I was almost never home. My wonderful mother-in-law took almost complete care of my baby.

I came home late one night and picked Jeff up from his grandmother's apartment on the third floor, took him home to our apartment, now in the basement, and he beat me in the face with his little fists and cried uncontrollably, as if to say, "Why have you thrown me away? I hate you for abandoning me! This is your punishment!" All I could do was hold him until he was all cried out and he fell asleep.

COMPLETING MY COLLEGE WORK

My goal was to accelerate collecting college credits so that I would be able to finish all of my course work by the end of summer 1956. Then I could apply for a teaching job with The Chicago Public Schools. The degree would not be awarded until summer, 1957, but I could get a job because I would have completed all of the requirements for the degree. In order to collect the credits I would have to go to the uptown campus.

Attending class on the uptown campus was as different from attending class downtown, as night is from day. In the first place, the uptown students were much younger than downtown, and they were almost all white. I don't remember seeing one other 'Negro' on campus. I felt very lonely—having no one with whom to relate—when I got the stare that said, "We don't want you here!" and I got that stare a lot! No one befriended me!

In the cafeteria, one young man showed downright hostility to me when I asked him to pass the sugar. After ignoring me through two requests, he shoved the sugar dispenser so hard that it toppled over and spilled. In a rare moment of choosing the right response, I got right up in his face and thanked him profusely, in the most syrupy fake voice I could muster. He turned red with embarrassment. He got my message!

After completing my courses on the uptown campus, I gathered all of my credits and went to the registrar's office to obtain a statement that I was eligible to graduate, and I would be in the next graduating class. The registrar was on vacation, but the person substituting for him (or her) issued the statement on DePaul University stationery. This was as useful as a degree at the Chicago Board of Education.

That September, I went to work as a first grade teacher at Forestville Elementary School, a school my mother had attended when she was a child.

DePaul notified me, around November, that my application for graduation was rejected, and that I would have to take two more courses because two of the courses that I had submitted were sophomore courses, but I had taken them when I was a senior. This meant that I wouldn't be able to graduate until the next year. So, instead of being able to graduate with the 1957 class, I would be in the 1958 class, provided I pass the two courses.

I was doing fairly well as a new teacher, in spite of the fact that I had not taken student teaching. Now that I had gained some status as a wage-earner, home life also improved I was also much happier with myself. I had made new friends and I wasn't required to write every purchase in the budget book.

I really shouldn't have been eligible to teach because teaching required a degree. I knew that I should have reported my situation to my principal, but I was too busy cringing in fear that I would be exposed, and enjoying the status and salary that went with the position. That is how I taught school for over a year before I got my degree.

GROWING, DEVELOPING

Jeffrey's motor skills developed at a normal pace. He sat up, crawled and walked at the same time that most babies did. In fact, he was somewhat ahead of the curve in motor development because he was unusually strong. He demonstrated his strength by knocking over a commercial-size floor fan in his grandmother's beauty shop before his second birthday. Jeffrey also spoke words at the same age (around 18 months) as other babies. The first true indication that his development was impaired was when he attempted to put words together in sentences. He would become extremely frustrated, cry and stop trying.

My brothers and sisters were growing and developing at their own paces. Daphne had married the guy who Ted introduced her to. He was fresh out of the navy. They fell madly in love, and married before they'd known each other six months. Their son, Charles, was born when Jeffrey was sixteen months old, just about the time that we were beginning to experience problems with Jeff. It was also the time that my lovely sister was seized with the ravishes of post-partum psychosis; and would probably, for the rest of her life, suffer with mental health issues.

She and her husband had two other children; Andrea and Michael. The youngest, Michael, inherited his mother's problem with mental illness to a far greater degree than she had experienced. He died at the tender age of forty-two.

Ted and his wife had three wonderful children, but their marital problems led them to divorce before the youngest reached school age. Bubby (now, Bob) had left home at sixteen. He was twenty-years-old when my son Jeffrey was born and he and his lady had a son who was a few months older than my Jeff. Arnold, Kenneth, and Sandra were young students who were still at home with Mom and Dad.

THAT AIN'T SAM COOKE!

Ted had teamed up with Sam Cooke's older brother, Walter, and started producing shows in the Southern part of the country. Sam Cooke was a rising young star at that time, and they were out to make as much money as they could by riding his stardom coattail. Sam and his family were well known in our neighborhood—even though they did not live in the project—and his father, Rev. Cooke, and my dad worked together at Reynolds' Aluminum Plant. They rode to work together for years. Sam worked there a short while before he became a big star. My dad told us how he'd be singing and composing songs in his dad's car on the long drive to and from the plant in McCook, Illinois. The other guys in the car wanted him to shut up but he never did. Sam did not work long at the plant.

In the fifties, there were very few 'Negroes' on television, so it was possible for a recording artist to have a big hit in the Black community and many people not know what he looked like. Ted and his partner counted on this by staging concerts with impersonators who could imitate the exact sound of popular recordings. Chicago provided excellent imitators for every recording artist with a hit. And the performers were eager to travel. The concerts were staged in school auditoriums, community halls, churches and other venues in the South, where segregation relegated 'Negro' artists to class 'B' halls.

With advance publicity and word-of-mouth advertising, Ted and his partner were able to pack these places for each concert. There were usually two or three big names featured on the bill—with fake Sam Cooke and Lenny Welch headlining most bills—and there was always popular local talent, too (not fakes) who would perform and warm up audiences before the "stars" were introduced.

In a town near Birmingham, Alabama, in a 'colored' high school auditorium, nearing the end of the concert, with "Sam" crooning his latest hit, a young man stood up, pointed his finger and announced in a booming voice, "THAT AIN'T SAM COOKE!"

It was with luck and Mother's Everyday Prayers that Ted and his posse made it out of the auditorium and back to Chicago before the infuriated crowd attacked them. That ended Ted's career as a big shot show producer.

DAPHNE; THE THESPIAN

At first, Daphne's health problems did not affect her in an overwhelming way. Before she got married she was able to graduate, teach school, and continue acting with her Windy City Thespians Group. She showed great promise as an actor and was often compared to Dorothy Dandridge. She had a friend, Ray, whose sister had made it to New York and was appearing in 'THE BLACKS' on Broadway. This guy had 'big eyes' for Daphne but she didn't return the feeling, he became her agent. She appeared in a few plays in the Black Community, but I don't know if Ray can be credited with steering her to them, I do know that she was very good.

In later years, with three pre-teens, a history of mental illness, a rocky marriage, and a failed career, Daphne would finalize her divorce and marry her very first sweetheart, Frank. This was kind of a re-run of the earlier Daphne except that she actually moved to California with her three children and Frank.

COPING WITH STRESS

These early years of coping with life's offerings found me living with stress on a daily basis. I had encouraged Manuel to become more friendly with guys on his job. I had met some of the newly-hired 'Negro' collection officers, and some of their wives. They all, pretty much, fit the same profile as my husband: college educated, embarking on a new career, married, home-owning (or saving for one). Each had a child or two and each was very ambitious to succeed on the job. The increased hiring of 'Negroes' to good government jobs was a direct result of stepped-up activism by The NAACP and other civil rights groups.

Little did I suspect that the first beer bash, which was held in our apartment, would result in 'Manny' (as he came to be known to his friends) becoming the lead 'swell' and drinking buddy of his group.

Manny and the 'Boys' began stopping off after work for an occasional drink. Then it became a couple of nights, then practically a daily thing. This became a four—out-of five nights a-week ritual of not making it home until after nine at night.

As years went on, this group took up tennis on Saturdays, and golf whenever they could wedge it in. They formed an investment club, then some of them took up flying planes, and yes, my Manny was an integral part of every adventure. Often, when he was so very late, Manny would use the excuse that he had to take 'Ol Charlie' home. Charlie lived on the West Side and he didn't drive. Of course, this caused many arguments between us, and it eventually got to the place where we argued almost all of the time.

I was stuck with all of the responsibilities of keeping the household going, raising our son and dealing with his special needs.

One time, when Manny used the excuse that he had to take Ol' Charlie' home, I had to ask, "How did you transport him, piggyback? Because I had the car!"

Many of my husband's activities began to be secretive. He knew that I would object, so he would just do as he pleased and not tell me. He became such an avid golfer that when I looked for my missing red nail polish, I found it among Manny's things. He used the polish to paint his golf balls red, so that he could find them in the snow.

FORMING BONDS TO COPE WITH MADNESS

The thing that probably saved me from completely going out of my mind was that I formed a tight bond with wives of his friends, and discovered that they were coping with the same madness. We were in agreement that the thing that was the hardest to take was the secrecy, how our husbands would make plans and not let us in on them.

One such plan was to play golf on a Friday afternoon, and then meet at our house for the monthly investment club meeting. I was well aware of the meeting because I had been preparing for it for weeks. What I didn't know about was the golf game. The guys had not yet been to our (new to us) house, and I had been cleaning, fixing, sewing and arranging for weeks. All of this, while I worked full time, did three hours of homework per night, took complete care of my four-year-old, cooked every night and made attempts at keeping up my social obligations.

The house was my focus when I came home from work the Monday before the meeting, and I took a bus to the loop to come home with three stacking serving tables. This was a much too heavy load, but I was motivated to fix up because we'd just moved from a four room apartment to a four bedroom house and some of our rooms were furnished with wall to wall echo. The house, though sparsely furnished, was decently decked out by Friday. And Friday was the day that, instead of having my lunch, I food shopped to be able to make the gumbo that would feed the investment club members when they came about six-o-clock that evening. I had left Manuel at home that morning taking the day off to cut our eight-inch-tall grass and to pick up Jeff from his school.

It was almost one-o-clock when I dashed into my house to refrigerate the groceries. I had to get back to school for the afternoon session, but I couldn't help noticing that the grass hadn't been cut. When I returned home after three-o-clock, Manuel still wasn't there and the grass still wasn't cut. I wondered where he could be with our son. Could Jeffrey have had an emergency? Could Manuel have had to rush him to the hospital?

I did what any independent married woman would do. I called my mother. "Why, yes, Betty Anne, I know where Manuel took Jeffrey, he brought him here. He's here now. Manuel dropped him off after picking him up from school, about 12:30; he said he was going to play golf with some of the guys from work."

I literally SAW RED! I went into a rage! I overturned every piece of furniture I could upset. I grabbed the newly-hung drapes that I had worked so hard to prepare, and left them dangling from their hooks. I went into the kitchen and threw all of the ingredients for the gumbo all over the floor. I opened a bottle of ketchup and poured it all over my freshly-scrubbed floor so that it looked like blood had been spilled. Then I went next door to my neighbor and friend, Sovilla's house—sobbing—that I needed a drink! Sovilla was married to Herman, a pediatrician, who worked many evenings. She welcomed company.

Sovilla was a great listener as she poured and I drank. By five-o-clock, I was soused!

In the meantime, my mother tried to reach me by phone to see when I was coming to pick up Jeffrey. Not being able to reach me, she got in her car with Jeffrey and came to my house. She had the key, so when I didn't answer the bell, she and Jeff came in and found the mess I'd made. When she saw the ketchup, she just knew it was my blood and that something terrible had happened to me. Mother ran next door to Sovilla's and, screaming at the top of her lungs, punched the bell frantically until Sovilla came to the door, followed by her tipsy guest, Betty Anne.

HUSBAND POWER

A few months before we bought our house, I wanted a new dress to wear to an important event. I usually designed and made my party dresses, but I didn't have time to make something for this particular occasion which was on a Friday evening. It was not unusual for me to dash down to the Loop on Saturday morning, buy the fabric and the pattern, come home, cut out and stitch up my garment and wear it to an event that same night. I did it several times.

For this very special event, I decided I would buy a dress, wear it, and then return it to the store for a refund. I knew many gals who did this. We were on a very tight budget because we were saving to buy our house. I had learned from a friend that I could take the label off with a razor blade, the price tag was always attached to the label. I would wear no perfume or cologne and I would simply sew the label, with the price tag back on before returning it. No one would be able to tell that I had worn the dress. I related this plan to my husband. He just shook his head and walked away without comment.

When I finally settled on a dress that I liked, I gave the clerk my credit card, which I had obtained on my own, in my own name using my credit—as a salaried person, a schoolteacher—earning a livable salary.

The clerk said I'd have to go to the office! I couldn't imagine what could be wrong. I had been very conservative, I hadn't abused my credit at all, I knew I was in good standing.

The clerk in the office seemed embarrassed to tell me that my husband had called the store and told her not to allow me to buy anything on credit, and they could not let the sale go through. The year was 1959, and husbands had that kind of power . . . or should I say . . . wives were that powerless!

A friend from school and her husband were among the early visitors to our new home. We had only a two-seater loveseat as furniture in our living room. When we needed additional seating we would pull up chairs from the kitchen.

When Lillian and her husband arrived, Manuel announced that we didn't have anything to drink, so he would go out to the liquor store and get a bottle. Manuel didn't like Lillian or her husband. She had the habit or ordering her husband around and we all found it rude and distasteful. Manuel was away well over an hour for something that should have taken fifteen minutes.

We were upstairs checking out the house when he returned. He was drunk, and he had no bottle for the company. He stretched out on the only seating in the living room, the loveseat, fell asleep, and snored.

About a year-and-a-half after we bought our one-family home, Manuel needed a loan in order to take care of some expenses on the apartment building that he owned with his mom and dad. He applied and took out the loan, using our one-family home; which he owned with me, as collateral. He did this without my knowledge and totally without my permission. I didn't find out about the loan until the late sixties; when we were ready to sell our house. This amounted to more than ten years of deceit, disrespect and humiliation.

THAT SQUEAK IS OUR BABYSITTER!

We were pretty excited when we closed on the house. It was in a safe area, with good schools, and the community of Chatham did a good job of keeping property values intact. We moved there in 1960, and today, it is still a viable community.

Jeffrey wasn't five-years-old, but he could play outside without constant supervision because the neighborhood was so safe. Mostly, he liked to ride his tricycle, which was probably his favorite activity. We, also, liked for him to ride it. He could go all around the long city block without either of us having to go and check on him because the tricycle had a loud squeak. As Jeff stretched his little legs to push against the pedals of that tricycle, we could tell, with great accuracy, just where he was by how loud the squeak sounded. When the squeak was faint, we knew he was on the other side of the block. When the squeak grew louder, we knew he was approaching home. That squeak was our babysitter.

One day, we were listening to the weak squeak, and mentally noting that our precious little boy was on the other side of the block, when the squeak stopped altogether. Manuel and I stared at each other, then we grabbed our keys and dashed out the door! We ran towards the other side of the block where we had last heard the telltale squeak. Before we got there, we saw Jeff, silently peddling his little tricycle along towards home, and there was our neighbor observing him, with his oil can still in his hand.

USING MADNESS TO COPE WITH BONDS

The frustration, humiliation, hurt and feelings of rejection, inflicted on me by my husband's behavior—which I lived with on a daily basis—sent me, along with other IRS wives, who were experiencing the same feelings, to seek solace in the bottle. I had been brought up around hard liquor, and it was taken for granted that socializing meant downing a few drinks, but most of my drinking had been confined to week-end partying. I took to having a drink or two after school. Usually I was with one or two of the wives who were also missing the feeling of being cherished by their IRS spouses. Our children would play together while two or three of us wives drowned our complaints and compounded our problems with our 'Pity Party' going from one house to the other.

One of the wives (I'll call her Rose) must have thought that I resorted to extreme methods to maintain my status as mother of only one child. Most of the couples had two children, a few had more. Rose and her husband had four. I never expressed to her my desire to have more children, and I certainly didn't let her know about the prolapsed uterus which was preventing me from becoming pregnant. We were not that close as friends.

I was very much surprised when Rose asked me to go with her to the doctor who was going to perform an abortion on her. She had no idea that I thought abortions were horrendous and that I was thankful to never have been in a situation where I needed to consider such a violent act for myself. She told me that she thought I would understand. I didn't challenge her to find out what she meant by that remark. I just went along with her assumption and said very little. She must have sensed that I really didn't want to go with her because the day before she was scheduled she telephoned me to cancel, saying that her relative (a cousin, I think) was going with her, instead. Rose and her family were Catholic.

WHO IS THIS HUSSY NAMED MERRILL LYNCH?

One of the IRS wives with whom I became quite friendly was Alma. Alma was very pretty, had been married before and had two children by her first husband. She was extremely suspicious of her present husband, Don, and allowed him no breathing room outside of her view. She was not aware that the investment club guys pooled their money, gave it to one single member each month for him to act as broker, research the stock, purchase the stock, and then report to the group. We all got such a good laugh out of the way Alma found out about the method used to make the purchase, that I wrote a short story about it. I dramatized the story, but the basic facts are true. Here it is:

DIATRIBE

"Oh, so you've finally decided to come on home! No, I don't want to hear any of your lame-brained excuses! This is the second time this week! You're supposed to be home by six-fifteen, and here it is, wh', oh, uh . . . well, so it is only six fifty-five, but you didn't call. You could have called!

"Yeah, I see. You don't have to act so silly. Pointing to your new haircut is so juvenile! "So maybe you did tell me you were getting your hair cut. It's a wonder I can remember anything, with the shock I got today! In the six years we've been married I've never had this kind of blow to my heart!

Now, I've told you this before, and I'm telling you again; the one thing I will not tolerate is an unfaithful husband! You know that's the reason I divorced Horace after seven years of marriage. Even though we had two young children, I couldn't live with him when I found out about him shacking up with that bitch! Sure it was hard, trying to work and raise two kids. Donna was only six, and Horace Jr. wasn't four yet, but I couldn't stand the sight of Horace when I found out!

When you proposed, I kept telling myself it won't be like that! Maybe Horace didn't get a chance to sow his wild oats since we got married soon out of high school and started having babies right away. Maybe he wasn't ready to be a real husband, but you were older, ready to appreciate a beautiful, good and faithful wife! You had been around!"

"But I will divorce your ass, too. I know I'm still attractive and desirable to many men. Getting another husband is the least of my worries! It's just that I thought we had a real bond, a good understanding, a real love thing!"

"Ever since you joined that group you call an investment club, you've been acting strange. Like I'm supposed to believe that EVERY member has to do research at the library and that EVERY member has to buy the stock. No club runs like that! The treasurer is ALWAYS the one who handles the money. He's the one with the responsibility. That's why he's called the treasurer, because he has the money! And you, going out all these Saturday afternoons, you and Charlie, telling me you're doing research! Research my ass! That's the same kind of cover Horace used. He was supposed to be registered in school but all the time he was sneaking around with his other woman.

"Don't say a word! I know you've been seeing someone! Because now, today, I have proof! Here's your cancelled check to prove that you've been sending money to your other woman. Yes, I went through your records, the ones you keep locked up. Your so-called business records for that ragged-assed pool hall, and that ghetto slum building you own with your ex-wife! The records I'm not ever expected to see, the ones you use for cover to do whatever in hell you want with the money, telling me the investment club monies are part of that account. Since Arthur is the treasurer, he's in charge of that account, not you!'

"I go out of here EVERY day, forty hours a week, and bring my money home to help with the expense of owning this house and to pay for that brand new Mustang in the garage! I don't really have to work, you know. I could live off of the child support I get from Horace, plus the house allowance from you and be quite comfortable. But I work to keep you from straining, to help you out with bills so that you can feel free enough to make a few investments, but in something sensible, not in the white folks' stock markets. How many Negroes buy stocks? I'll bet you could count them on one hand! This is 1963, and our people have made a lot of progress, but you can bet that white folks aren't about to let Negroes in on their big moneymaking deals!

"If I hadn't gotten your checks from Mrs. Hudson, next door, who got them from that new mailman, who delivered them to the wrong address, I wouldn't know that you gave your bitch almost two thousand dollars last month! Two thousand is more than my ex sends his kids in SIX months! I didn't say much when it was only your time you were wasting out there in the streets, but now I see it's your time AND your money, and YOUR money is MY money!"

"Don't say a word! I caught you red-handed! This check tells the whole story! You'll see that two can play that game. There's this cute new guy in the office next to mine at work who has invited me to lunch a few times, and I know he has big eyes for me, but I never encouraged him, being the faithful, married woman that I am, I've only flirted with him in a teasing way, not seriously, but now, maybe I'll look him over in a new light since you have screwed up our marriage!

"I could adjust to being a kept woman, just like your bitch. I could sit home, paint my nails every day, go to the beauty parlor twice a week and live a pampered life just like your woman. I could get me a sugar daddy, too!

"That bitch doesn't cook for you, wash your dirty drawers, shop for you, take care of you when you're sick, play hostess to your boring friends and even pretend to respect ol' fresh Wally! Yes, FRESH Wally. You heard me right! Wally!

"I can tell by your expression that it shocks you to find out that your so-called best friend has gotten fresh with your wife. I wasn't going to tell you, but twice, on those Hollywood type kisses, Wally tried to slip me some tongue. Not once, but TWICE! And I should have known that if your best buddy has a taste for playing around on his lovely wife, Jeannie, YOU, bird-of-a-feather, would too!

"I wouldn't ever have told you about Wally, except that I am so devastated to find out about you and your other woman!

"There's no way you can deny it. Here, in your OWN handwriting is the check for almost two thousand dollars, made out to your bitch! And now that I've got her name, I'm gonna find her, and we'll see how much you still want her when I get through with her! I can track her down. I have ways! Didn't I find Horace's bitch? Got her name, address AND social security number. I Found out when she was born and when she expected to die. I have ways. All I have to do is smile at a certain guy I know and make him think he's got a chance with me. That's all it takes and he'll get any information I want!"

"This is 1963, the double standard is dead! You men can't continue to have your cake and eat it, too! Like the song says, "Who's making love to your old lady while you are out making love?" That's why I'm gonna get me a sugar daddy. Two can play that game! A good-looking woman can always attract enough men to satisfy whatever needs she has! How do you think I survived between my marriages, those years when I was single?

So, don't play me for a fool. If you think you can still keep on seeing your WHITE BITCH and hold on to me, you've got another think coming! And the way I know she's white? Because she's got a white-sounding name! No BLACK woman would ever be named, MERRILL LYNCH!"

The story has been fictionalized for dramatic impact but the basic fact remains; Alma really did think her husband was giving money to a woman whose first name was Merrill and whose last name was Lynch.

WHO WERE THOSE WOMEN AT OUR TABLE?

Our guys were no saints, but women did chase after them in a frenzy. They were all nice-looking, college educated, and good wage-earners. A few of their wives didn't work. My husband reminded me quite often that I didn't have to work. Every time I brought up the subject of how he should help out around the house, he would invite me to stay home and be a housewife. I had worked hard to become a teacher. I didn't want to give up the prestige of being somebody to just focus on the needs of our family. I was beginning to find teaching interesting, even though it had not been my first career choice. I was, also, getting pretty good at it.

I considered myself only a social drinker. On weekends, it was scotch and soda at the various club affairs we attended. My husband and I were usually the last to arrive at our table because I had used up the time perfecting my one-of-a-kind outfit. When we got there, we felt pressured to drink two or three stiff drinks in order to catch up with our friends at the table; otherwise, we couldn't stand them. We would drink so much on weekends that I wouldn't get completely sober until about Thursday.

At one of the dances, at the Parkway Ballroom (where most of the club events were held) two women showed up and sat down at our table. The husbands seemed to know one of them. They all spoke to the women but no one introduced them to the wives! They didn't dare! We wives did a lot of speculating as to whose girlfriend the familiar one was, but we had no clue and the men did not help out in the least. We silently dared anyone to dance with them, and the men did a good job of ignoring them. The only thing my husband said, afterward, was that he thought one of the women worked in their office.

I went to work every day, taught my class, picked up my son, drove around and did the errands that were required to keep us going. I always cooked a full dinner, marked several sets of classroom assignments, and attended to the needs of my son, all in a kind of alcoholic stupor for much of the week. I recall Thursday as being the best day of any week. By then, I was usually alcohol free. With the new routine of sorrow-drowning drinking, Thursdays were no longer guaranteed good days. Even Thursdays became hangover days on occasion. And no one experienced worse hangovers than the ones I suffered through.

DRINKING BUDDY: JACKIE

Eventually, I narrowed my weekday consumption down to drinking with one friend. Jackie was not one of the IRS wives, but she socialized with that group, she was my number one buddy, another one of my best friends! She had two sons near Jeff's age, and our boys played very well together. Jackie and her husband were both educators. He was head teacher at his school, took courses in administration, and eventually became a principal. His ambitions allowed Jackie to have as much un-husbanded time as my stay-out-after-work husband. This was during the period when Manuel never made it home from his nine-to-five job until well after nine at night.

Jackie was a champion drinker. She could down five or six drinks to my two or three. We both smoked the same brand of cigarettes; Newport. We sometimes smoked nearly a pack of cigarettes while drinking gimlets. It was, tragically, a trip to the store to buy cigarettes when Jackie had a minor accident and hit her head. A huge bump rose on her forehead, and stayed there for months. Jackie started acting strange then became psychotic to the extent that she had to be institutionalized. She got worse, and slipped into a coma. She remained in that vegetative state for many months. When she briefly awoke from the coma, she was completely incoherent. After only a few hours of being awake, she slipped back into the coma, remained for a few more months, and at age fifty-one, she passed away.

A NEW COCKTAIL TABLE

Before we moved into our house, Manuel had a unique idea for a cocktail table. He would glue several small pieces of wood together for a platform, and then have glass cut to cover the creation and complete the much-needed cocktail table. The sample pieces that he had worked on looked very promising, so I encouraged him to go to our local community center to take a woodworking class. This was before he developed the pattern of not making it home before nine o-clock at night. He went to the center one evening, but never made it to the class. When he saw the sexy-looking older woman shaking her hips while teaching her dance class, he joined the dance class. It wasn't long before the dance teacher was calling my house and he was speaking to her in hushed tones, because, ". . . she had problems with her taxes and asked me to help her out!"

That teacher must have had a very complicated tax problem because my husband spent many an evening ". . . helping her out!" He also wore out our rug practicing his dance steps

It wasn't until my dear mother-in-law urged me to join the dance class, too—coming to my rescue, by babysitting with Jeffrey—that I was able to put into practice that age-old notion of befriending the woman who was threatening my marriage. I also learned several fancy ballroom steps and danced with my husband in the spring showcase performance. I wish we had won a trophy. We could have displayed it on the beautiful new cocktail table I bought that summer from Marshall Field's Department Store.

WE COULD CATALOG OUR ARGUMENTS

My husband's habit of staying out after work was taking a terrible toll on our marriage. We constantly fussed and argued, to the point where I would actually turn off my brain and, by rote, recite my points of contention. During one light moment, when we discussed our arguments, I suggested that we label them: Argument 1.) "You Don't Come Home After Work." 2.) "You Don't Help Out Around The House." 3.) "You Treat Me Like A Second Class Citizen" 4.) "You Practice a Double Standard", etc. Then we could just mention the number of the argument, and that would save us time and energy.

Jeffrey was weaned on his parents' arguments. Parental discord was so much a part of his life that he seemed to accept it as normal. He would show emotion and fear during the rare times when Manuel and I were loving and tender toward each other. If we kissed, danced, or embraced, Jeff would try to separate us, and sometimes he would actually cry.

WHAT'S BURNING ON THE LAWN?

Union Pier, Michigan, is a quiet little resort village about two-and-a-half hours' drive from Chicago. Its main attraction is its wonderful beach on the shore of Lake Michigan.

During the early sixties, there was an increase in the number of black people visiting the area. It became the 'in' place to vacation. Union Pier had always been integrated, with a small number of Blacks owning homes there. It was also known to be Klu Klux Klan territory.

My very pushy friend, Jeannie, organized a group of five couples to spend a whole week, without our kids, in a house she rented in Union Pier. Manuel and I were excited to go, since we hadn't been on a trip since our visit to Detroit when Jeffrey was still taking milk from a bottle, and that trip included Jeff.

I remember the Detroit trip so well because we stayed with a cousin of Manuel's who seemed to be a very popular guy, judging by the number of people who kept dropping by his house. Cousin would introduce the guest to us and then Cuz' and guest would close the kitchen door behind them as they 'visited' for a short while. This pattern repeated itself with each guest but we didn't think much about it.

It was when I went into the kitchen on my own to rinse out Jeff's bottle, that I became aware of the three faucets at the sink. I reached for the middle one—thinking it must be warm water (since the other two had the standard 'C' and 'H labels')—when Cuz' shouted, "Don't touch that faucet!" That's how we found out Cuz' was a bootlegger. He made and sold 'white light'nin', (homemade corn liquor) and did such a brisk business that he had a special faucet to dispense it.

Anxious to go on the trip to Union Pier, we packed everything we would need, including half-gallon bottles of booze. The very first night we were there, we were playing loud music, drinking, laughing, dancing and having a wonderful time when someone looked out the window and shouted, "What's that burning on the lawn?!"

The thing that was burning on the lawn was a cross, standing about eight feet high!

Air had been let out of all five of our cars' tires; they were all completely flat! We never found out who had done it but it didn't make us leave. We completed our week's vacation in Union Pier, Michigan. After all, how rare were the times when we, as parents, were able to get away from our kids for a whole week! We'd take cross-burning over child-rearing anytime!

JEFFREY'S SCHOOL YEARS

During Jeffrey's young years, he was probed, diagnosed and evaluated very often because his development didn't allow him an easy fit into any of the known categories, such as: retarded or psychotic. He seemed very self-sufficient, had unusually advanced hand-to-eye coordination, could work almost any puzzle given to him, made a lot of sense when answering questions and eschewed overly demonstrative shows of affection. Yet he made little progress in academics. One of the questions he was asked was, "If a superball was dropped from an airplane, would it be able to bounce all the way back up to the plane?" The superball was a ball that its makers claimed, could bounce back to the height from which it was dropped. Jeffrey didn't have to think hard and long on that question, he answered; "No, the airplane would have moved on away, so the superball couldn't reach it." Jeff's response showed his ability to think. His diagnosis at Dr. Bettelheim's Behavioral Analysis Clinic at the University of Chicago, was inconclusive. Dr. Bettelheim was the world's leading child psychologist at that time.

Schooling for Jeff was difficult. Our neighborhood school expelled him in the middle of the day. It was political. The teacher's enrollment was over the legal class load, she complained, and Jeff was the victim. I had to scurry around and find a sitter for him for the afternoon, so that I could return to my job at a neighboring school.

When I protested that such an abrupt expulsion was unfair, I was told that the school had accepted Jeff only as a professional courtesy to me because he was not yet eight-years-old (the mandatory age for enrollment); yet, none of this was mentioned at the time I registered him.

Jeff had been a misfit in the expensive pre-school he attended. The psychologist diagnosed him as being 'emotionally retarded' and urged Manuel and me to seek counselling for our 'troubled relationship'. I thought this was hogwash! In fact, most of the professionals who evaluated my son put the onus on us. At that time, it seemed to be the style, and, oh boy, did it give me massive guilt! Yet, on Jeff's birth record, there was the answer, ". . . forceps!" It wasn't until Jeff became a teenager that we realized how damaging forceps had been. The strange marks on both sides of his head had never been the focus of any of the evaluations done on him before then. He had languished in classes for the mentally retarded, acted-out in regular graded classes, and solidified a general resistance to, and hatred for, academics, from my prodding and attempts to tutor him.

Until age ten, when he started attending the outrageously expensive, private Blueberry School in Brooklyn, Jeffrey hated school. He spent seven years at Blueberry, and for what it cost, we could have sent him to Harvard for a PhD! Although Blueberry didn't make a scholar out of Jeff, it provided him with experiences that helped him develop life skills and self-confidence.

MEANWHILE; IN THE
HENNINGS HOUSEHOLD

Mom and Dad found a house in the preferred community of Chatham that they could afford, and they were buying it on contract. The house had been vandalized because it had sat empty for years. The radiators had been removed in almost every room so my parents were out shopping for radiators during the heating season. The three, still-at-home children, Arnold, Kenneth and Sandra, were very much against the idea of getting a house with no radiators but Ted and Bess knew what they could afford.

The other objection the kids had to buying the house was that there were pipes running from the house to a cement platform in the back yard. The platform had once had some kind of metal apparatus attached to it which was no longer there.

The basement had been cemented over so that the original floor was covered up, and the height reduced to where, if you were over five and-a-half feet tall, you had to stoop to walk around down there, otherwise your head would bump the wooden beams. The space under the front steps (where most houses of this type had open latticework) had been very sloppily cemented to obscure something!

My brothers imagined that bodies were buried in the basement and under the front stoop, which accounted for the cement overlays. The truth was that the house had been one of a network of houses used during prohibition by Al Capone and his organization as a still and as a distribution station for bootleg liquor. The cement work had been done to cover over what remained of the still.

When Sandra sold the house in in 2002, and the new owner had all of the cement dug up, there were no remains of body parts found anywhere on the property. Shortly after they bought the house in 1958, my family had gotten rid of the pipes and the platform in the yard. The house had been in the family for forty-four years before it was sold to the present owner who did extensive re-modeling, and transformed it into a showplace!

TESTING THE WATERS

Since Manuel's response to my pleadings for him to do more around the house was always the same, "If you can't stand the heat, get out of the kitchen!" By that, he meant, "Quit your job! I can afford to take care of you!" This had become his mantra. He was doing very well on the job, and had positioned himself to be promoted. This would probably mean that we would have to re-locate. I had mixed feelings about moving away from Chicago. Things hadn't gotten better between us so I viewed moving as an opportunity to make a new start. I thought I'd test the waters by taking the first step. After teaching just five and a half years, I quit my job!

Within a few weeks, I was miserable! My self-esteem had no place to land! I was no longer an insider, nor did I want to hear the stories and gossip told by my former co-worker buddies. The worst part was that I was drinking far more than usual and arguments had just about replaced any love life the two of us had left.

One miserable evening, after a particularly ugly knock-out, drag-down argument, I left the house in a fury and went to a bar all by myself. I stayed only a little while, just long enough to have a couple of drinks. I went home and tried to arouse my husband so that we could continue the argument. He had retired for the night but he wasn't asleep.

I was suffering from PMS and my nerves were totally on edge. I was feeling so desperate that I started ranting that I just might commit suicide!

I was in our master bathroom trying to drink water from a glass. The glass slipped out of my hand and broke on the tile floor. I continued ranting and crying. Manuel (later on, claiming that I attempted to cut my wrist, which was not true, I had not broken the glass on purpose) dashed into the bathroom (to save me from killing myself, I guess), stepped on a piece of glass and cut his foot! Then, in his fury, he followed me—bleeding foot and all—out of the master bedroom suite into the dining room. Upon noticing that my husband was responding to me, I became even louder. After all, this is what I wanted, some kind of attention from him. He ordered me to shut up but I continued to sob, shout, and threaten. Then he tackled me like a defensive end which dislocated my left shoulder. All of this took place in just a few seconds.

WHY DID YOU ATTEMPT SUICIDE?

I was in the hospital for about a week answering psychiatrists' questions about why I wanted to kill myself. There were a couple of members from the Chicago Bears' Football Team in the same hospital—also with dislocated shoulders—they and some visiting team members, (six in all) came to my hospital room to meet me and sign my twenty-two pound cast. Those six huge white men stayed only a few minutes but their presence lingered and felt like trees in a forest, as they teased me by asking what team I played on because, they said, my injury was one that only football players got.

The injury was in the fall of sixty-three and the Civil Rights Movement was on all the news reports. I had been the babysitter for the people in my family who attended the March on Washington. I had participated whenever I could, but my son's needs did not allow me to attend many marches and demonstrations. Malcolm X was a haunted man and Cassius Clay had recently changed his name to Mohammad Ali.

The group called The Nation of Islam had been written and talked about in the media and a rumor became a roar, that these Islamic people were contracting to buy the block-long property (a Catholic girls' high school and convent) across the street from our house.

Fear turned into resentment and resentment turned into resistance at the thought of these robe-wearing, head-wrapped, chanting people, roaming our streets with their strange religious practices and their ex-con members.

Their leader, Elijah Mohammad, was cousin to my Aunt Anna's husband, Joe, and Joe was no one to be proud of. He drank heavily, never seemed to work, was cruel to his wife (my mother's sister) and children (sixteen in all). If these Islamic people were like Joe, I wanted nothing to do with them. In our ignorance, we neighbors met, traded stories and made plans, but nothing happened. The Nation bought another property a few miles away and we missed the chance to revise our closed-minded views about them. We missed the chance to learn, close up, about their healthy lifestyle, or their dedication and discipline. It took the media quite a few years to portray the Nation of Islam from a perspective that was balanced enough to be considered outside the realm of propaganda.

WE MOVE TO BOSTON

Manuel's big promotion came in spring of sixty-four and we moved to Boston. Mohammad Ali was training for a fight in Boston and Malcolm X was often in town. This gave me a new fear: my husband, although better looking, resembled Malcolm X. What if killers mistook Manuel for Malcolm? I lost a few hours of sleep worrying about this.

The apartment building we moved into in the Brighton section was new and luxurious although the neighborhood was quite old. There were several vacant lots that became small lakes when it rained. Most of the people were first or second generation Italians. Ours was the only Negro Family in the entire neighborhood, but there was a single Negro man who lived in our building. He was a ballplayer with the Boston Red Sox—a pitcher, who had pitched a no-hitter—his name was Earl Wilson, and the kids in the neighborhood would swarm around him in a frenzy, begging for his autographs any time he came in or went out.

We didn't get to know him well, just well enough for him to borrow our vacuum cleaner a few times. He, of course, being a professional ballplayer, traveled a lot.

One day, my family (the three of us) were trying to get past the crowd outside our apartment when one of the kids asked

Manuel if he played ball, too. I jokingly told him, "Yes, he's Willy Mays." The crowd of kids turned on Manuel, demanded his autograph, and Manuel stood there signing Willy Mays' name for about half an hour.

There were loads of kids for Jeff to play with, and his social skills took an enormous leap forward as he did more than just the parallel play which he was accustomed to doing. The negative side was that his toys went missing almost every time he took them outside. We lived there only eleven months but Jeff had two bicycles stolen from him during that time.

One day, Jeff came home crying and soaking wet. When I questioned him, he was reluctant to say what had happened. My list of multiple choices got a nod to; 'some boys pushed you down in the vacant lot that became a lake?' I became furious! I wanted to know more because I was sure it must be racism since Jeff was the only brown boy for blocks around. I was ready to do battle in the name of the Civil Rights Struggle!

As I coddled my eight-year-old, fed him hot chocolate and fumed about racially motivated attacks, his dad quietly took him aside, closed his bedroom door—shutting me out—and I could hear the two of them talking. Pretty soon, they were laughing hysterically.

What had actually happened, Jeff had found an old door in the flooded lot. He had also found a long stick. He was using the stick to move the 'door-raft' as he gave a ride to two girls. The door hit a rock, turned over and they had all fallen into the water.

After the shoulder dislocation, I had weighed my options before making my decision to stay married to Manuel. I weighed them again when I made the choice to move to Boston. My overwhelming motivation for hanging-in there was that I fervently rejected the status of single-parenthood for myself. There was no way that I was going to raise a child all by myself! I was raised in a two-parent home and that's the way it would be for Jeff! With Jeffrey having learning disabilities and needing to have special placement in school, I knew that I needed support on a continual basis.

Boston proved to be somewhat good for our marriage and interesting for my career. Manuel and I had to cling to each other since neither of us had anyone else to drink with, so things got a little better. Manuel had only two buddies in Boston, one that he mentored, Tim, and new buddy, Lem. Tim was newly married, and Lem was married with seven children. Neither was the kind of man who'd go out drinking after work. For months, my husband and Tim's wife, right in front of my face, carried on a merciless flirtation. This behavior challenged my marriage, but, oddly enough, she and I became friends. Perhaps it was because there were few other women to relate to, and because I quickly sensed the enormous mound of insecurity behind which she functioned.

I signed up to do some substitute teaching and Boston Public Schools proved to be unbelievably backward. The same DICK AND JANE readers, copyrighted the year I was born, were still being used as basal readers. The principal at the school, a block from my house, refused to let me teach in her school because I was black. Later, I learned that she had made a public declaration to that, effect before I was sent there by the school board. She kept me sitting in the office, doing paperwork all day. Eventually, I was assigned to a first-grade class in South Boston, where parents had defied the bussing plan with such vehemence that rioting had occurred, and it was reported on national media.

Sometimes parents stood outside my classroom door and peeked in. On one occasion, I deliberately went over to the door, swiftly opened it and offered my hand to the mother standing there. "I'm Mrs. Jackson, You are ___'s mother?" I asked. The poor woman became so flustered, she said, "I'm glad to meet ME".

I was barely able to finish the semester before we had to relocate to New York because the Internal Revenue Service had merged the Boston Office with the one in New York. I had done a great job with my class that semester and had gained the confidence of the parents to the place where no one stood outside my classroom door any longer. Before I left, I received a lovely gift from each one of my students, with cards thanking me for excellent teaching.

WE BECOME NEW YORKERS

The best thing about moving to New York was THE NEW YORK WORLD'S FAIR. Our Flushing, Queens, New York apartment was about twenty minutes away from the fair grounds. The only people we knew in New York were the two IRS men and their families who moved with us from Boston, a few friends of friends and my dear friend, Jackie's sister, Dotti. As a result, we spent a great deal of our time at the fair. Jeffrey was thrilled that I took him there every chance I could. We had moved in late May, the school suggested I keep Jeff out until the fall session. I don't think they wanted to deal with a student whose records indicated that he was a special needs student. I was delighted to have something so appealing to Jeff, that I enjoyed, too. Later, when we told Jeff the fair was closing, he cried.

There were several boys in our neighborhood close in age to Jeffrey so he gained many friends right away. He became the envy of the kids on the block, where he was known as, ". . . the new kid who doesn't have to go to school and his mother takes him to the World's Fair almost every day!"

There was a wooded area in back of our second floor apartment where we took our dog, Shep, off her leash and allowed her to walk herself. The kids in the area had built a tree house in the woods. Jeff loved it, and spent many happy hours up in the tree house.

It was also in this same wooded area—about a block away—where the bodies of the two Crimmins Children were found. The mother of the children (a boy and a girl) in a sensational case (which for months, was all over the media) was later convicted of killing them. The neighborhood was so rural that from the yard of the house across the street, roosters awakened us each morning. Our landlord and his wife lived on the first floor, and it wasn't long before they brought her sick mother to live with them.

With a nine-year-old boy, a dog, two healthy adults, lots of juvenile company; up and down the un-carpeted stairs, we were soon asked, for the sake of the sick mother, to find another place to live.

BROOKLYN

Brooklyn was a wonderful Borough of New York City to live in during the late sixties. Protests against the Viet Nam War were held on a daily basis right across the courtyard from our fifteenth-floor apartment, as we overlooked Pratt Institute from our terrace. Something was always fermenting: whether it was a flag-burning, a flag flown upside-down, a musical group singing protest songs or direct action to protest the long-lasting teacher strike by cutting locks to open up school buildings. I was in the thick of it all! My activist muscles got exercised almost every day!

I was on my second teaching assignment in Brooklyn, and the school, P.S. 20, was just a couple of blocks from our apartment. Students from our building attended the same school, and a girl in my fifth grade class lived two floors down. The great jazz saxophonist, Sonny Rollins, lived two floors above us.

One of the drawbacks about that kind of closeness was that I had no privacy. Kids from my class were in the grocery store, on the elevator, at the Laundromat. One day, my husband roused me from my sick bed to a living-room full of my students who'd come to check on me. I had been out sick with the flu for most of the week.

I had tried my hand at teaching CRMD (children with retarded mental development) on my first teaching assignment when we still lived in Flushing. The school, P.S. 306, was in a much quieter section of Brooklyn, but I had not liked it. Dealing with my son's learning problems at home was enough! I had requested a transfer when we moved, and gotten appointed to an inner-city school where the principal claimed that her school was so well-functioning and high-achieving that she had "reverse integration".

REVERSE INTEGRATION

What the principal called reverse integration, was white parents clamoring to get their kids enrolled in her school, where the school population was predominately black. And that was true, there was a waiting list and the kids on the list were white. This was a complete departure from what was happening in other schools where black parents were seeking to enroll their kids in white schools, as intense disputes over integration and bussing were raging in many parts of the country.

Upon closer look at the situation, I found that the reason white parents wanted their kids transferred into our school was that it would almost guarantee placement in an IGC (intellectually gifted children) class. In their own neighborhood schools, these students could achieve placement only in a regular-grade class. In their own neighborhoods, they didn't qualify for IGC. The only white kids who were not in IGC classes at P.S. 20, were a few low-achieving kids from our apartment buildings. This building complex provided the only racially integrated housing in the entire Fort Green/Clinton Hill section of Brooklyn that I knew of, and most of the white kids populating the IGC classes were bussed in.

The principal wanted the white kids on her enrollment list so that she could claim her school was racially integrated. In truth, the school was run like a plantation. The IGC classes had all of the privileges available in the school and the rest of the students got what was left. When monitors were needed, kids from IGC were selected; they were usually white. When an IGC class had to be broken up, instead of students being distributed among other classes on the same grade level, they were sent to other IGC classes of various grades. The IGC classes had their own separate lunch schedule and when guest speakers arrived for an assembly, the IGC classes were the greeters and were given first preference on seating. New text books went first to the IGC classes, then to others. IGC classes also got to go on more and better field trips than children in the other classes. But the greatest transgression was that the IGC classes received intensive test-tutoring with the actual standardized tests that would provide students' official standardized test scores, such as the Iowa or the California achievement tests. Scores from these tests were recorded on pupils' cumulative records, which were maintained throughout high school. These records had the power to direct the arc of a student's life.

I couldn't help thinking how I would feel if I were a child in that school, in a regular class and was constantly exposed to what amounted to white privilege being continually flaunted in my face. I believe the principal did more harm than good with her reverse integration policy.

The reason I know so much about what went on in IGC is that when I was newly assigned to P.S. 20, I taught fifth-grade IGC. The experience was so against my egalitarian ideals that, for the next term, I requested assignment to a class of under-achievers. Many teachers considered IGC a preferred assignment, and requested it, but I did not like how the concept of challenging gifted children (which was why IGC was formed) was being mishandled to produce whiny, over-privileged, obnoxious know-it-alls and to re-enforce racial stereotypes.

The day after Dr. Martin Luther King was assassinated, an early dismissal was ordered because gangs were roaming streets in Brooklyn, looking for anybody who was white to beat up. I got my students on the bus just in time! As the bus drove away from the curb, the mob of angry, young black men and boys came around the corner.

WAYNE'S WAY vs. MY WAY!

There were some tough, streetwise, hoodlum-type students in the sixth-grade class I taught after my IGC experience, but no student was tougher than Wayne Bryant. Rules meant nothing to Wayne, and to him, class assignments were a joke. He was accustomed to doing what he wanted, when he wanted, and that did not include class work, or homework. Wayne left his seat, roamed around the classroom disturbing other children at will. His records showed he had acted-out since kindergarten. I pulled out every trick in my bag, but nothing seemed to work with Wayne.

I always allowed my sixth-graders to get up and go to the bathroom whenever they had the need. I felt that by the time you are old enough to be in sixth grade (and some of my children were thirteen-years-old) you needn't have to raise your hand and ask permission like a first-grader. We had established rules for bathroom usage. You had to sign the bathroom book (a bound composition book) with your name, date, and the time you leave. You had to take a bathroom pass (this prevented more than two students out at the same time). You had to record the time you returned.

I regularly monitored the bathroom book and the system worked fairly well. Most children went and came back within a reasonable time. I noticed that Wayne's name was all over the bathroom book. He didn't stay an inordinate length of time and he knew that I'd come and pull him out if he had, but he had gone frequently.

I sent a note to Wayne's mother asking if Wayne had a problem. She returned a note to me, very promptly, stating that, ". . . he do have a problem, if fact he still wet the bed . . ." This was all the ammunition I needed. That note provided me with a way I could communicate with the number one-bully in the class; the kid who made me feel like I was teaching in a prep school for Attica.

The next time Wayne did something outrageous, I called him up to my desk and quietly told him, "If you don't sit down and do your work, I'm going to tell everybody in this class that you still wet the bed". When I showed him the note, he became furious and called his mother all kinds of profane names. That explosion revealed he not only had no respect for school authorities, but no respect for his own mother.

When he calmed down a bit, he did go back to his seat and he didn't even stop to menace the cute little Puerto Rican girl he was so crazy about. Wayne's behavior was subdued for most of the day but towards the end of the afternoon, he was up out of his seat hovering over a boy and making threatening gestures. I called out to him, "Hey B.W., sit down and finish your work!" In a belligerent tone, he answered me back, "My initials are W.B. Not B.__". His voice abruptly stopped as he realized what the reversal of his initials indicated, and, as if he were a marionette whose strings had been cut, he twisted himself back into his assigned seat and lowered his head into his social studies textbook.

Wayne didn't become an A student, but he did make some progress, especially in math, a subject in which he had been very deficient.

During my years of classroom teaching (the world's hardest job), I developed many strategies to deal with children who displayed pathological behaviors. None of the strategies I found successful were in the college textbooks which are supposed to teach you how to teach. On many occasions I employed modified techniques of meditation (which I learned in Yoga) with my students, and these techniques proved to be effective.

I tried to always employ the positive approach to discipline. For instance; most teachers, or their monitors, listed the names of acting-out kids for punishment, I listed the names of the most well-behaved students for a reward rather than a punishment. By emphasizing the positive and teaching students to control their anger and be responsible for their own actions, children made improvements that were intrinsic. This approach allowed children to be free of 'authority bullying' (the implied threat of punishment for rule-infraction) without having to have discipline and control super-imposed on them. Of course, the 'Waynes of the world' required heavy applications of skullduggery, street smarts and 'whatever works'! Many were beyond being reached by the positive approach.

Before the term ended, Wayne and I became friends. He was the leader of the group of students from my class, whom our doorman allowed to come up to my apartment and check on my health. And it was Wayne who asked, "Hey Miz Jackson, where was you at. You been sick?"

By the time I left that school for P.S. 99 in the Bronx, I had increased my arsenal of psychological weaponry, tenfold. Every day had been a challenge, and I had gained a reputation as being a tough but fair teacher who got students to learn, no matter what were their problems. And one of the proudest moments of my life was when parents chipped in and surprised me with a pair of gold and jade earrings. The card read, simply: "Thank you Mrs. Jackson, for all you do for our children." That was well over forty years ago, but I still wear those earrings, and always with a smile in my heart.

I.R.S. TRAINING SESSIONS

The Civil Rights Movement was in full force, the three Mississippi workers, Chaney, Schwerner and Goodman were missing and presumed murdered. Their bodies had yet to be found. The Internal Revenue Service, anxious to take advantage of the newly integrated conference centers and hotels, conducted 'business as usual' in their staff training programs. They utilized these venues with no regard for the racial make-up of their employees. My husband was sent to one of the training sessions in Texas for two weeks. He was the only black person in his class at the recently integrated conference center.

One day, as the class re-convened after lunch, one guy asked, "Hey Manny, did you hear about the black guy they fished out of the river in Mississippi? He had ten bullet holes in his body, a noose around his neck, chains around his hands and weights on his feet?" Manuel froze. He told me that he had no idea how to answer, but he didn't have to, the guy went on . . ." They asked the sheriff about it and he said, "It was the worst case of suicide I ever did see!" Everybody in the class broke out in tension-relieving laughter, including my husband. He was greatly relieved to know it was a joke, even though it was in the worst possible taste, considering the circumstances.

When Manuel was sent to Baltimore for a training session, Jeff and I went with him. We spent a few days together and Jeff and I flew home without Manuel. It was Jeff's first airplane ride.

Ours was the first black family (we were later told) to stay as guests in the hotel since its integration a few months before. We found out, after our stay; that the black people of Baltimore had sat-in, marched, picketed and negotiated long and hard to bring about the integration we were enjoying and taking for granted. The only clue we had of their struggle was the overwhelmingly superior service we received every time we ate in the dining room. Two or three waiters would rush to serve us. They would wave to us, smile at us and bring extra everything to our table. As we left, they stood in groups staring, smiling, and waving. The entire dining room staff was black.

It became increasingly difficult to endure the long separations required by the employee training sessions for the Internal Revenue Service. Very often I felt like a single parent because I was forced into being one by my husband's absences. After training was over and Manuel was promoted again, he was sent to the regional office. He was with the new data processing division in Hartford, Connecticut where he was able to come home on week-ends. But two days home, verses five days away did little to alleviate my angst, and we often spent much of our together-time bickering.

WE BUY THE HOUSE IN NEW ROCHELLE

Buying the house gave us a temporary boost in our marriage in that we had a mutual project on which to work. The previous owner was obviously not content with the contract because she took many of the things which she was supposed to leave when she moved out. She took almost all of the custom made radiator covers, all of the fireplace utensils and the grate. She dumped a whole package of hairpins down the drain in the master bathroom. I think she was unhappy about the price. She had obviously bought the house on speculation because she sold it right away. She had asked to re-negotiate the contract but I wouldn't hear of it and let her know it in very unfriendly tones.

On the first Saturday after we moved in, Manuel worked on the plumbing problem all day. He tried everything he knew; and, having done so much plumbing when he operated the apartment building in Chicago, he knew a lot. He was about to give up when he said to me, "Betty Anne, go get that 'Jinx Removing spray' my mother gave us about ten years ago. Nothing else has worked, maybe that'll unplug whatever is stopped up in this damn drain!"

Dotti and Charlie (our favorite couple) had come by to see our new house, so I went upstairs to get the spray, just to show off for our visitors and go along with the gag. We all laughed as Manuel profusely sprayed the pipes in the basement with the mist from the can marked, 'Jinx Removing Spray' which my mother-in-law had bought from one of those stores that sells powders, candles, spirit-blessed waters and scents as potions for good luck and to remove bad spirits.

When our laughter died down we could hear a gurgling, rumbling sound coming from the pipes, I turned on the water and the drain was open! A few minutes later, Manuel fished out the huge wad of hairpins all matted and rusty.

TEACHING IN SOUTH BRONX

Shortly after moving to New Rochelle, I transferred to a school in the South Bronx which had as its community, a population of very poor black and Latino people. The school was old and dilapidated; the principal was a narrow-minded bureaucrat who was a stickler for record-keeping and getting reports in on time, but offered no leadership, guidance or supervision to the staff. He sat in his office all day, and treated me with impatience and dis-interest. When I had questions that pertained to the job, he would always refer me to the assistant principal.

When I refused to fill out a questioneer that asked for all kinds of personal information; having nothing to do with the job, that little man became livid and threatened me. I didn't budge from my position, I refused to divulge personal information because I was sure the information was being used for commercial purposes, and I suspected other teachers felt the same. It also robbed children of a half day of class because they were dismissed for the afternoon to give staff the opportunity to complete the form. I felt that was immoral. I worked in my classroom during the free afternoon.

This period, during the Viet Nam War, was a time of enlightenment. Extreme polarization of citizens (those who favored the war, vs. those against it) became a catalyst to examine many decisions of people in authority. I was flexing my newly-strengthened awareness when I refused to submit the form. Mr.Pompell, the principal, became furious and made threats that were never carried out. For years, I continued to not submit the form. As I talked about it with my colleagues I discovered that I was not the only one who refused. Eventually, the requirement to fill out the form was dropped for all teachers.

Working in the Bronx, which is the only part of New York City located on the mainland, (the other four boroughs are on islands) was a real challenge. Our house is also on the mainland, thirteen miles north of the Bronx. I didn't have to cross any bridges or tunnels to get to work. At the time, that part of the Bronx (South Bronx) was a blighted area with many burned-out buildings. Today, it has gentrified into some rather choice neighborhoods, but then, most of our children were so poor that for many, school was the brightest spot in their lives.

My class of fifth-grade under-achievers read on first to third grade levels. I started an incentive program of taking four of my students home each week-end as a reward for making the most progress for the week. My house had two guest rooms with two twin beds each. I would take all boys one week, all girls the next. I had full approval of their parents (in most cases only a mother), and they would return with me on Mondays.

For the most part, these under-privileged pre-teens had never been in a private home. They were impressed with the large yard, the dog house and the apple trees on our property. During art period they all drew my house, the big yard, the apple trees and the dog house (and, of course, they all labeled the dog house). After seeing so many almost identical pictures, I made the off-hand comment, "Why do you all draw the same thing, can't someone draw something a little different?"

One girl took me up on my request, and proudly displayed her picture. In it sat my house, the big yard, the apple trees and the little house clearly labelled, "Cat House".

Many of our children came to school hungry, this was before the government provided breakfast programs, I conducted my own breakfast program in my classroom. The daily school milk was picked up early and some of it was mixed with cocoa in my crock pot to make hot chocolate. Oatmeal cookies, that I supplied, were served with it. Later, dry cereal was supplied in abundance by General Mills, from only one appeal letter which I wrote.

My in-class breakfast program had one flaw; almost every day, one or two students would throw up after eating. I carefully checked the ingredients for freshness. I had students change their cereal choices. I double-checked the milk each day. I didn't figure out the reason they were throwing up until years later. After the government breakfast program was operating, children didn't have to eat in close quarters (like a section of a classroom) as mine had.

In those days, my favorite scent was Norell by Revlon (a very strong perfume). I don't consider myself fully dressed until I spritz on a bit of perfume. I sprayed it on so heavily in those days, that when I entered the office to punch in each morning, the clerk would say, "Good morning, Mrs. Jackson" without lifting her head from the work at her desk. In retrospect; I figured out, it had to be my perfume making my children throw up.

JEFFREY AND THE 'SLOW SQUIRREL'

Jeffrey blossomed as never before. He was able to freely travel on his bike, all over town. His excellent sense of direction was put to good use. He enjoyed the house and the yard, and one of his favorite activities was chasing the squirrels in our yard . . . until, one day, he caught one . . . and it bit him!

When we got to the emergency room, the staff was amazed! "How do you catch a squirrel?" asked the doctor who checked on the tiny wound, cleaned it agan and advised us not to force Jeff to take the rabies shots. Jeff's answer was, "The squirrel was going slow."

As parents, the decision to not subject our precious young teenager to the series of painful, sickening rabies shots which would assure that he wouldn't come down with rabies, (if the squirrel had been infected) was the most agonizing decision we ever had to make. We frantically researched the incidences of known rabies cases in our area, and consulted with medical authorities before deciding he would not have the shots. The three days after the squirrel bite, checking Jeff for symptoms, were pure agony. I never prayed more in my life! Of course, he was fine!

I ADVANCE ON MY JOB

The school district where I worked was in the throes of decentralization and fighting for community control. This opened up opportunities for me to advance in ways I had never dreamed of. My dear friend, Nola, worked in district office on the superintendent's staff. She recommended that I be brought on staff after I distinguished myself in the growing field of Black Studies. Students from colleges and universities all over the country were demanding that Black Studies be made part of their school's curriculum. They were holding sit-ins and taking offices hostage to strengthen their demands.

Being brought up in Chicago meant that learning the history of our people was infused into our everyday experiences. There was a lot of living history all around us as well. Ida B. Wells' grandchildren, The Dusters, were some of my best friends in high school. I took advantage of the increased availability of printed materials (book jackets, calendars, workbooks, charts and even comic books) to formulate an ethnic studies' program. It greatly expanded learning in my classroom when students could read about role-models with whom they could relate.

It wasn't long before I was asked to present my program to the entire school, then to the district. Our students were very anxious to learn about people who looked like themselves, and that is what my ethnic studies program presented; people of color, for children of color.

Programs similar to mine were being established throughout the entire city. Coordinator of ethnic studies positions opened up in practically every one of the newly de-centralized thirty-two school districts in New York City. When all of the Bronx coordinators and their staffs met, there was hardly standing room in the large library of the school where the meetings were held. Less than eight years later, we were so few; we could meet in a mid-sized office.

Enthusiasm ran high at that time. There were training sessions, curriculum development committees, conferences (with paid expenses for travel) lots of grant monies for proposals and many special events.

One of the most important special events that I handled was The Martin Luther King Jr. Program sponsored by our district. During my career, I had produced many assembly programs but none on the scale of the district-wide productions we gave in the late seventies and early eighties. This was even before Dr. King's birthday became a national holiday. District sponsored events, which were always popular and well-attended by people in our community, began to attract city-wide attention, and even celebrities. Jimmy Breslin, the well-known newspaper columnist, actually attended and wrote a review of 'Charlotte Street', (one of the productions I coordinated) which appeared in a major New York daily.

The Dr. King productions gathered many factions in the community together which had the effect of unifying them so that they could work together.

One of the psychologists, who worked with the children in our district, was a life-long friend of Coretta Scott King, wife of Dr. King. Her name was Fran Lucas. She brought Dr. King's daughter, Yolanda, to speak at more than one of our productions. She also gave me pictures of the Kings and some early pictures of Coretta. Many of the pictures—there were about twenty of them—were autographed.

Using the skills I learned from my 'display' days at The Chicago Public Library, I displayed the pictures beautifully on two giant easels, with the appropriate text for our audience to view during the reception that followed the performance. When we gathered in the foyer for the reception, all of the pictures were gone! They had been removed—stolen—from the easels!

A DREAM FULFILLED; I STUDY IN AFRICA

I had been awarded a Fulbright scholarship to study in Africa. It was upon completion of my entire summer's study in Nigeria, in 1973, that I had moved completely out of the classroom and into District Office Twelve. Politics was the name of the game on that level. There were people vying for each other's jobs, sexism, racism, one-up-man-ship, stealing of ideas, others taking credit for work someone else did, and long working hours. Deference for the superintendent, which took the form of buying tickets for every dinner (and there were many) where he was honored, was an unspoken demand that I felt financially.

The most painful part of working in district office was attending the interminable meetings. When the superintendent wanted to introduce a methodology, a new procedure, a proposed idea or practically anything that required staff cooperation, a meeting was held. He rarely came out and stated his aim in calling the meeting. He would talk all around the subject, present speakers (usually other staff members who had been briefed) and go on and on until he obtained consensus. If he had gathered us together and announced his aim, answered a few questions and passed out a memorandum he could have saved thousands of dollars in work hours. The average meeting lasted about two hours. I got the impression that our superintendent had attended encounter training sessions (which were very popular at the time) and he was determined to practice his skill, but he had failed to get the true hang of it. His inept handling just wasted our time, built up resentment, and kept us from being as productive as we might have been.

Working as teacher-assigned in district office carried a lot of prestige, and a raise was promised to me, but I never got it. What I did receive in abundance was an education in office politics, what to put in my C.Y.O.A. (cover your own ass) file, adult skulduggery and how to survive a hostile environment. In Summer, 1976, I returned to Nigeria, this time on a Ford Foundation Grant, to complete my field work for a Master's in Ethnic Studies administration.

MAKING IT ALONE

By 1976 my husband and I were separated. Our marriage was not able to survive physical violence, nor did I want it to. Jeffrey's problems were no closer to being solved and I had gotten myself into a whole lot of debt. The thing I had feared the most; being a single parent, had come true.

After obtaining my master's degree, (which wasn't in ethnic studies, but a M.A. with specialty in teaching remedial reading) I taught night school at Borough of Manhattan Community College (BMCC). One summer, I had three jobs; BMCC at night, P.S. 54 in the morning and I worked in a private library during the middle of the day. The regular school year provided an after school job in the disastrous after-school program and the Welfare to Work Program (W.E.P.). Both of these programs were bogus. They were poorly supervised, lacking in substance and light on evaluation and student progress. I do not list my work in these two programs as successes in my life, even though I tried to make a difference.

When I was still teaching classroom and getting phenomenal results with my incentive program of four visiting students per week-end, I was told by the assistant principal (after only half of the class had participated) I could no longer take students home with me. It was against the rules and there was no insurance to cover them if someone should get hurt. Jeff was terribly disappointed because he didn't make friends easily and he had enjoyed being with the children and going places with them. It was as close as he came to having brothers and sisters.

I had escaped P.S. 99 by volunteering to be one of the teachers in a newly opened experimental school project. It consisted of tandem schools: one; lower grades, the other; upper grades, with a supervising principal overseeing both schools. Each school had two assistant principals. There were seven supervisory personnel always interfering with teaching by interrupting our lessons with visitors who were usually from textbook companies. Sometimes the visitors were from test-making companies, and many were from colleges and universities which were conducting educational studies of one kind or another.

The school was brand new, state-of-the-art 'seventies' modern, but we had no textbooks. For months we had to rely on teacher-gathered or made materials. Many of the teachers were inexperienced young men who were avoiding being drafted to fight in the Viet Nam War and using the teaching deferral. Most of their degrees were in fields other than teaching, and overall, they enriched our staff with diversity and intelligence. Most were lacking in ability or will to apply enough discipline to control their classes. They were generally referred to as 'hippies'. One of the outstanding things I noticed about the hippies on our staff was that they were much better at math than many seasoned teachers.

During the early part of my teaching career, it had been my observation that many of the men who chose to go into teaching were the ones who couldn't make it in other fields. They were often lacking in math skills and so they took their 'vows of poverty' in the low-paying field of education where advanced computational skills were not required. These were the men who proved the Peter Principal; "In a hierarchy, employees tend to rise to the level of their incompetence". With assistance from prevailing and persistent sexist attitudes, the 'old boys network' and aided by antiquated union rules, they disproportionately occupied supervisory positions which inflicted the 'Mr. Pompells' on our school systems. It was unfortunate that many of the hippies left teaching after the war ended.

RODNEY READS

In a school with delayed shipment of books, I had to rely on the donated books from some of our community resources for supplemental reading for my sixth-graders.

One day, it came to my attention that there was one fought-over book which seemed to be more popular than any other, Even Rodney (who read on about a 2.3 level) would sit and read it for the entire forty-five minute period. I had not had time to check on the contents of these community-donated books. The assistant principal had provided them so it never even occurred to me that any could be unsuitable.

One of the girls came up to me and shyly told me that Rodney had torn pages from one of the books and that he had the pages in his desk. When I checked, there they were! Several pages of pornographic pictures, which had surely been torn from a book, were stuffed in Rodney's desk. I confiscated the book and the pictures. The book was rife with descriptive passages of sex scenes. So, without commenting on it to the class I locked the book and the pictures up in my closet with intentions of taking the matter up with the assistant principal. As any caring teacher would, I stayed late checking the rest of the books for unsuitable content. I did not find any other.

Rodney, at thirteen-years-old, had been left back (failed a grade) twice. He had developed the habit of not attempting to try. It is true that from kindergarten to third grade, students learn to read. From fourth grade through high school, students read to learn. Rodney had obviously met with little success in learning to read so he had given up trying. He spent his class time fumbling through stuff in his desk or bothering other students who were trying to study. He wasn't a mean person, but he was a disruptive influence in the classroom. Fortunately, Rodney qualified for one-on-one tutoring so he was picked up twice a day and taken into one of the small offices which were especially designed for that purpose.

When Rodney's hippie tutor was replaced by the sexy-looking, young beginning teacher who wore her skirts well above her knees and her hair well below her shoulders, tutoring Rodney gave Rodney more problems than it solved. He may have just been a young boy to her but when he returned from tutoring, he required several trips to the bathroom to 'recover from tutoring'.

With days of Rodney's disruptive behavior, and the supervisory staff away at a conference, I remembered how Rodney had focused on reading that book, how it had engrossed him to the point that I had observed him moving his lips in order to sound out words on his own, so I slipped the offensive book (without the torn out pictures) back onto the supplemental reading bookcase, and called Rodney's row as first to go up and select books. It didn't take a minute for him to discover the re-admitted book. I made sure the book was not available to any of the other students. Rodney's reading improved during the school term. He even got to a level where he would attempt to read to learn.

THE WHOLE CLASS WORKING TOGETHER

I had established and polished my reputation as a tough, no-nonsense teacher who could handle the most under-achieving class of sixth-graders in the school. And that's the kind of class I was assigned almost every year. The way I got the group to work as one, was to present 'The Christmas Carol' play every year. I would assign parts in September as soon as I learned the names of my students. The starring part of Ebenezer Scrooge was always assigned to the most acting-out boy in the class. This would, generally, bring him into line and usually the others would follow. Then we'd pull together as a team with a common goal. This attitude of cooperation was carried over to our studies, and resulted in spectacular learning progress.

One Christmas season, the class performed the play so well that I wanted to give them a special treat. When a monitor came to my class to take orders for Christmas Candy, I ordered three large fancy boxes of a candy listed as; 'BA-BA-AH RHUM'. There were enough pieces for each child to have four or five. The candy was delivered to my classroom just in time for our in-class Christmas party. I selected monitors to pass out the 'BA-BA-AH RHUM' and instructed them to keep on passing it out until their boxes were empty.

It wasn't long after eating the candy that my class became unruly. They jumped onto seats with their feet, some ran around the room, they all became extremely loud, and fights broke out. It was impossible to control them, no matter how loud I shouted, or how much I threatened. It was only when the principal came in to wish everyone a Merry Christmas, that I retrieved an empty box from the waste basket, read the fine print, to discover that 'BA-BA-AH RHUM' was made with real rum! I had unintentionally made the whole class drunk!

FAMILY UPDATE

KENNETH

At home in Chicago, my siblings were establishing their own active lives. My youngest brother, Kenneth, became a founding member of Jesse Jackson's Operation Breadbasket, the precursor to Operation Push. He had earned his master's degree in business administration and helped to start the Chicago chapter of the Black M.B.A.'s.

I never had a prouder moment than when I read the featured article (with pictures) of him, his partner and their business in the Sunday Business Section of the New York Times Newspaper. Theirs was the first frozen soul food company established in the country. The company, Soul Chef, has expanded and is still functioning today.

THEODORE

By this time, Theodore and I had buried the hatchet and become the best of friends. He had become one of Chicago's leading liquor salesmen. His enormous personal charm and good looks translated into wealth, so that he was able to afford a new wife, a house with a pool, a boat and to travel extensively.

Things went well for Theodore for a number of years, until Theodore (now called Ted) began cheating on his wife with a woman who was not from a social class with which we were familiar. This led to a costly and long drawn-out divorce battle. Ted developed a heart condition that forced him to retire earlier than he had wanted. He bought a house in which he and the woman lived. It was only a five minute drive from the house he owned with his wife, Odessa. He took Daddy (now fully Alzheimered) to live with them.

After Daddy died in 1996, and when Ted's divorce was finally obtained, Ted called me up to ask me if he could move in with me. He and the woman had married by then, but he was distrustful of her and he was very unhappy. I assured him that he could move to New York and live with me, but he never took me up on it. He became sick enough to require regular out-patient care and then hospitalization.

When Ted died in 2008 relations were so strained with the family that his widow wouldn't allow his sisters and brothers (under threat of summoning security) to even sit on the front row bench at his funeral.

DAPHNE

Daphne was struggling with her illness and accepting a lot of help from Mom and Dad in raising her children. She divorced her husband and married her childhood sweetheart, Frank. Frank's sister was the first Black woman to appear as a regular actor in a T.V. series. 'Star Trek' was the series, Nichelle Nichols was the actress. Frank owned a jewelry store and my sister wore diamond rings on all but her thumbs. Frank bought her a house but they soon moved to Hollywood (probably to advance Daphne's career), where they didn't last long, and soon bounced back to the comforts and support offered in Chicago.

ARNOLD

Arnold, the brother most like Dad, had been the one whom the Nun (Arnold's sixth grade teacher) had asked my father to come to school to see about. As she explained to Dad, she felt Arnold was mocking her in class in front of the other students. She said, "Arnold has a way of giving a little laugh before he answers my questions, he's not a bad boy, but I find it most annoying that he seems to be mocking me and I take it as a sign of disrespect which can undermine my authority with the class. Mr. Hennings, can you tell me why he does this? Is there any way we can break him of this habit?"

Dad mustered all of his fatherly concern before he answered; with, "Ah, ha, hum, Sister . . ." But he didn't get the chance to verbally expound as the Nun cut him off with, "Never mind, Mr. Hennings!"

Arnold was my only brother to serve full term in the military. He had the loquacious personality of a salesman, attended college for over three years and became one of the leading salesmen in a cosmetics firm. At one time, he out-earned us all. His lovely, classy wife, Sarah, bore a striking resemblance to the singer-actress Barbara McNair. With help from Big Brother Ted, Arnold became one of the first black men to run a business on Rush Street in Chicago. His photography shop became party headquarters for visiting celebrities—and home grown ones, too—like members of The Chicago Bears' Football Team, but his success didn't last long.

SANDRA

Sandra had married a young Jamaican businessman and was living in Montego Bay. She had graduated with a degree in education, but found that assisting her husband in his island touring business was far more rewarding than teaching school. It was her idea to use a large Egyptian-style eye as the logo for 'Forsythe's Tours' which brought in a lot of additional business as people could readily distinguish their buses with the big eye from all the rest of the competition.

BOB

Bubby, now called Bob, worked in the insurance industry all of his life. Before he died in 2003, he had worked his way to the top echelon of his international company. As an executive, he and his wife, Evelyn, were able to afford a penthouse apartment near Navy Pier that was so high, it looked down on flying airplanes. Bob was, by far, the smartest sibling, but he was the one who got the least amount of schooling. Bob never liked submitting to the confines and rules of institutions like schools. Bob was, by far, the best joke-teller in the family. He knew and told more jokes than anyone else, yet I never heard him tell a dirty one.

MOM AND DAD IN RETIREMENT

Mom and Dad maintained the homestead on eighty-eighth place where we got together as often as we could. There were some wonderful parties held there and each was a feast with daddy's homemade wine and mother's home-grown vegetables.

Daddy took great pride in his lawn, and when, in 1967, he saw a man walking across it, he called out to him, intending to scold him. The man had his head down and seemed to be concentrating on something other than where he was strolling. When the man looked up, Daddy recognized him as Dr. Martin Luther King. Daddy rushed over to Dr. King, shook his hand and declared, "Dr. King, you are the ONLY man I allow to walk on my lawn!" It was summer, and the King children were staying with Mom and Dad's next door neighbors, Rev. and Mrs. Thurston, while their parents lived in the worst project in Chicago. Rev. King was obviously visiting his children.

Dr. and Mrs. King and the SCLC were conducting a campaign against the practice of wholesale warehousing of poor black people into low-income government housing projects. Their contention that these projects were breeding places for crime, drug abuse, gang violence, and other societal ills was borne out in daily police reports. Finally, some attention was being focused on the brutal quality of life endured by the families who had to live there.

The patch of lawn where Daddy encountered Dr. King is the same patch where, a few years later, he saw his neighbor, Mrs. Smith, traverse to get to the alley. It was dusk so Dad couldn't see very well but he wondered why Mrs. Smith was crossing near his house when she could access the alley from her own house a few houses down the block. Dad went to the back of his house, looked out the window and saw Mrs. Smith meet up with Mr. Ford, Daddy's next door neighbor. Daddy told me later, "I hadn't seen Mr. Ford in about a week, he and his wife had been suffering with the flu, so I went out to greet him, and I also spoke to Mrs. Smith, but it looked like they didn't hear me, so I called to them, but they still didn't seem to hear me. So I went over to Mr. Ford's car and knocked on the window and finally got their attention before they drove off."

Mom's version was a little more explanatory, "Your father had been drinking when he saw Mr. Ford sneaking off with Mrs. Smith. He was too boozed-up to know that they didn't want to be recognized. Since he retired, your dad stays high all the time. You remember when we were visiting your office in New York, and one of the women said to me, 'So, you have been married to the same man for almost fifty years?' And I said to her, 'Not really, because when he retired a whole different man emerged that I had never met before."

We gradually came to realize that there was a lot more than 'getting high' going on with Daddy. Every day, he was slipping further into Alzheimer's and every day brought new challenges to our family of how to deal with it. Mother had undergone open heart surgery and was facing her own challenges trying to heal. Mom and I spoke by phone every day, and she would describe the things my father did, some were hilarious.

One of the stories she told me was about Dad wanting her to have sex with him, but she knew her own healing from open heart surgery would suffer a setback. Since Dad didn't remember anything, anyway, she told him that they had already done it. He accepted this, but asked how it was. She said she described it and graded it as wonderful! She said that Dad's hydraulic system had stopped working years ago so sex was only in his mind. But he became quite content when she asked him, "Don't you remember, Ted?" Then, over the phone, she and I fell out laughing,

Unlike Brady and Mildred's dad (childhood friends of ours) who was so addicted to drinking that he would lay in bed all day and drank his booze from a baby bottle with a nipple on it, our dad functioned. He did all that he needed to do to maintain order and support the lifestyle he and Mom were used to. But he, nevertheless, was alcoholic during the later years of his life. As loving and possessive as Daddy had almost always been towards Mom, when she passed away, his Alzheimer's shielded him from knowing she had gone. At her funeral, he told Theodore, "This is the best party I've ever been to!" Then he proceeded to leave the funeral parlor along with my best friend, Bootsie, and her sister, Ruth, two pretty women who had to leave early. Daddy always liked pretty women and Mom was a very pretty in her day. We had to go half a block to catch up with Dad and bring him back (in January, Chicago weather) to the funeral parlor. He wore no overcoat, only his suit jacket.

PART IV
MY MATURE YEARS

FAMILY AFFLICTIONS

My father and three of his siblings developed Alzheimer's disease. That's four out of twelve, which is one third; a very high percentage. My dad was in his late sixties when symptoms appeared. His sister, Catherine, was well into her nineties. Aunts, Ruby and Audrey, displayed symptoms when they were in their eighties.

Heart disease is the killer on Mother's side of the family. The statistics are even worse for her and her siblings. They are all deceased. Most of them died of heart disease. Outside of a wonderfully fit aunt, Doris Humphries (my Uncle Rick's widow who is a professional dancer at age 88), I am the oldest person on Mom's side of the family.

Aunt Catherine, Daddy's one-hundred-two year-old sister, lived with Alzheimer's for about six years until she passed away in February, 2013.

There are three sisters still living, ranging in age from eighty-five to ninety-six. Ruby (ninety-four-years old) slips in and out of the dementia that characterizes Alzheimer's. Audrey (ninety-six years old) has a full blown case of Alzheimer's. Mary, the youngest sister, is well, sharp and Alzheimer's free.

Dad lived with Theodore and Theodore's (eventual) third wife, until he died in 1996. Mom had passed away in 1992; she had been cared for by Sandra. Sandra and Theodore were excellent caregivers which was very fortunate because both had dreaded going into nursing homes. I wasn't able to physically be in Chicago with them but I sent money, offered advice and counsel, and visited whenever I could.

My health has improved to the place where I suffer far less (thanks to nine operations) in my old age than I did in my youth.

UPDATE ON JEFFREY

Jeffrey graduated from New Rochelle High School with a certificate of completion, not a diploma, and for his first job, he worked as a volunteer on the animal preserve in our town. He worked part-time and spent much of his free time swimming at the YMCA. He travelled on his bicycle and was so self-sufficient that I was able to concentrate on my career and work the long hours that success required. Jeff—with great urging from me— joined our town's recreation program for developmentally disabled people, and it opened up a new world for him. Never one to make many personal friends, he has over a dozen 'program' friends who form the basis of his social life. He still attends the program which offers respite for me and trips and activities for him.

Jeff, always the animal lover—through the years—took almost complete responsibility for the dogs we owned as pets. He was always the dog-walker, and, in any kind of weather, the dog-feeder and trainer. The constant performance of these tasks helped prepare him to 'man-up' to whatever challenges he has had to face in adulthood. And he has faced many: losing his grandparents, his best friend drowning in a water

312

reservoir in a Boston suburb, losing two good jobs due to company re-locations, his dog being killed by a car, another dog strangulating in our backyard, his parents' separation and divorce. He has undergone rigorous psychological testing (even though his problem was brain damage) and most of all—in the early years—being bugged by his Mom to improve his reading, when the capacity to do so just didn't seem to be there!

He has become a man in full. I am very proud of him. He is generous, compassionate, extremely helpful, even-tempered, consistent, reliable, totally honest and has no bad habits.

Jeff will soon embark on a new adventure: independent living. He has always lived with me but it is time for us to separate which, for him, must be like a divorce because we've never known any other arrangement. It is time for him to establish his own living space. I know he will do well on his own and we are fortunate that I still have enough good health to assist him in the transition.

I have been asked why Jeff was not forced out of the nest earlier. When he was a young adult I surveyed the available offerings but did not find them up to our standards so I kept delaying and avoiding facing the issue.

MR. WEBSTER

Jeff was working on his first real job when we met Mr. Webster's son, Paul, who was a few years older than Jeff and who also had special needs. That is when I started, in earnest, to envision how Jeff could follow in Paul's pattern. Webster was not Paul's father's real name; his was a hard-to-pronounce Italian name.

He was my upholsterer and people called him Mr. Webster because Webster was the name of his shop on Webster Ave. The young man had recently started a new job and he was living in a group home.

Whenever I saw Mr. Webster, I would ask about his son. I had started to plan in my mind—and Jeff and I had even gone out and looked at some residences—how it would be. I was hopeful that the right situation would come along, where Jeff would be offered suitable living space (not just the standard one-half bedroom), and that he would become adjusted just like Mr. Webster's son, Paul.

One day, I was in the lottery-playing line at our local deli when Mr. Webster came in. We spoke and I asked about his son. He turned his back to me and walked out of the store. I thought this was very strange as he was always so friendly. A few minutes later, he came back in. He said to me, "Mrs. Jackson, my son is dead! He got depressed. He didn't like the job. He never got used to the group home and one day he went up on the roof of the place and jumped off!"

I was saddened but transformed by this revelation. I became determined that there is nothing more important that I had to do in this life than care for the child I brought into this world! For many years, I stopped looking for placement for Jeff. I concentrated on providing the best life and home for him that I could. We still travel together and often eat out together. We attend shows and do a lot of shopping together. Now that I am a senior citizen, I am aware that it's time for him to become adjusted to living without me. The agency assisting us in this pursuit is Taconic Innovations. His father is also trying to be helpful.

LOOKING BACK ON MY CAREER

Teaching black studies did not endear me to many of my white colleagues. Their prevailing attitude was, 'your ethnicity was like your underwear. 'You know you've got it, but you don't bring it out in the open and talk about it.' Conversely, those of us working in that area, held that learning about ones ancestors and discovering heroes and sheroes to admire and emulate as role-models was essential to the development of proud, healthy, achieving students. There are few or no places for Black students to learn about their history, other than in school. And, if taught honestly, the study of slavery had to be a large part of the curriculum even though just bringing up the subject was anathema to some of my colleagues.

These white colleagues were not racists. Many of them had participated in various Civil Rights marches and had amassed impeccable credentials for being on the right side of history. Many were the products of Yeshiva training in their Shuls, where they were taught their ethnic studies, which became the undergirding for the development of their own self-esteems. Yet they were unable to see how ethnic studies, taught to black students, could not be anything other than indoctrination and teaching race-hatred.

My position as coordinator of ethnic studies for Community School District Twelve was personally challenging. It required constantly using my gifts of ingenuity and creativity and to avoid stepping on white supervisory toes, which proved not always to be possible.

I was responsible for devising curriculum and implementing programs in African and African-American Studies. The work was engrossing and I felt that all my life had prepared me to do this job. My attendance at The South Side Art Center, when I was a child, opened my mind to Black Heroes. There, I was exposed to live leaders in the 'Negro' community, such as Roy Wilkins, Walter White, Etta Molten, Rosella Laws Smith, and Maudelle Bousfield. My study trips to Africa and the efforts I expended in producing ethnic studies materials; especially a workbook for middle grade children; entitled, "AFRICAN ACTIVITIES, NIGERIA" contributed to the feeling that I was made for the position!

When I was honored with "Outstanding Ethnic Coordinator Award" from Morrisania Education Council I was thrilled and further convinced I was in the right job.

I wrote articles that appeared in community newspapers, and the article I sold to Essence Magazine; "How I Almost Became Wife Number Six" (their edited title, not my original one) paid me well. It was the story of how I received a proposal in Nigeria to join a polygamous marriage

The study guide I wrote for Kwanza was circulated only among teachers in my program. One was stolen and offered for publication by a teacher substituting in one of our schools. It was accepted and published under his name almost exactly as I wrote it.

I was invited to be part of several book-selling events, but the one I was most delighted to participate in was when Alex Haley introduced his much talked-about, monumental, novel of faction (fiction based on facts), ROOTS, at The African Heritage Studies Association's Book Party. I was allowed to sell my workbook at a table opposite to where Alex Haley was signing his book.

What a thrilling evening that turned out to be! In all the T.V. guest appearances where I had seen Alex Haley telling the story of how he traced his ancestry back to Africa, I became convinced that his story was my story too. It was because he was born and raised in Henning, Tennessee, and from slavery time, my dad's family was from that same town. That's how we got our last name, Hennings. It was my father who added the final 's'.

When I got the chance to speak with Mr. Haley and his assistant, George Sims, I found out the Haleys had come from Virginia to Henning late in the nineteenth century. My great-grandfather had been born in Henning in 1850. In the book, ROOTS, There is mentionof our families' paths crossing when Rev. Cyrus Henning (my ancestor) performed the marriage ceremony for Alex Haley's relatives early in the twentieth century.

ROOTS, THE BOARD GAME

During my conversation with Mr. Haley, I learned that he was planning to publish ROOTS JR. for schools. This revelation motivated me to try to get in on the sale of ancillary materials. To make sure that it would be greatly in demand by teachers, I worked on devising a game which followed the book. I spent many, many hours developing, polishing and test-marketing my game. I presented my game at a special session during a conference of Black Studies Professors in Washington, D.C. It was a disaster. None of the seventeen professors had read ROOTS and the game was based on having read the book. I was totally shocked that none of them had bothered to read one of the most monumental works of the twentieth century. All of them had seen the film.

I revised my game, and polished some more, and then secured a copyright and trade-marks. Next, (after assurance from Parker Bros. that they were interested in publishing it), I set out to get an endorsement from Alex Haley. I arranged a meeting with Donald Bogle, who represented Haley, and I paid my Madison Ave. lawyer a handsome fee to accompany me. That was when I discovered there was a plagiarism lawsuit pending against ROOTS.

Large passages had been lifted from works by Harold Courlander (a well known African scholar and author) and used in ROOTS without giving credit. This doomed chances of any ancillary materials making money. The response from Alex Haley was that he was not able to endorse my work, but I could go ahead and publish it if I wished. Parker Bros. had said that they would publish my game if I got an endorsement. This put me in a 'Catch 22' position. The game still sits in my front hall closet. The thousands of dollars I envisioned making on it will just have to wait for another big project.

THIS IS THE RIVER CALLED NIGER! is the title I gave to the next creation I figured would make me rich. It is a cumulative rhyme, written for children of all ages. Very young children can enjoy the pictures, words, rhythm, story line, and rhyme when the story is read to them. Older children can read it themselves. The language in a cumulative rhyme is very prescribed (think of THE HOUSE THAT JACK BUILT). Change one word and the entire work has to be re-written. I cannot count the times I have re-written it, and I plan to do it again, because my finished, copyrighted version was rejected by publishers to whom it was sent.

AFRICAN ACTIVITIES, NIGERIA is the workbook I wrote after my study abroad, It was published by inexperienced Heritage Publications in Philadelphia in '74. Tim, the president, had a law degree but didn't practice law. He saw the possibility of making a lot of money by supplying the educational community with its latest demand: ethnic heritage materials. My work may have been his first publication because he did a lot of things wrong. After I signed the contract, I heard no more from Tim until he called to see if I was planning to attend the conference for The Association for the Study of African American Life and History, (ASAALAH) being held in his town.

I was indeed, planning to attend the conference. It was imperative for Black Studies educators to come together in order to develop strategies that would enable us to obtain what we were all seeking: state mandates to include Black Studies in our curriculums.

It was a special project of mine (and others on the committee) to attempt to standardize the Black Studies curriculum, by proposing a core set of structured courses which would designate what should be taught at each grade level; kindergarten through high school.

ASAALAH was the organization that probably had the best chance to succeed at curriculum standardization. Its members were all well-respected scholars in the field. Most were college professors, many had earned doctorate degrees.

Unfortunately, my committee's proposal never even got on the agenda. The thing we hadn't factored into our plan was the enormous egos of the members. They had been in the organization for years, and they wouldn't allow us newcomers to fashion any policy they had not proposed themselves. And all they proposed were many reasons why our plan was unworkable.

Tim said that he wanted me to sign copies of my workbook at the conference. I was very surprised that it would be ready. He had never even given me a proof copy, but I could see why he'd want to have it available so educators from all over the country could peruse it and order in large quantities.

The ink was, literally, wet when I signed those first copies, I had to go to the ladies' room and scrub the ink off of my wrist, arm, and hand. Then it hit me, the title of the book had a misspelling of its most important word! 'ACTIVITIES' was spelled 'ACTIVITES'. There were other problems with the content and there were some additions that I had not submitted under my copyright. I learned many years later that the original run was for one hundred-thousand copies. My contract said ten-thousand. That would explain why ads for my book appeared in two major teacher periodicals long after I had received my last royalty check. No reprints were ever made. I assume all of the workbooks Tim sold had the misspelling in the title!

The first generation of published materials for Black studies was, by and large, not quality stuff. Most had been hastily prepared with little appeal to students. The quality of most I'd seen was so poor that instead of enhancing the black image, they probably had a reverse effect. I had carefully crafted my work to have appeal and quality. The misspelling was so disappointing that I skipped dinner, sat in my hotel room and cried.

SUMMATION

As a single person, my personal life was undergoing many changes. I was finding out how fragile was my sense of confidence, and how much it depended on external things. The mood swings I experienced were not only because I had unknowingly started early menopause, but also dependant on how things went at work or in my personal relationships. I was balancing increased career responsibilities, single parenthood (with special needs requirements), trying to date, and attempting to get out of debt. I had amassed more debt than I could handle because I was still trying to live the life to which I had become accustomed when I was married. Expensive weekends away were frequent. As a single person, most were bought by credit card.

Never one to stay in a morass for long, I had assessed the problem and determined that I needed more income than I was earning from my primary job and the editing work I was doing for Heritage Publications. The in-service human relations course I taught and the various after-school and vacation teaching jobs I worked, did not bring in enough income for my life style. I further enhanced my income by renting out the guest room in my house. I was lucky. Charles fit right in. He was like a second son. Subsequent roomers showed how lucky we had been with Charles.

When I became single, I had to tackle and defeat my drinking problem as my first challenge. I figured that getting high was a luxury I could no longer afford. It took months of drinking only one or two glasses of white wine spritzers, whereas before, it had been gin gimlets. I had a lot of support from family and friends—even one of our favorite couples (and their daughters)—Manuel's cousin Zeno, his wife Jean, and their daughters, Debra and Denise supported me as if I were their relative. I like to say that I got custody of Manuel's relatives in our divorce. I have no idea how Jeff and I would have made it through many holidays without the Richardsons.

A surprise supporter was my mother. She said she was proud of me for getting out of a marriage that had soured. She said that she had wanted to leave my father many times, but was always prevented by circumstances and fear. She said it made her proud to know that I had the courage to refuse to take the kind of treatment she had endured.

DATING

Dating wasn't the thrill I had hoped for. Mores had changed. If a man took you out for lunch, he seemed to expect to become intimate with you. And if he took you to dinner, he expected to move in with you! As far as I was concerned, the sexual revolution had not done dating any favors.

When Betty Friedan's book, THE FEMININE MYSTIQUE (which started the sexual revolution) was published in 1963, I was too busy doing my housewife, mother, and career woman thing to read it. It was my husband who read it, and it was he who quizzed me about my level of fulfilment as a woman. He asked me to tell him what my goals were, what I wanted out of life. And, for the life of me, I could not come up with an answer that didn't include the three of us. I had become incapable of thinking of myself as a separate entity. Becoming suddenly single required that I regard myself as an individual because, I certainly had become one. The dating scene could not provide me with what I wanted: a long term, committed relationship. Most of the men I encountered were itinerant lovers who were incapable of bonding with me and my son. I discovered that I had not evolved much and I never became a true member of the sexual revolution. I have never been what I regarded as sexually free, therefore I did not do well in the short term dating department either. I had never before experienced such loneliness.

RELATIONSHIPS

When I did manage to acquire a real boyfriend I hung in there much too long. Our relationship lasted (off and on) for over twenty years, but the quality of the relationship did not warrant that kind of time. Nick's appeal was that he supported me in my various ventures, had a real affection and respect for my son, and he was tolerant of my moods. There were elements of a good relationship which were missing, like fidelity.

It was also quite a revelation to me that my status as mother to a special needs son, was a definite hindrance to being able to attract and sustain a long term relationship. These conditions still prevail. How sweet life would be for me if we all aged out of needing the warmth, companionship, and love of another individual. Conversely, those needs grow stronger with age; they don't lessen.

A ninety-year-old recently demonstrated that even he still practices ruthless deceit, two-timing and pain infliction on his loyal lady. Perhaps Alzheimer's, instead of being such a great affliction, is really a blessing for the person who has it. He or she feels no emotional pain. The victims are the loved ones of the afflicted.

TIPS FOR VINTAGE WOMEN . . .

The humorous paperback book I wrote and illustrated, TIPS FOR VINTAGE WOMEN WITH YOUNG LOVERS (which I still have available for sale) will occasionally generate questions by some people about my proclivities. When those queries lead to sales of my book, I don't discourage them, but it's not the real me. I am no cougar, I only write the rules for them.

In this, 'THE UNIVERSITY OF LIFE', my worst subject has been 'MEN, AND RELATIONSHIPS WITH THEM'. However; I've learned many lessons from them: 1.) The double standard is alive and well! 2.) Emotional courage and honesty are in very short supply 3.) He's only as faithful as his options.

My sister thinks that my extreme independent streak and inability to allow a man to know how much I care about him (thus displaying my vulnerability) have not served me well in the many relationships I've attempted over the long course of my single life.

THE THUNDERBOLT

Most women I know, including my sisters, have had the 'thunderbolt' kind of love relationship at least once in their lives. That's the kind of love that is all consuming, strong, and blinding to all other forces. It's the kind of love that makes a woman abandon her goals and principles, forget her mother's warnings, and readily give up everything to be with him. I have never experienced the 'thunderbolt' kind of love.

I have secretly wanted to unleash my fertile imagination by inventing a good story and perhaps creating something even more salacious than "FIFTY SHADES" . . . to express myself as capable of being 'thunderbolted'.

Years ago, I had the desire to explain my singed pubic hair with an exotic tale of ritual sexual practices, or initiation rites, or anything that I had yet to dream up. But alas, I couldn't come up with a good story, and if I had, I wasn't in a relationship that was intimate enough to share the fantasy. I had to chuckle alone at my stupidity.

What actually happened; I was home, getting ready for work. I looked at my fingernails, and then at the clock. I figured I had enough time to get rid of a worn-out manicure, do all I had to do, and still make it out the door on time.

Sitting on the toilet in my morning routine, I removed the old nail polish, lifted one cheek to drop the cotton in the toilet, reached over to pick up whatever I was reading, then proceeded to light my cigarette. I lifted the same cheek to deposit the lighted match into the toilet. The highly flammable fluid, nail polish remover—being lighter than water—formed a film in the toilet and ignited immediately! In my haste to rise, my foot slipped on the slick mat in front of the toilet and deposited me back down onto the seat for an additional burn before I had the chance to flush. Singed pubic hair was the result of careless stupidity, rather than some exotic practice.

REFLECTIONS

I have been blessed with extraordinarily gracious, true and lasting friendships from some wonderful people during my tenure here on earth, and I have no idea how I could have made it through much that I have experienced without them

Working with and within organizations has occupied much of my time during this; the latter half of my life. I credit the YMCA with providing me with a wholesome place to hang out in my youth, and a place in my senior years to practice the life-sustaining exercises that keep me fit. I have come full circle with the Y, because—just as when I was in my teens—much of my social life is centered around friendships I made there.

Travel has been a mainstay of my existence as well. I have been fortunate enough to check off as 'been there' every state in the union except New Mexico, Idaho (no black female who knows Ebonics wants to claim this state) and the state of Washington. I have been to Mexico more times than I can count. I have crossed the Atlantic Ocean eight times just to Africa, (plus twice more to Europe) for a total of ten times. And I have sailed on more cruise ships than I can remember. I have been to almost every major island in the Caribbean (even twice to Cuba). South America, Alaska, and Hawaii have welcomed me, and I am happy to say; on more than half of these trips, Jeff was right there beside me. He is a seasoned travel companion.

I am, and have been, a member of some wonderful groups; The Harlem Writers Guild, The Coalition of One Hundred Black Women and a group that did a great job of bringing awareness to the public about the ugliness of apartheid in South

Africa during the eighties. The group was called B.R.A.I.N. (Black Resources and Issues Network). There were many more, but these are some of the most outstanding organizations with which I have worked.

CONCLUSION

I have led a full and (mostly) happy life. During my young days, I experienced a lot of pain. My current life is managed well, so that I have very little pain. I have endured nine operations and rid myself of abdominal cramps; which I've traded for leg cramps. I try to tell at least one good joke a day. I may have to tell my 'joke du jure' many times to make sure all who wish to hear it may do so. I consider laughter as essential to my well-being as the eighteen vitamins and other nutritional supplements I take each day, on recommendation from my nutritionist. In fact, members of my water aerobics class have taken to quoting my adage: "You haven't fully exercised until you've also exercised your funny bone".

I am, and have always been, a voracious reader. I read about five books a month and about eight periodicals. I have been a member of a book club for over twenty years.

My hobby is collecting lighthouses. I have lighthouse lamps, lighthouse curtains, lighthouse bedspreads, and clothes with lighthouses on them. The many replicas of actual working lighthouses, rendered in miniature, which decorate my house, are to become mementos of me when I have passed away.

I am an excellent cook and I usually serve my specialty, New Orleans Style Gumbo at the two house parties I give (almost) every year. My Martin Luther King Day Party started before the holiday was established. During the years when funds were being raised to erect the memorial in Washington, D.C., I used my party as a fundraiser. I requested donations from my guests, which I sent off to the memorial committee. I feel proud to have contributed over three-thousand dollars to that effort.

The other annual party which I (along with the Harlem Writers Guild) host, is a picnic in my yard in early September. My yard is large enough to accommodate over a hundred people, and I have, so far, managed to have enough gumbo for everybody.

I am very charitable. My donations are not huge, but they reflect my commitments: The Children's Aid Society receives the largest amount because of how it rescued my mother and her siblings when they were children. Many Native American groups receive my contributions, because they were the people this country (as an official policy) designated for genocide, and their needs are enormous. There are others (like the Alzheimer Fund, and The Heart Association) to which I give. I hold memberships in and donate to many black causes. I have been a charter member of The Schomberg Center for Research in Black Culture for over twenty years. And my loved ones are eager to open Christmas and birthday cards from me which contain my personal checks. I am also, a volunteer in the Read-A-Loud program at Grimes Elementary School in Mount Vernon, New York.

One of the nicest surprises I've received lately, was to be presented with The International Excellence in Education Award, given to me by The National Association of Negro Business and Professional Women's Clubs, Inc. at the United Nations on

October 14, 2013 at their Twenty-Fifth Annual Luncheon. I was nominated by International Governor, Dr. Beryl Dorsett. And, to sweeten the pot, A proclamation, issued by State Senator Andrea Stewart Cousins, named that day: Betty Anne Jackson Day.

My religious beliefs are fervent, private, and more spiritual than ritualistic. My pattern has always been that I will attend church weekly in spurts of several months, then not go at all for quite a few weeks.

I have had many challenges in life, and I am proud to say I have overcome most of them. One of the most difficult was quitting smoking after thirty years of puffing away.

I have been divorced since 1982, but I have been single since 1974. We were fully emotionally divorced before we were legally divorced.

By the time I retired, I had attained a master's degree, plus thirty-three hours over. This allowed me to receive the maximum in pension benefits; which put me in good financial shape until taxes began to eat me alive.

At this stage of my life I have no more personal goals to reach other than seeing my 'GRANDCHILD' published, and settling Jeff in his new apartment. I have accepted the fact that a long-term relationship, with a caring gentleman, where I would be chief mourner at his funeral (or he, at mine) was not 'in the cards' for me. I suppose just being mother to Jeffrey has been my major pursuit in this life.

When I die, I want to be spoken of as having "FINISHED LIVING" because I'm not leaving anything undone. I may not have done it all, but I have certainly done enough! And if I were asked to give account for things that have shaped my life, one of the things I would point to is my mother's caution: "Girl, don't you jump rope!" and be grateful for the restriction. Because, in the denial of something I desired, I discovered discipline. In re-focusing my activities, I developed my creative side. By following Mother's directive, I practiced the diligent obedience which undergirds all successful endeavors.

So you see, Mom, by not jumping rope, I jumped higher! I jumped out of the circumstances of being brought up in the project and became FROM the project, not OF the project. I jumped out of being a victim of poverty and want. And I jumped out of the trap of un-fulfilled potential.

So, for a girl who couldn't jump rope, this child from the project has had her share of life, and has gobbled it up with gusto!